The Uda

&

The Itivuttaka

The Udāna

Inspired Utterances of the Buddha

&

The Itivuttaka

The Buddha's Sayings

Translated from the Pali by

John D. Ireland

Published in 1997
Reprinted 2007

Buddhist Publication Society
P.O. Box 61
54, Sangharaja Mawatha
Kandy, Sri Lanka

ISBN 10: 955-24-0164-X
ISBN 13: 978-955-24-0164-0

National Library of Sri Lanka- Cataloguing in Publication Data

The Udāna & the Itivuttaka/ tr. John D. Ireland. - Kandy: Buddhist Publication Society Inc. - p. 258; 22cm

ISBN: 955-24-0164-X Price:

i. 294.3 DDC 21 ii. Title

iii. Ireland, John D. - tr.

1. Buddhism 2. Udāna

3. Itivuttaka

Typeset at the BPS

Cover art by Martha Aitchison

Printed in Sri Lanka by

Creative Printers & Designers,

Bahirawakanda, Kandy.

In memory of my mother

Brahmā ti mātāpitaro pubbācariyā ti vuccare
āhuneyyā ca puttānaṃ pajāya anukampakā

Itivuttaka, 106

Contents

List Of Sutta Titles

Part I. The Udāna

1. The Bodhi Tree *(Bodhivagga)*

2. Mucalinda *(Mucalindavagga)*

3. Nanda *(Nandavagga)*

2. The Section of the Twos *(Dukanipāta)*

3. The Section of the Threes *(Tikanipāta)*

KEY TO ABBREVIATIONS

A	Aṅguttara Nikāya
BPS	Buddhist Publication Society
Bv-a	Buddhavaṃsa Commentary
Comy	Commentary on Udāna or Itivuttaka
D	Dīgha Nikāya
DN	Dīgha Nikāya Sutta
Dhp	Dhammapada
Dhp-a	Dhammapada Commentary
It	Itivuttaka
J-a	Jātaka Commentary
M	Majjhima Nikāya
MN	Majjhima Nikāya Sutta
Nett	Nettippakaraṇa
Peṭ	Peṭakopadesa
PTS	Pali Text Society
Pv	Petavatthu
S	Saṃyutta Nikāya
Sn	Sutta-nipāta
Th	Theragāthā
Thī	Therīgāthā
Ud	Udāna
Vin	Vinaya Piṭaka
Vism	*Visuddhimagga*
Vv-a	Vimānavatthu Commentary

References to Vism are to the chapter and section number of Bhikkhu Ñāṇamoli's translation, *The Path of Purification*, followed in parenthesis by the page number of the PTS edition. Unless indicated otherwise, other textual references are to volume and page number of the PTS edition.

Part I

The Udāna

Inspired Utterances of the Buddha

INTRODUCTION

The Udāna, or "Inspired Utterances of the Buddha," belongs to the Sutta Piṭaka of the Pali Canon. It is the third book of the Minor Collection (Khuddaka Nikāya), found between the Dhammapada and the Itivuttaka. The Minor (or Lesser) Collection, although it is actually quite bulky, is given this name because it is an assortment of miscellaneous texts most of which were not included in what are regarded as the four main collections (*nikāya*).

The Udāna consists of eighty discourses, mostly short, divided into eight sections or chapters (*vagga*). The title "Udāna" refers to the pronouncement, usually in verse, made at the end of each discourse and prefaced by the words: "Then, on realizing its significance, the Lord uttered on that occasion this inspired utterance" (*atha kho bhagavā etam atthaṃ viditvā tāyaṃ velāyaṃ imaṃ udānaṃ udānesi*). Thus *udāna* means an inspired or solemn utterance spontaneously evoked, literally "breathed forth" (*udānesi*), by the understanding or realization (*viditvā*) of the significance (*etam atthaṃ*) of the situation or event that occasioned it (*tāyaṃ velāyaṃ*). Here it is the Buddha who pronounces these utterances although others are sometimes so inspired (e.g., in 2.10 and 3.7). Such utterances also occur elsewhere (e.g., M I 508; II 104–5, 209; S I 20, 27–28, etc.).

The Udāna was first translated into English by D.M. Strong (1902). A second and better translation was made by F.L. Woodward and, together with his translation of the Itivuttaka, was published in *Minor Anthologies of the Pali Canon*, Vol. II (*Sacred Books of the Buddhists*, London: PTS, 1935). The present translation was attempted because a certain dissatisfaction was felt with Woodward's rendering and style, which is now somewhat dated. The present translator has had the advantage of being able to consult the much improved translations of Pali texts published in recent years, especially those of the late Miss I.B. Horner and the Ven. Bhikkhu Ñāṇamoli. These and other scholars have made great strides in our understanding of Pali and general Buddhist terminology.

The translator was, moreover, able to consult several printed editions of the text. The PTS edition of the Udāna, made by Paul Steinthal in 1889 and used by Woodward, contains so many errors that there is hardly a page without fault. Therefore, during the preparation of this translation, besides Steinthal's text, increasing use was made of the Sinhalese Buddha Jayanti edition and the Nālandā Devanāgarī text. Neither Steinthal nor Woodward gives titles to the discourses: I have adopted these and the numbering from the Sinhalese edition for easier reference. Several other works were consulted, in particular the Commentary (*Paramatthadīpanī*) composed by Ācariya Dhammapāla in perhaps the sixth century C.E., which was useful when difficulties were encountered and for help in preparing many of the notes. Ven. Ñāṇamoli's translation of the *Nettippakaraṇa*, entitled *The Guide*, was quite invaluable. The *Netti* quotes nearly a third of the *udānas*, and Ven. Ñāṇamoli's renderings were a great help in understanding several obscure passages (see 3.10).

Some remarks must be made regarding a number of terms used in the discourses. The title "Buddha" has mostly been rendered as "the Awakened One," but occasionally left untranslated. He is usually referred to as "the Lord" (*bhagavā*) and addressed as "revered sir" (*bhante*), but non-believers refer to him as "the good Gotama" (*bho Gotama*) or "the recluse Gotama" (*samaṇa Gotama*). The word "Tathāgata" is obscure in meaning. It is briefly explained as "he who has thus (*tathā*) come (*āgata*) or gone (*gata*)" to enlightenment, or "he who has arrived at (*āgata*) the Truth (*tatha*)" as former Buddhas have done. It is most often used by the Buddha when referring to himself obliquely, but here in our text it is several times used by the Venerable Ānanda. For another use see 6.4 and note. The Buddha is also referred to as the Sugata (literally, "Well-gone").

Brahmin is the name for a member of the priestly caste in Indian society. In another, specifically Buddhist sense, it is used of an enlightened person, an arahat, a perfected one, one who has realized the goal. The Buddha is occasionally referred to as a brahmin.

A *bhikkhu* is an ordained member of the Buddhist Sangha (the monastic order); the word could possibly have been rendered as "monk." *Bhikkhunī* (an ordained woman, a nun) is mentioned only at 4.5 and 6.1.

A group of words left untranslated are those referring to non-human beings: *devatā* (occasionally *deva*), *nāga, yakkha* (see Chapter 6, note 2), *asura, gandhabba,* etc., for which there are no real equivalents in English. *Devatā* could perhaps be translated as "god," but these are not immortal gods; they are, rather, beings who are born and die like other beings, and although they may live much longer and have greater powers than humans, they are still "of this world." *Sakka* is the ruler of the devas and lives in great splendour with his consort *Sujā* (see 3.7) in the *Tāvatiṃsa,* "the heaven of the Thirty-three." *Asuras* live in the ocean (see 5.5) and are said to be at war with the devas. *Gandhabbas* are a kind of heavenly musician.

Names of persons and places have often been left untranslated, or only partly translated, as is the usual practice. By far the largest number of discourses occur at Sāvatthī, either in the Jeta Wood or in Migāra's mother's mansion. Jeta Wood was donated by Anāthapiṇḍika, a rich merchant of Sāvatthī who bought the land from Prince Jeta and built the monastery where the Buddha spent the greatest number of rains retreats. Migāra's mother's mansion was donated by the woman lay follower Visākhā, who often visited the Buddha when he was staying there. The mansion (or palace) was given to her by her father-in-law, Migāra, another rich merchant of Sāvatthī.

Dhamma is a word of wide meaning the sense of which cannot be adequately conveyed by a single equivalent, for it means different things in different contexts; such meanings as truth, reality, natural state, law, norm, ideal, morality, the teaching of the Buddha, and religion in general indicate its wide range of applications. In the discourses of the Buddha it most often means the Buddha's teaching, and specifically the doctrine of dependent arising (*paṭicca samuppāda*), the uniquely Buddhist theory of conditionality. This doctrine holds that things arise and cease, not from one cause, but from the presence or absence, the influence or cessation, of several conditioning factors. Formally expressed in the formula found in the first three discourses of the Udāna (1.1–1.3), the doctrine is referred to obliquely elsewhere and actually permeates and underlies all the teachings of the Buddha.

There are a number of technical terms that have been translated but need some further explanation. The largest number occur in the formula of dependent arising, which offers a detailed exposition of the second and third of the Four Noble Truths, the origination and cessation of suffering (*dukkha*).

Ignorance (*avijjā*) is not knowing the Four Noble Truths concerning suffering, the origin of suffering, the cessation of suffering, and the Noble Eightfold Path leading to the cessation of suffering. It is the non-knowledge of enlightenment and of the practices for realizing it. Due to this ignorance there arise "volitional activities" (*saṅkhārā*): good and bad, wholesome and unwholesome, deeds or actions (*kamma*)—physical, verbal and mental—which lead to results (*vipāka*, literally "ripening") proper to the moral quality of the action. According to the Buddha it is the conscious impulse or volition (*cetanā*) that is the actual kamma.

As a result of past volitional activities there arises consciousness (*viññāṇa*), beginning with the first moment of consciousness linking the past and present lives, and dependent upon this arises "name-and-form" (*nāmarūpa*) or mind-and-body, i.e., feeling, perception, and other mental states along with physical form composed of the four elements—earth, water, fire, and air (extension, cohesion, heat, and motion)—and their derivatives. The "sixfold base" (*saḷāyatana*) consists of the five sense faculties and the mind, which exist and function in dependence on name-and-form. Contact (*phassa*) is the coming together of an internal sense faculty with its respective external base or sense object—visible forms, sounds, etc., ideas being the object of the mind-base: "Dependent upon the eye and visible objects visual consciousness arises; the coming together of these three is called contact," and similarly with the other senses (S IV 32). Feeling (*vedanā*), which may be pleasurable, painful, or neutral, arises through contact.

Dependent upon feeling there arises craving (*taṇhā*), which is threefold: sensuous craving (*kāma-taṇhā*) or the desire to experience sense objects, craving for continued being (*bhava-taṇhā*), and craving for non-being (*vibhava-taṇhā*). The next factor, grasping (*upādāna*), is the seizing and clinging to what was craved, and thus the natural outcome of craving. There are four kinds of grasping: at sense pleasures, views, external religious observances, and the idea of self. From grasping arises being (*bhava*), becoming or existence in the three realms of existence: the sensuous, form, and formless realms.

Craving, grasping, and being are the present activities (*kamma*) that lead to future birth and the repetition of the whole process, the round (*vaṭṭa*) of births and deaths, *saṃsāra*. The Udāna mentions "cutting the round" (7.2), and the point at which it is cut is feeling, by not allowing craving to arise in response to feeling.

Another important word is *Nibbāna*, the final aim of all Buddhist endeavour. By studying the contexts in which it occurs (e.g., 8.1–8.4) some idea may be formed of what it signifies. *Parinibbāna*, "final Nibbāna," is the term used to describe the death of the Buddha and the enlightened disciples (see especially 8.5, 8.9–8.10).

One who is enlightened, the *arahat*, is said to have gotten rid of the taints (*āsavā*) of sensual desire (*kāma*), being (*bhava*), views (*diṭṭhi*), and ignorance (*avijjā*). The four taints are also called the four bonds (*yogā*) and the four floods (*oghā*)—see the expression "crossed over the flood" (7.1, 8.6). Similar to the taints are the four (poisonous) darts or barbs (*sallā*) of passion, hate, conceit, and delusion. Defilements (*kilesā*) is another term for various mind-defiling things, as are the fetters (*saṃyojanā*), hindrances (*nīvaraṇā*), swellings (*ussadā*), etc. All these terms are to be found in the Udāna.

Besides the arahat there are three other types of noble disciple (*ariyasāvaka*) who are progressing on the path towards this final stage: the stream-enterer, who is said to be reborn seven times at most before realizing Nibbāna; the once-returner, who will be reborn in the sense sphere only one more time; and the never-returner, who makes an end to *saṃsāra* after taking rebirth in the "pure abodes" of the form realm.

This then is a brief explanation of some of the terms that will be met in the translation. Others will be explained in the notes.

The prose passages which precede the "inspired utterances" of the Udāna may be regarded as a type of commentary, supplying the introductory circumstances to the essential teachings found in the utterances themselves. The latter, being so brief and concise and most often in verse, present numerous difficulties to the translator. Being expressions of the Buddha's teaching, they allow for a wider interpretation than the circumstances surrounding them suggest. Sometimes the utterances do not appear to fit neatly into the context in which they are set (e.g., 5.2, 5.5), though in other cases (4.5) the story and the *udāna* are integral to each other. Some *udānas* can be interpreted at different levels, and some have multiple meanings and allusions that tend to be lost in translation.

As well as being uplifting and inspiring, the stories from the Udāna also reveal much humour. For example, the response of Nanda on being asked to compare those pink-footed nymphs with that Sakyan girl, "the loveliest in the land." Again, in the story of Suppavāsā, when the Buddha elicits from her the response that she would like another seven sons, despite the trouble and pain she had to undergo to produce just one—all forgotten in the pride of motherhood! And then there is the incongruity of a new-born baby being able to hold a conversation. These, and other subtle touches, reveal the inspiration, humour, joy, and delight—and devout faith too—of those ancient and unknown story-tellers who collected and put together this literature. Also noticeable is their love of puns and allusions, the word-play and the ingenuity involved. Thus in 1.8, the pun on Sangāmaji's name, and, in the "Bull Elephant" story (4.5) the play on the word *nāga*, meaning both perfected one and elephant. In this last is also the charming touch of the elephant bringing water "for the Lord's use" with his trunk. Then there are the similes and parables, like that of the blind man and the elephant (6.4), that are both entertaining and instructive. Although this parable may be better suited to Jainism than to Buddhist doctrine—a theory of partial truth being somewhat un-Buddhistic—the story is probably older than both and is still used today by modern Hindu teachers.

The thought processes of the compilers of the Pali Canon are also revealed when it is discovered that there is a connection between two adjacent suttas, although this may not be obvious at first sight. One example in the Udāna is between suttas 5.8 and 5.9 where a reference to Devadatta's schism is followed in the next sutta by the inclusion of a verse that is found elsewhere (e.g., Vin I 349) in the context of the Kosambī rift. Other examples may be found in the Aṅguttara Nikāya. These connections are often so well hidden that great ingenuity is needed to discover them. They would also constitute necessary aids to memory in an oral literature and an indication of how it was gradually put together, a word or phrase in one sutta acting as a cue or trigger for the next. Also to be found are connections and allusions within the same sutta that are not at first obvious, some so subtle that one could be forgiven for thinking they are accidental rather than deliberate. An example is contained in Ud. 5.4. What is more natural for little boys, caught out in some misdemeanour ("tormenting fish in a pond") by a passerby, than to attempt to run away, as is suggested in the last line of the verse:

> *If you have done a bad deed or do one now,*
> *You will not escape pain, though you try to flee.*

Another device the ancient compilers of the Canon have employed is the occasional interposing of lines of explanatory narrative prose with verse that repeats what was previously said in prose. This has been done in the Cunda Sutta (8.5), heightening the solemnity of the events being described with dramatic effect. This sutta also has a number of curious features. It consists of four separate pieces, actually four short suttas that have been strung together.

Could the *udānas* have once existed as a collection apart from the introductory discourses, like the verses of the Dhammapada? These verses are also described as *Buddha-udānas*, but the stories supplied to explain when and where they were spoken are found in the commentary and are not reckoned as the Word of the Buddha. In the first chapter of the Udāna, the *udāna*-utterances form a group united by the common word "brahmin," which is obvious when they are read apart from the introductory discourses. So this chapter could well have been called *Brāhmaṇa-vagga*, following on from the last chapter of the Dhammapada. Similarly, the second chapter, has the unifying theme of *sukha*: happiness, bliss. However, in the subsequent chapters there is often no discernible theme linking the utterances.

The Udāna is an anthology, many pieces being taken from elsewhere in the Pali Canon, with no obvious systematization except for that mentioned above. However, the beginning of the first chapter does deal with the start of the Buddha's career beneath the Bodhi Tree and the last chapter contains material also to be found in the Mahāparinibbāna Suttanta (DN 16), which recounts the last days of the Teacher before he passed away. And the final *udāna*-utterance (8.10) is a fitting ending to the whole work.

Note to the Second Edition

Since the first edition of this translation appeared (1990), the Pali Text Society has published Peter Masefield's careful and extremely literal translation of the Udāna (1994) and his translation of the massive Udāna Commentary itself (1994–95)—see Bibliography. Masefield's approach to translation, adhering almost to the syntax of the Pali and closely following the commentary, is quite different from the one which I have taken, but a study of his translations has helped me to correct several errors in the first edition of this work. A number of changes were also proposed by Ven. Vanarata Ānanda Thera and Ven. Bhikkhu Bodhi; the latter has also kindly added several new notes for this edition.

John D. Ireland

Namo tassa bhagavato arahato sammāsambuddhassa

CHAPTER 1

THE BODHI TREE
(Bodhivagga)

1.1 The Bodhi Tree (1) *(Paṭhamabodhi Sutta)*

Thus have I heard. At one time the Lord was staying at Uruvelā, beside the river Nerañjarā at the foot of the Bodhi Tree, having just realized full enlightenment. At that time the Lord sat cross-legged for seven days experiencing the bliss of liberation. Then, at the end of those seven days, the Lord emerged from that concentration and gave well-reasoned attention during the first watch of the night to dependent arising in forward order, thus:[1]

"This being, that is; from the arising of this, that arises. That is: with ignorance as condition, volitional activities come to be; with volitional activities as condition, consciousness comes to be; with consciousness as condition, name-and-form comes to be; with name-and-form as condition, the sixfold base comes to be; with the sixfold base as condition, contact comes to be; with contact as condition, feeling comes to be; with feeling as condition, craving comes to be; with craving as condition, grasping comes to be; with grasping as condition, being comes to be; with being as condition, birth comes to be; with birth as condition, ageing-and-death, sorrow, lamentation, pain, grief, and despair come to be. This is the origin of this whole mass of suffering."

Then, on realizing its significance, the Lord uttered on that occasion this inspired utterance:

When things[2] become manifest
To the ardent meditating brahmin, [3]
All his doubts then vanish since he understands
Each thing along with its cause.

1.2 The Bodhi Tree (2) *(Dutiyabodhi Sutta)*

Thus have I heard. At one time the Lord was staying at Uruvelā … for seven days experiencing the bliss of liberation. Then, at the end of those seven days, the Lord emerged from that concentration and gave well-reasoned attention during the middle watch of the night to dependent arising in reverse order, thus:

"This not being, that is not; from the cessation of this, that ceases. That is: from the cessation of ignorance, volitional activities cease; from the cessation of volitional activities, consciousness ceases; from the cessation of consciousness, name-and-form ceases; from the cessation of name-and-form, the sixfold base ceases; from the cessation of the sixfold base, contact ceases; from the cessation of contact, feeling ceases; from the cessation of feeling, craving ceases; from the cessation of craving, grasping ceases; from the cessation of grasping, being ceases; from the cessation of being, birth ceases; from the cessation of birth, ageing-and-death, sorrow, lamentation, pain, grief, and despair cease. This is the ceasing of this whole mass of suffering."

Then, on realizing its significance, the Lord uttered on that occasion this inspired utterance:

When things become manifest
To the ardent meditating brahmin,
All his doubts then vanish since he has known
The utter destruction of conditions.

1.3 The Bodhi Tree (3) *(Tatiyabodhi Sutta)*

Thus have I heard. At one time the Lord was staying at Uruvelā … for seven days experiencing the bliss of liberation. Then, at the end of those seven days, the Lord … gave well-reasoned attention during the last watch of the night to dependent arising in both forward and reverse order, thus:

"This being, that is; from the arising of this, that arises; this not being, that is not; from the cessation of this, that ceases. That is: with ignorance as condition, volitional activities come to be; … with birth as condition, ageing-and-death, sorrow, lamentation, pain, grief, and despair come to be. This is the origin of this whole mass of suffering.

"But from the complete disappearance and cessation of ignorance, volitional activities cease; ... from the cessation of birth, ageing-and-death, sorrow, lamentation, pain, grief, and despair cease. This is the ceasing of this whole mass of suffering."

Then, on realizing its significance, the Lord uttered on that occasion this inspired utterance:

When things become manifest
To the ardent meditating brahmin,
He abides scattering Māra's host
Like the sun illumining the sky. [4]

1.4 The Banyan Tree *(Nigrodha Sutta)*

Thus have I heard. At one time the Lord was staying at Uruvelā, beside the river Nerañjarā beneath the Goatherds' Banyan Tree, having just realized full enlightenment. At that time the Lord sat cross-legged for seven days experiencing the bliss of liberation. And when those seven days had elapsed the Lord emerged from that concentration.

Then a certain haughty brahmin[5] approached the Lord. Having approached, he exchanged polite greetings with him and stood to one side. Standing there that brahmin said to the Lord: "How, good Gotama, is one a brahmin and what are the things that make one a brahmin?"

Then, on realizing its significance, the Lord uttered on that occasion this inspired utterance:

A brahmin is one who has discarded evil states;
Not haughty, free from stains, self-controlled,
Perfect in knowledge, one who has lived the holy life;
He might rightly use the word "brahma"
Who has no swellings [7] *anywhere in the world.*

1.5 The Elders (*Thera Sutta*)

Thus have I heard. At one time the Lord was staying near Sāvatthī in the Jeta Wood at Anāthapiṇḍika's monastery. At that time the Venerable Sāriputta, the Venerable Mahāmoggallāna, the Venerable Mahākassapa, the Venerable Mahākaccāyana, the Venerable Mahākoṭṭhita, the Venerable Mahākappina, the Venerable Mahācunda, the Venerable Anuruddha, the Venerable Revata, and the Venerable Nanda were approaching the Lord.[8] Seeing those venerable ones coming, the Lord said to the bhikkhus: "Those are brahmins who are coming, bhikkhus, those are brahmins who are coming."

When this was said a certain bhikkhu, who was a brahmin by birth, asked the Lord: "How, revered sir, is one a brahmin and what are the things that make one a brahmin?"

Then, on realizing its significance, the Lord uttered on that occasion this inspired utterance:

Those who have expelled evil states
And who fare ever mindful,
The awakened ones who have destroyed the fetters—
They are the brahmins in the world.

1.6 Mahākassapa (*Mahākassapa Sutta*)

Thus have I heard. At one time the Lord was staying near Rājagaha in the Bamboo Wood at the Squirrels' Feeding Place. At that time the Venerable Mahākassapa, while staying in the Pipphali Cave, became sick, afflicted, grievously ill.[9] Then after a while the Venerable Mahākassapa recovered from that sickness and thought, "What if I should enter Rājagaha for almsfood?"

At that time five hundred devatās were busily preparing almsfood for the Venerable Mahākassapa. But having refused the offerings of those five hundred devatās, the Venerable Mahākassapa robed himself in the forenoon, and taking his bowl and outer cloak, entered Rājagaha for almsfood, going to those streets occupied by the poor and needy, the streets of the weavers.

Now, the Lord saw the Venerable Mahākassapa in Rājagaha walking for almsfood in those streets occupied by the poor and needy, the streets of the weavers.

Then, on realizing its significance, the Lord uttered on that occasion this inspired utterance:

Not supporting another and unknown,[10]
Controlled, set firm in the essential,
With taints destroyed and rid of faults,[11]
Him I call a brahmin.

1.7 Ajakalāpaka *(Ajakalāpaka Sutta)*

Thus have I heard. At one time the Lord was staying at Pāvā, at the Ajakalāpaka Shrine, the dwelling place of the yakkha Ajakalāpaka.

It happened that the Lord was seated in the open air on a pitch-black night while it was gently raining. Then the yakkha Ajakalāpaka, desiring to cause fear and consternation in the Lord and to make his hair stand on end, approached the Lord and close to him emitted three times a terrifying cry, saying: "That is a goblin for you, recluse!"[12]

Then, on realizing its significance, the Lord uttered on that occasion this inspired utterance:

When a brahmin has gone beyond
In things pertaining to himself,[13]
Then he has surpassed the reach
Of this goblin and his noisy din.

1.8 Saṅgāmaji *(Saṅgāmaji Sutta)*

Thus have I heard. At one time the Lord was staying near Sāvatthī in the Jeta Wood at Anāthapiṇḍika's monastery. On that occasion the Venerable Saṅgāmaji had arrived at Sāvatthī to see the Lord. The former wife of the Venerable Saṅgāmaji, hearing that master Saṅgāmaji had arrived at Sāvatthī, took her child and went to the Jeta Wood.

Now at that time the Venerable Saṅgāmaji was sitting at the foot of a certain tree to rest during the middle of the day. Then the former wife of the Venerable Saṅgāmaji approached him and spoke these words: "I have a little son, recluse, support me." When this was said the Venerable Saṅgāmaji remained silent. A second time and a third time she said: "I have a little son, recluse, support me." And a third time the Venerable Sangāmaji remained silent.

Then the former wife of the Venerable Saṅgāmaji put the child down in front of him and went away, saying: "This is your son, recluse, support him." But the Venerable Saṅgāmaji neither looked at the child nor spoke to him. Then the former wife of the Venerable Saṅgāmaji, having gone a short distance, looked back and saw that he was neither looking at the child nor speaking to him. On seeing this she thought: "This recluse does not even want his son!" She returned, took the child, and went away.

With the divine eye which is purified and superhuman the Lord saw that discourteous behaviour[14] on the part of the Venerable Saṅgāmaji's wife.

Then, on realizing its significance, the Lord uttered on that occasion this inspired utterance:

He had no pleasure in her coming,
Nor grief when she went away;
Saṅgāmaji, freed from ties,[15]
Him I call a brahmin.

1.9 The Jaṭila Ascetics *(Jaṭila Sutta)*

Thus have I heard. At one time the Lord was staying near Gayā on Gayā Head.[16] At that time, during the cold winter nights between the "eights" in the season of the snowfall, many Jaṭila ascetics[17] at Gayā were plunging in and out (of the water), pouring water (over themselves), and performing the fire sacrifice, thinking that by these practices purity is obtained.

The Lord saw those Jaṭila ascetics ... plunging in and out (of the water), pouring water (over themselves), and performing the fire sacrifice....

Then, on realizing its significance, the Lord uttered on that occasion this inspired utterance:

Not by water is one cleansed,
Many people bathe in this.
In whom is truth and Dhamma,
He is cleansed, he is a brahmin.

1.10 Bāhiya *(Bāhiya Sutta)*

Thus have I heard. At one time the Lord was staying near Sāvatthī in the Jeta Wood at Anāthapiṇḍika's monastery. At that time Bāhiya of the Bark-cloth was living by the seashore at Suppāraka. He was respected, revered, honoured, venerated, and given homage, and was one who obtained the requisites of robes, almsfood, lodging, and medicines.[18]

Now, while he was in seclusion, this reflection arose in the mind of Bāhiya of the Bark-cloth: "Am I one of those in the world who are arahats or who have entered the path to arahatship?"

Then a devatā who was a former blood-relation of Bāhiya of the Bark-cloth understood that reflection in his mind.[19] Being compassionate and wishing to benefit him, he approached Bāhiya and said: "You, Bāhiya, are neither an arahat nor have you entered the path to arahatship. You do not follow that practice whereby you could be an arahat or enter the path to arahatship."

"Then, in the world including the devas, who are arahats or have entered the path to arahatship?"

"There is, Bāhiya, in a far country a town called Sāvatthī. There the Lord now lives who is the Arahat, the Fully Enlightened One. That Lord, Bāhiya, is indeed an arahat and he teaches Dhamma for the realization of arahatship."

Then Bāhiya of the Bark-cloth, profoundly stirred by the words of that devatā, then and there departed from Suppāraka. Stopping only for one night everywhere (along the way),[20] he went to Sāvatthī where the Lord was staying in the Jeta Wood at Anāthapiṇḍika's monastery. At that time a number of bhikkhus were walking up and down in the open air. Then Bāhiya of the

Bark-cloth approached those bhikkhus and said: "Where, revered sirs, is the Lord now living, the Arahat, the Fully Enlightened One? We wish to see that Lord who is the Arahat, the Fully Enlightened One."

"The Lord, Bāhiya, has gone for almsfood among the houses."

Then Bāhiya hurriedly left the Jeta Wood. Entering Sāvatthī, he saw the Lord walking for almsfood in Sāvatthī—pleasing, lovely to see, with calmed senses and tranquil mind, attained to perfect poise and calm, controlled, a perfected one, watchful with restrained senses. On seeing the Lord he approached, fell down with his head at the Lord's feet, and said: "Teach me Dhamma, Lord; teach me Dhamma, Sugata, so that it will be for my good and happiness for a long time."

Upon being spoken to thus, the Lord said to Bāhiya of the Bark-cloth: "It is an unsuitable time, Bāhiya, we have entered among the houses for almsfood."

A second time Bāhiya said to the Lord: "It is difficult to know for certain, revered sir, how long the Lord will live or how long I will live. Teach me Dhamma, Lord; teach me Dhamma, Sugata, so that it will be for my good and happiness for a long time." A second time the Lord said to Bāhiya: "It is an unsuitable time, Bāhiya, we have entered among the houses for almsfood."

A third time Bāhiya said to the Lord: "It is difficult to know for certain … Teach me Dhamma, Sugata, so that it will be for my good and happiness for a long time."

"Herein, Bāhiya, you should train yourself thus: 'In the seen will be merely what is seen; in the heard will be merely what is heard; in the sensed will be merely what is sensed; in the cognized will be merely what is cognized.' In this way you should train yourself, Bāhiya.

"When, Bāhiya, for you in the seen is merely what is seen … in the cognized is merely what is cognized, then, Bāhiya, you will not be 'with that.' When, Bāhiya, you are not 'with that,' then, Bāhiya, you will not be 'in that.' When, Bāhiya, you are not 'in that,' then, Bāhiya, you will be neither here nor beyond nor in between the two. Just this is the end of suffering."[21]

Now, through this brief Dhamma teaching of the Lord the mind of Bāhiya of the Bark-cloth was immediately freed from the taints without grasping. Then the Lord, having instructed Bāhiya with this brief instruction, went away.[22]

Not long after the Lord's departure a cow with a young calf attacked Bāhiya of the Bark-cloth and killed him.[23] When the Lord, having walked for almsfood in Sāvatthī, was returning from the alms round with a number of bhikkhus, on departing from the town he saw that Bāhiya of the Bark-cloth had died.

Seeing this he said to the bhikkhus: "Bhikkhus, take Bāhiya's body, put it on a litter, carry it away and burn it, and make a stupa for it. Your companion in the holy life has died."

"Very well, revered sir," those bhikkhus replied to the Lord.

Taking Bāhiya's body, they put it upon a litter, carried it away and burnt it, and made a stupa for it. Then they went to the Lord, prostrated themselves, and sat down to one side. Sitting there those bhikkhus said to the Lord: "Bāhiya's body has been burnt revered sir, and a stupa has been made for it. What is his destiny, what is his future birth?"

"Bhikkhus, Bāhiya of the Bark-cloth was a wise man. He practised according to Dhamma and did not trouble me by disputing about Dhamma. Bhikkhus, Bāhiya of the Bark-cloth has attained final Nibbāna."

Then, on realizing its significance, the Lord uttered on that occasion this inspired utterance:

Where neither water nor yet earth
Nor fire nor air gain a foothold,
There gleam no stars, no sun sheds light,
There shines no moon, yet there no darkness reigns.
When a sage, a brahmin, has come to know this
For himself through his own wisdom,
Then he is freed from form and formless.
Freed from pleasure and from pain. [24]

This inspired utterance was spoken by the Lord also, so I did hear.

Chapter 2

Mucalinda
(Mucalindavagga)

2.1 Mucalinda *(Mucalinda Sutta)*

Thus have I heard. At one time the Lord was staying at Uruvelā beside the river Nerañjarā at the foot of the Mucalinda Tree, having just realized full enlightenment.

At that time the Lord sat cross-legged for seven days experiencing the bliss of liberation. Now, it happened that there occurred, out of season, a great rainstorm and for seven days there were rain clouds, cold winds, and unsettled weather. Then Mucalinda the nāga-king left his dwelling place and having encircled the Lord's body seven times with his coils, he stood with his great hood spread over the Lord's head (thinking) to protect the Lord from cold and heat, from gadflies, mosquitoes, wind, sun, and the touch of creeping things.[1]

At the end of those seven days the Lord emerged from that concentration. Then Mucalinda the nāga-king, seeing that the sky had cleared and the rain clouds had gone, removed his coils from the Lord's body. Changing his own appearance and assuming the appearance of a youth, he stood in front of the Lord with his hands folded together venerating him.

Then, on realizing its significance, the Lord uttered on that occasion this inspired utterance:

Blissful is detachment for one who is content,
For one who has learnt Dhamma and who sees;
Blissful is non-affliction in the world,
Restraint towards living creatures;

Blissful is passionlessness in the world,
The overcoming of sensual desires;
But the abolition of the conceit "I am" —
That is truly the supreme bliss.

2.2 The Kings *(Rāja Sutta)*

Thus have I heard. At one time the Lord was staying near Sāvatthī in the Jeta Wood at Anāthapiṇḍika's monastery. On that occasion after the meal, on returning from collecting almsfood, a number of bhikkhus had gathered together in the assembly hall when this topic of conversation arose: "Which of these two kings, friend, has greater wealth, greater possessions, a greater treasury, greater territory, conveyances, army, prosperity, and power: Seniya Bimbisāra the king of Magadha or Pasenadi the king of Kosala?" And this conversation of those bhikkhus continued without coming to an end.

Then the Lord, emerging from seclusion in the evening, went to the assembly hall and sat down on the seat prepared for him. Sitting there the Lord asked the bhikkhus: "What were you talking about just now, bhikkhus, while gathered here together? What was the topic of discussion that you had left unfinished?"

"After the meal, revered sir, ... this topic of conversation arose: 'Which of these two kings has the greater wealth ... Seniya Bimbisāra the king of Magadha or Pasenadi the king of Kosala?' This, revered sir, was our discussion that was left unfinished when the Lord arrived."

"It is not right, bhikkhus, that you sons of good family who have gone forth out of faith from home to the homeless state should talk on such a topic. When you have gathered together, bhikkhus, you should do one of two things: either engage in talk on Dhamma or maintain noble silence."[2]

Then, on realizing its significance, the Lord uttered on that occasion this inspired utterance:

Whatever bliss in the world is found in sensual pleasures
And whatever there is of heavenly bliss,
These are not worth a sixteenth part
Of the bliss of craving's destruction.

2.3 The Stick *(Daṇḍa Sutta)*

Thus have I heard. At one time the Lord was staying near Sāvatthī in the Jeta Wood at Anāthapiṇḍika's monastery. On that occasion, between Sāvatthī and the Jeta Wood, a number of boys were hitting a snake with a stick. Now the Lord, having put on his robe in the forenoon and taken his bowl and outer cloak, was going to Sāvatthī to collect almsfood when he saw those boys between Sāvatthī and the Jeta Wood hitting a snake with a stick.

Then, on realizing its significance, the Lord uttered on that occasion this inspired utterance:

Who harms with a stick beings desiring happiness,
Though he himself seeks happiness,
He does not obtain it after death.
Who harms not with a stick beings desiring happiness,
While he himself seeks happiness,
He obtains it after death.

2.4 Respected *(Sakkāra Sutta)*

Thus have I heard. At one time the Lord was staying near Sāvatthī in the Jeta Wood at Anāthapiṇḍika's monastery. At that time the Lord was respected, revered, honoured, venerated, and given homage, and he obtained the requisites of robes, almsfood, lodgings, and medicines. And the Order of bhikkhus was also respected.... But the wanderers of other sects were not respected, revered, honoured, venerated, and given homage, and they did not obtain the requisites of robes, almsfood, lodgings, and medicines. Then those wanderers of other sects, unable to tolerate the respect shown to the Lord and the Order of bhikkhus, on seeing bhikkhus in the village and the forest, reviled, abused, provoked, and annoyed them with insults and harsh words.

Then a number of bhikkhus approached the Lord, prostrated themselves, and sat down to one side. Sitting there those bhikkhus said to the Lord: "At present, revered sir, the Lord is respected, … and the Order of bhikkhus is also respected, … but the wanderers of other sects are not respected…. And now, revered sir, those wanderers, unable to tolerate the respect shown towards the Lord … on seeing bhikkhus … provoke and annoy them with insults and harsh words."

Then, on realizing its significance, the Lord uttered on that occasion this inspired utterance:

> *When affected by pleasure and pain in the village and forest,*
> *One should not ascribe them to oneself or another.*
> *Contacts affect one dependent on clinging.* [3]
> *How can contacts affect one without clinging?*

2.5 The Lay Follower *(Upāsaka Sutta)*

Thus have I heard. At one time the Lord was staying near Sāvatthī in the Jeta Wood at Anāthapiṇḍika's monastery. On that occasion a certain lay follower from Icchānaṅgala had arrived at Sāvatthī on some business or other. Then, when that business in Sāvatthī had been completed, the lay follower approached the Lord, prostrated himself, and sat down to one side. As he was sitting there the Lord said to that lay follower: "At last, lay follower, you have found an opportunity to come here."

"For a long time, revered sir, I have wanted to come and see the Lord, but being involved with various affairs of business that had to be done I was just not able to come personally and see the Lord."

Then, on realizing its significance, the Lord uttered on that occasion this inspired utterance:

Blissful indeed is it to own nothing
When one is learned and has mastered the Dhamma.
See how people who own things are afflicted,
For people are strongly bound to people.

2.6 The Pregnant Woman *(Gabbhinī Sutta)*

Thus have I heard. At one time the Lord was staying near Sāvatthī in the Jeta Wood at Anāthapiṇḍika's monastery. On that occasion the young wife of a certain wanderer said to the wanderer: "Go and fetch some oil, brahmin, I will use it at my delivery."

When this was said that wanderer replied to the woman wanderer: "But where can I get oil for you?"

And a second time and a third time that woman wanderer said to the wanderer: "Go and fetch some oil, brahmin, I will use it at my delivery."

At that time at the storehouse of King Pasenadi of Kosala there was being given to any recluse or brahmin as much as he wanted of ghee or oil to drink, but not to take away. Then that wanderer thought: "At the storehouse of King Pasenadi of Kosala there is being given to any recluse or brahmin as much as he wants of ghee or oil to drink, but not to take away. What if I went to the storehouse and drank as much oil as I wanted, and having returned home and vomited it up, should offer it to my wife for use at her delivery."

So that wanderer went to the storehouse of King Pasenadi of Kosala and having drunk as much oil as he wanted, he returned home, but was able neither to bring it up nor make it pass through him. Experiencing feelings that were acute, painful, sharp, and severe, he rolled about in agony.

Now the Lord, having put on his robe in the forenoon and taken his bowl and outer cloak, was going to Sāvatthī to collect almsfood. And the Lord saw that wanderer rolling about in agony.

Then, on realizing its significance, the Lord uttered on that occasion this inspired utterance:

They are happy indeed who own nothing at all;
Those with highest knowledge own nothing at all.
See how people who own things are afflicted,
For people are strongly bound to people.

2.7 The Only Son *(Ekaputta Sutta)*

Thus have I heard. At one time the Lord was staying near Sāvatthī in the Jeta Wood at Anāthapiṇḍika's monastery. At that time the dearly beloved only son of a certain lay follower had died. Then a number of lay followers with wet clothes and hair approached the Lord in the middle of the day, prostrated themselves, and sat down to one side. As they were sitting there the Lord said to those lay followers: "Why have you come here in the middle of the day, lay followers, with wet clothes and hair?"[4]

When this was said that lay follower replied to the Lord: "My dearly beloved only son, revered sir, has died. That is why we have come here in the middle of the day with wet clothes and hair."

Then, on realizing its significance, the Lord uttered on that occasion this inspired utterance:

Devas and most men are truly fettered
By what they hold as dear and pleasant.
Worn out with grief (when their dear ones die),
They fall into the power of the King of Death. [5]

But those who are heedful day and night,
Who abandon whatever is dear—
The bait of Death so hard to overcome—
They dig up the root of grief.

2.8 Suppavāsā *(Suppavāsā Sutta)*

Thus have I heard. At one time the Lord was staying at Kuṇḍiyā in the Kuṇḍiṭṭhana Wood.[6] On that occasion Suppavāsā the Koliyan daughter had been pregnant for seven years and for seven days had experienced difficult labour.[7] But although she experienced feelings that were acute, painful, sharp, and severe, her mind was occupied with three thoughts: "The Lord is indeed a Fully Enlightened One, who teaches Dhamma for abandoning such suffering as this; the Order of the Lord's disciples is indeed progressing on the right path, following a path to abandon such suffering as this; Nibbāna is indeed perfect bliss, where such suffering is not found."

Then Suppavāsā the Koliyan daughter said to her husband: "Come, master, go to the Lord and approaching him in my name, worship the Lord with your head at his feet, and ask concerning his health and well-being, fitness, strength, and comfort, saying: 'Suppavāsā the Koliyan daughter, revered sir, worships the Lord with her head at his feet and asks concerning his health and well-being....' And also say: 'Suppavāsā, revered sir, has been pregnant for seven years and for seven days has experienced difficult labour. But although she experiences feelings that are acute ... her mind has been occupied with three thoughts; "The Lord is indeed a Fully Enlightened One ... Nibbāna is indeed perfect bliss, where such suffering is not found."'"

"Very well," replied the Koliyan son[8] to Suppavāsā, and he approached the Lord, prostrated himself and sat down at one side. Sitting there he said to the Lord, "Suppavāsā the Koliyan daughter, revered sir, worships the Lord with her head at his feet ... But although she experiences feelings that are acute ... her mind has been occupied with three thoughts...."

"May Suppavāsā the Koliyan daughter be well and healthy and give birth to a healthy son."

When the Lord had spoken these words, Suppavāsā the Koliyan daughter became well and healthy and gave birth to a healthy son.

The Koliyan son, saying, "So be it, revered sir," pleased and appreciative of the Lord's words, arose from his seat, prostrated himself to the Lord, and keeping his right side towards him returned home.

And the Koliyan son saw that Suppavāsā was well and healthy and had given birth to a healthy son. On seeing this he thought: "It is indeed wonderful, it is indeed marvellous, the great supernormal potency and power of the Tathāgata![9] When those words were spoken by the Lord, Suppavāsā became well and healthy and gave birth to a healthy son." And he was pleased and delighted and became joyful and happy.

Then Suppavāsā said to her husband: "Come, master, go to the Lord and approaching him in my name, worship the Lord with your head at his feet and say: 'Suppavāsā the Koliyan daughter, revered sir, worships the Lord with her head at his feet.' And also say: 'Suppavāsā, revered sir, was pregnant for seven years and for seven days experienced difficult labour. She is now well and healthy and has given birth to a healthy son. She invites the Order of bhikkhus to a meal for seven days. Please consent, revered sir, to Suppavāsā's providing seven meals for the Lord together with his Order of bhikkhus.'"

"Very well," replied the Koliyan son to Suppavāsā, and he approached the Lord ... and said: "Suppavāsā the Koliyan daughter, revered sir, worships the Lord with her head at his feet ... She is now well and healthy and has given birth to a healthy son. Please consent, revered sir, to Suppavāsā's providing seven meals for the Lord together with the Order of bhikkhus.'"

Now, at that time a certain lay follower had invited the Order of bhikkhus headed by the Buddha to a meal the next day, and that lay follower was the supporter of the Venerable Mahāmoggallāna. Then the Lord called the Venerable Mahāmoggallāna and said: "Come, Moggallāna, go to that lay follower and say: 'Friend, Suppavāsā the Koliyan daughter invites the Order of bhikkhus headed by the Buddha to a meal for seven days. Allow Suppavāsā to give her seven meals.' Your supporter can give his afterwards."

"Very well, revered sir," the Venerable Mahāmoggallāna replied to the Lord, and he went to that lay supporter and repeated what the Lord had said.

"If, revered sir, the noble Mahāmoggallāna will be my surety for three things—for wealth, life, and faith—then let Suppavāsā the Koliyan daughter give her seven meals and I will give mine afterwards."

"For two of these things, friend, I will be your surety, for wealth and life; but as for faith, you are your own surety."

"If, revered sir, the noble Mahāmoggallāna will be my surety for two things, for wealth and life, I allow Suppavāsā to give her seven meals. I will give mine afterwards."

Then the Venerable Mahāmoggallāna, having obtained the consent of that lay follower, approached the Lord and said: "That lay follower of mine has consented, revered sir. Let Suppavāsā the Koliyan daughter give her seven meals. He will give his afterwards."

So Suppavāsā the Koliyan daughter, with her own hand, served and satisfied the Order of bhikkhus headed by the Buddha with sumptuous solid and soft food for seven days. And she made her child pay homage to the Lord and the whole Order of bhikkhus. Then the Venerable Sāriputta said to the child: "Are you well, child? Are you healthy? Have you any pain?"

"How, revered Sāriputta, can I be well? How can I be healthy? I have spent seven years in a cauldron of blood." [10]

Then Suppavāsā, (reflecting) "My son is conversing with the general of the Dhamma," [11] was pleased and delighted and became joyful and happy. Then the Lord said to Suppavāsā: "Do you wish you could have another such son?"

"I wish, Lord, I could have seven more such sons!"

Then, on realizing its significance, the Lord uttered on that occasion this inspired utterance:

Discomfort in the guise of pleasure,
The unloved in the guise of love,
Suffering in the guise of bliss
Overpower the heedless one.

2.9 Visākhā *(Visākhā Sutta)*

Thus have I heard. At one time the Lord was staying near Sāvatthī in the Eastern Park at Migāra's mother's mansion.

On that occasion Visākhā, Migāra's mother,[12] was involved in some business with King Pasenadi of Kosala, and this the king did not conclude as she intended. So Visākhā approached the

Lord in the middle of the day, prostrated herself, and sat down to one side. As she was sitting there the Lord said to her: "Well, Visākhā, where have you come from in the middle of the day?"

"I was involved in some business, revered sir, with King Pasenadi of Kosala, and this the king did not conclude as I had intended."

Then, on realizing its significance, the Lord uttered on that occasion this inspired utterance:

All subjection to another is painful;
All sovereignty is bliss.
Partners share in affliction,
Bonds indeed are difficult to overcome.

2.10 Bhaddiya *(Bhaddiya Sutta)*

Thus have I heard. At one time the Lord was staying at Anupiyā in the Mango Orchard. At that time the Venerable Bhaddiya, Kāligodhā's son, on going into the forest to the foot of a tree or to an empty place, constantly uttered, "Ah, what bliss! Ah, what bliss!"

A number of bhikkhus heard the Venerable Bhaddiya ... constantly uttering, "Ah, what bliss! Ah, what bliss!" and the thought came to them: "No doubt, friend, the Venerable Bhaddiya, Kāligodhā's son, is dissatisfied with leading the holy life, since formerly when he was a householder he enjoyed the bliss of royalty. And when recollecting that, on going into the forest ... he utters, 'Ah, what bliss! Ah, what bliss!'"

Then a number of bhikkhus approached the Lord, prostrated themselves, sat down to one side, and reported this to the Lord.

Then the Lord addressed a certain bhikkhu: "Come, bhikkhu, in my name tell the bhikkhu Bhaddiya, 'The Teacher calls you, friend Bhaddiya.'"

"Very well, revered sir," the bhikkhu replied and approaching the Venerable Bhaddiya, Kāligodhā's son, he said, "The Teacher calls you, friend Bhaddiya."

"Very well, friend," the Venerable Bhaddiya replied, and approaching the Lord he prostrated himself and sat down to one side. The Lord then said to him: "Is it true, Bhaddiya, that on going into the forest ... you utter, 'Ah, what bliss! Ah, what bliss!'?"

"Yes, revered sir."

"But, Bhaddiya, what do you see that prompts you to do so?"

"Formerly, revered sir, when I was a householder and enjoyed the bliss of royalty, inside and outside my inner apartments guards were appointed; inside and outside the city guards were appointed; inside and outside the district guards were appointed. But, revered sir, although I was thus guarded and protected, I lived fearful, agitated, distrustful, and afraid. But now, revered sir, on going alone into the forest, to the foot of a tree or to an empty place, I am fearless, unagitated, confident, and unafraid. I live unconcerned, unruffled, my needs satisfied, with a mind become like a deer's.[13] Seeing this, revered sir, prompts me, on going to the forest ... to utter constantly, 'Ah, what bliss! Ah, what bliss!'"

Then, on realizing its significance, the Lord uttered on that occasion this inspired utterance:

In whom exist no inner stirrings,
Having passed beyond being this or that,
Free from fear, blissful and sorrowless,
The devas are not capable of seeing him. [14]

CHAPTER 3

NANDA
(Nandavagga)

3.1 Former Action *(Kamma Sutta)*

Thus have I heard. At one time the Lord was staying near Sāvatthī in the Jeta Wood at Anāthapiṇḍika's monastery. On that occasion a certain bhikkhu was sitting cross-legged not far from the Lord, holding his body erect, mindful and clearly comprehending, enduring without complaint feelings that were painful, acute, sharp and severe, the ripening of former action.

The Lord saw that bhikkhu sitting cross-legged not far away ... enduring without complaint feelings that were painful, acute, sharp and severe, the ripening of former action.

Then, on realizing its significance, the Lord uttered on that occasion this inspired utterance:

A bhikkhu who has left behind all action,
Shaking off the dust of former deeds.
The stable one, unselfish, steady,
Has no need to address people. [1]

3.2 Nanda *(Nanda Sutta)*

Thus have I heard. At one time the Lord was staying near Sāvatthī in the Jeta Wood at Anāthapiṇḍika's monastery. On that occasion the Venerable Nanda, the Lord's (half-) brother,[2] the son of his maternal aunt, informed a number of bhikkhus thus: "I am discontented with leading the holy life, friends. I am unable to endure the holy life. I will give up the training and return to the low life." [3]

Then a certain bhikkhu approached the Lord, prostrated himself, sat down to one side, and said: "The Venerable Nanda, revered sir, the Lord's (half-) brother, the son of his maternal aunt, informed a number of bhikkhus thus: 'I am discontented with leading the holy life.... I will give up the training and return to the low life.'"

Then the Lord addressed a certain bhikkhu: "Come, bhikkhu, in my name tell the bhikkhu Nanda, 'The Teacher calls you, friend Nanda.'"

"Very well, revered sir," that bhikkhu replied, and approaching the Venerable Nanda, he said, "The Teacher calls you, friend Nanda."

"Very well friend," the Venerable Nanda replied, and approaching the Lord he prostrated himself and sat down to one side. The Lord then said to him: "Is it true, Nanda, that you informed a number of bhikkhus thus: 'I am discontented with leading the holy life ... I will return to the low life'?"

"Yes, revered sir."

"But why, Nanda, are you discontented with leading the holy life?"

"On departing from home, revered sir, a Sakyan girl, the loveliest in the land, with her hair half-combed, looked up at me and said, 'May you return soon, master.'[4] Recollecting that, revered sir, I am discontented with leading the holy life.... I am unable to endure the holy life. I will give up the training and return to the low life."

Then the Lord took the Venerable Nanda by the arm, and just as a strong man might extend his flexed arm or flex his extended arm, even so did they vanish from the Jeta Wood and appear among the devas of the Tāvatiṃsa heaven. Now, on that occasion about five hundred pink-footed nymphs had come to minister to Sakka, ruler of the devas. And the Lord said to the Venerable Nanda, "Do you see those five hundred pink-footed nymphs?"

"Yes, revered sir."

"What do you think, Nanda, who is more beautiful, more fair to behold, and more alluring—that Sakyan girl, the loveliest in the land, or these five hundred pink-footed nymphs?"

"Revered sir, compared to these five hundred pink-footed nymphs, that Sakyan girl, the loveliest in the land, is like a mutilated[5] she-monkey that has had its ears and nose chopped off. She does not count; she is not worth a fraction compared to them; there is no comparison. These five hundred nymphs are far more beautiful, more fair to behold, and more alluring."

"Rejoice, Nanda, rejoice, Nanda! I guarantee that you will obtain five hundred pink-footed nymphs."

"If, revered sir, the Lord guarantees that I will obtain five hundred pink-footed nymphs, I shall be content in living the holy life under the Lord."

Then the Lord took the Venerable Nanda by the arm ... even so did they vanish from among the devas of the Tāvatiṃsa heaven and appear in the Jeta Wood.

The bhikkhus heard: "It is said that the Venerable Nanda, the Lord's (half-) brother, the son of his maternal aunt, is living the holy life for the sake of nymphs. It is said that the Lord has guaranteed that he will obtain five hundred pink-footed nymphs."

Then the bhikkhu-friends of the Venerable Nanda went about calling him "hireling" and "menial," saying: "The Venerable Nanda is a hireling! The Venerable Nanda is a menial! He is living the holy life for the sake of nymphs! It is said that the Lord has guaranteed that he will obtain five hundred pink-footed nymphs!"

Then the Venerable Nanda was humiliated, ashamed, and dismayed by his friends calling him "hireling" and "menial." Living alone, secluded, diligent, ardent, and resolute, he soon realized even here and now through his own direct knowledge that unequalled goal of the holy life for the sake of which sons of good family rightly go forth from home to the homeless state, and entering into it he abode in it. And he knew: "Finished is birth, lived is the holy life, done is what had to be done, there is no more of this state." And the Venerable Nanda became one of the arahats.

Then, when the night was far advanced, a certain devatā of surpassing beauty, illuminating the whole Jeta Wood, approached the Lord, prostrated himself and stood to one side. Standing there that devatā said to the Lord: "The Venerable Nanda, revered sir, the Lord's (half-) brother, the son of his maternal aunt, by the ending of the taints has realized here and now through his own direct knowledge the taintless mind-deliverance and wisdom-deliverance, and entering into it, he abides in it."

The knowledge also arose in the Lord: "Nanda, by the ending of the taints, has realized here and now the taintless mind-deliverance and wisdom-deliverance, and entering into it, he abides in it."

When that night had ended the Venerable Nanda approached the Lord, prostrated himself, sat down to one side, and said to the Lord: "Revered sir, as to the Lord's guarantee that I will obtain five hundred pink-footed nymphs, I release the Lord from that promise."

"But, Nanda, comprehending your mind with my mind, I knew: 'Nanda has realized here and now the taintless mind-deliverance and wisdom-deliverance.' Also, a devatā told me: 'The Venerable Nanda, revered sir, has realized here and now the taintless mind-deliverance and wisdom-deliverance.' When, Nanda, your mind was released from the taints without grasping, I was then released from that promise."

Then, on realizing its significance, the Lord uttered on that occasion this inspired utterance:

That bhikkhu who has crossed the mire,
Crushed the thorn of sensual desire,
And reached the destruction of delusion
Is not perturbed by pleasures and pains.

3.3 Yasoja *(Yasoja Sutta)*

Thus have I heard. At one time the Lord was staying near Sāvatthī in the Jeta Wood at Anāthapiṇḍika's monastery. On that occasion about five hundred bhikkhus headed by Yasoja had arrived at Sāvatthī to see the Lord. As these incoming bhikkhus were exchanging greetings with the resident bhikkhus and lodgings were being arranged and bowls and robes put away, there was a loud noise, a great noise. Then the Lord addressed the Venerable Ānanda, "Ānanda, what is that loud noise, that great noise? It sounds like fishermen landing a catch of fish."

"About five hundred bhikkhus headed by Yasoja, revered sir, have arrived at Sāvatthī to see the Lord. And as these incoming bhikkhus were exchanging greetings ... there was a loud noise, a great noise."

"Well then, Ānanda, in my name tell those bhikkhus, 'The Teacher calls the venerable ones.'"

"Yes, revered sir," the Venerable Ānanda replied, and approaching those bhikkhus he said, "The Teacher calls the venerable ones."

"Very well, friend," those bhikkhus replied to the Venerable Ānanda, and approaching the Lord they prostrated themselves and sat down to one side. The Lord then said to those bhikkhus: "Bhikkhus, why was there that loud noise, that great noise, which sounded like fishermen landing a catch of fish?"

The Venerable Yasoja replied: "These five hundred bhikkhus, revered sir, have arrived at Sāvatthī to see the Lord. As these incoming bhikkhus were exchanging greetings ... there was a loud noise, a great noise."

"Go away, bhikkhus. I dismiss you. You ought not to stay near me."

"Very well, revered sir," those bhikkhus replied to the Lord. Then, rising from their seats, they prostrated themselves before the Lord keeping their right side toward him. Having set their lodgings in order and taking their bowls and robes, they departed on tour for the Vajjī territory. Walking on tour by stages among the Vajjīs, they approached the river Vaggumudā. And beside the river Vaggamudā they constructed leaf-huts and commenced the rains retreat.[6]

Then the Venerable Yasoja addressed those bhikkhus who were commencing the rains retreat: "Friends, the Lord dismissed us out of compassion, wishing our good, wishing to benefit us, being compassionate. Come, friends, let us so abide that the Lord will be pleased with our way of living."

"Very well, friend," those bhikkhus replied to the Venerable Yasoja. And living secluded, diligent, ardent, and resolute, those bhikkhus within that very rains retreat all realized the three knowledges.[7]

Then the Lord, having stayed at Sāvatthī as long as he wanted, departed on tour for Vesālī. Walking on tour by stages, the Lord arrived at Vesālī and stayed there near Vesālī in the Great Wood in the Hall of the Gabled House. Then the Lord, comprehending the minds of those bhikkhus beside the river Vaggumudā with his mind and having given consideration to it, addressed the Venerable Ānanda: "This direction, Ānanda, seems to me as if it has become light. This direction, Ānanda, seems to me as if it has become radiant. It is agreeable for me to go and consider that direction where those bhikkhus are staying beside the river Vaggumudā. Ānanda, you should send a messenger to the bhikkhus beside the river Vaggumudā to say: 'The Teacher calls the venerable ones; the Teacher wishes to see the venerable ones.'"

"Very well, revered sir," the Venerable Ānanda replied to the Lord. Approaching a certain bhikkhu, he said to him: "Come, friend, go to the bhikkhus beside the river Vaggumudā and tell them, 'The Teacher calls the venerable ones; the Teacher wishes to see the venerable ones.'"

"Very well, friend," that bhikkhu replied to the Venerable Ānanda. Then, just as a strong man might extend his flexed arm or flex his extended arm, even so did he vanish from the Hall of the Gabled House in the Great Wood and appear before those bhikkhus beside the river Vaggumudā. He said to them, "The Teacher calls the venerable ones; the Teacher wishes to see the venerable ones."

"Very well, friend," those bhikkhus replied. Then, having set their lodgings in order and taking their bowls and robes, just as a strong man might extend his flexed arm ... even so did they vanish from beside the river Vaggumudā and appear before the Lord in the Great Wood in the Hall of the Gabled House. At that time the Lord was sitting in imperturbable concentration.[8] Then those bhikkhus thought, "Iṇ what state is the Lord now abiding?"

Then those bhikkhus thought, "The Lord is abiding in the state of imperturbability," and they too all sat in imperturbable concentration.

Then, when the night was far advanced and the first watch had ended, the Venerable Ānanda arose from his seat, arranged his robe over one shoulder, raised his folded hands, and said to the Lord: "The night is far advanced, revered sir, the first watch has ended and the incoming bhikkhus have been sitting for a long time. Revered sir, let the Lord greet the incoming bhikkhus."

When this was said the Lord remained silent. When the night was (still further) advanced and the middle watch had ended, a second time the Venerable Ānanda arose from his seat ... and said to the Lord: "The night is far advanced, revered sir, the middle watch has ended and the incoming bhikkhus have been sitting for a long time. Revered sir, let the Lord greet the incoming bhikkhus."

For a second time the Lord remained silent. When the night was (yet further) advanced and the last watch had ended, when dawn was approaching and the night was drawing to a close, a third time the Venerable Ānanda arose from his seat ... and said to the Lord: "The night is far advanced, revered sir, the last watch has ended, dawn is approaching and the night is drawing to a close. The incoming bhikkhus have been sitting for a long time. Revered sir, let the Lord greet the incoming bhikkhus."

Then the Lord emerged from that concentration and addressed the Venerable Ānanda: "If you knew, Ānanda, you would not speak in such a way. These five hundred bhikkhus and I, Ānanda, have all been sitting in imperturbable concentration."

Then, on realizing its significance, the Lord uttered on that occasion this inspired utterance:

Who has mastered the thorn of sensual desire,
Abuse, punishment, imprisonment,
That bhikkhu stands steady as a mountain,
Desireless, not perturbed by pleasures and pains.

3.4 Sāriputta *(Sāriputta Sutta)*

Thus have I heard. At one time the Lord was staying near Sāvatthī in the Jeta Wood at Anāthapiṇḍika's monastery. On that occasion the Venerable Sāriputta was sitting cross-legged not far from the Lord, holding his body erect, having set up mindfulness before him.

The Lord saw the Venerable Sāriputta sitting cross-legged not far away, holding his body erect, having set up mindfulness before him.

Then, on realizing its significance, the Lord uttered on that occasion this inspired utterance:

Just as a mountain made of solid rock
Stands firm and unshakeable,
Even so, when delusion is destroyed,
A bhikkhu, like a mountain, is not perturbed.

3.5 Mahāmoggallāna *(Mahāmoggallāna Sutta)*

Thus have I heard. At one time the Lord was staying near Sāvatthī in the Jeta Wood at Anāthapiṇḍika's monastery. On that occasion the Venerable Mahāmoggallāna was sitting cross-legged not far from the Lord, holding his body erect, having mindfulness with regard to the body well established within him.

The Lord saw the Venerable Mahāmoggallāna sitting cross-legged not far away, holding his body erect, having mindfulness with regard to the body well established within him.

Then, on realizing its significance, the Lord uttered on that occasion this inspired utterance:

With mindfulness of the body established,
Controlled over contact's sixfold base,
A bhikkhu who is always concentrated
Can know Nibbāna for himself.

3.6 Pilindavaccha *(Pilindavaccha Sutta)*

Thus have I heard. At one time the Lord was staying near Rājagaha in the Bamboo Wood at the Squirrels' Feeding Place. On that occasion the Venerable Pilindavaccha went about calling the bhikkhus outcasts. Now, a number of bhikkhus approached the Lord, prostrated themselves, sat down to one side, and told him: "Revered sir, the Venerable Pilindavaccha is going about calling the bhikkhus outcasts."

Then the Lord addressed a certain bhikkhu saying, "Come, bhikkhu, in my name tell the bhikkhu Pilindavaccha, 'The Teacher calls you, friend Pilindavaccha.'"

"Very well, revered sir," that bhikkhu replied to the Lord, and approaching the Venerable Pilindavaccha he said, "The Teacher calls you, friend."

"Very well, friend," the Venerable Pilindavaccha replied, and approaching the Lord he prostrated himself and sat down to one side. The Lord then said to the Venerable Pilindavaccha: "Is it true, Vaccha, that you go about calling the bhikkhus outcasts?"

"Yes, revered sir."

Then the Lord, on giving consideration to Pilindavaccha's former lives, addressed the bhikkhus: "Do not be irritated, bhikkhus, with the bhikkhu Vaccha. It is not with inner hatred that Vaccha goes about calling the bhikkhus outcasts. For five hundred births without interruption the bhikkhu Vaccha has been born in the brahmin caste, and thus for a long time he has been habituated to calling others outcasts. It is because of this that Vaccha goes about calling the bhikkhus outcasts."[9]

Then, on realizing its significance, the Lord uttered on that occasion this inspired utterance:

In whom there is neither fraud nor conceit,
Who is without greed, unselfish, desireless,
With anger quelled, his mind quenched—
He is a brahmin, he is a recluse, he is a bhikkhu.

3.7 Kassapa *(Kassapa Sutta)*

Thus have I heard. At one time the Lord was staying near Rājagaha in the Bamboo Wood at the Squirrels' Feeding Place. On that occasion the Venerable Mahākassapa was staying in the Pipphali Cave, sitting cross-legged for seven days having attained a certain (state of) concentration. Then at the end of those seven days the Venerable Mahākassapa emerged from that concentration. After emerging the Venerable Mahākassapa thought: "What if I should enter Rājagaha for almsfood?" [10]

At that time five hundred devatās were busily preparing almsfood for the Venerable Mahākassapa, but having refused the offerings of those five hundred devatās the Venerable Mahākassapa robed himself in the forenoon, and taking his bowl and outer cloak, entered Rājagaha for almsfood.

On that occasion Sakka the ruler of the devas, wishing to give almsfood to the Venerable Mahākassapa, assumed the appearance of a weaver weaving at a loom, while Sujā the asura-maiden filled the shuttle. Now, the Venerable Mahākasapa, walking for almsfood in Rājagaha on an uninterrupted alms round,[11] came to the dwelling of Sakka the ruler of the devas. Seeing the Venerable Mahākassapa coming from afar, Sakka the ruler of the devas came out of the house and went to meet him. Taking the bowl from his hand and going into the house, he took boiled rice from a pot, filled the bowl, and gave it to the Venerable Mahākassapa. And this almsfood included various kinds of curry, various kinds of sauce, curry of various kinds of (excellent) tastes and flavours.

Then the Venerable Mahākassapa thought: "Who is this being who has such supernormal potency and power?"

Then the Venerable Mahākassapa thought: "Is it not Sakka the ruler of the devas?" Realizing it was, he said: "This is your doing, Kosiya;[12] do not do such a thing again."

"We too need merit, revered Kassapa. We too should make merit."

Then Sakka the ruler of the devas, having prostrated himself to the Venerable Mahākassapa, keeping his right side towards him, rose into the sky. While suspended in the sky, three times he uttered this inspired utterance: "Ah, the best almsgiving! On Kassapa alms is well donated!"

The Lord, with divine hearing purified and surpassing that of humans, heard Sakka the ruler of the devas suspended in the sky uttering three times this inspired utterance.

Then, on realizing its significance, the Lord uttered on that occasion this inspired utterance:

The devas hold dear such a bhikkhu
Who collects his food on alms round,
Self-sufficient, supporting no other,
Who is calm and ever mindful.

3.8 The Almsfood Collector *(Piṇḍapātika Sutta)*

Thus have I heard. At one time the Lord was staying near Rājagaha in the Jeta Wood at Anāthapiṇḍika's monastery. On that occasion after the meal, on returning from collecting almsfood, a number of bhikkhus had gathered together in the kareri-tree pavilion when this topic of conversation arose: "An almsfood-collecting bhikkhu, friends, while walking for almsfood, from time to time gets to see agreeable forms with the eye, from time to time gets to hear agreeable sounds with the ear, from time to time gets to smell agreeable odours with the nose, from time to time gets to taste agreeable flavours with the tongue, from time to time gets to touch agreeable tangible objects with the body. An almsfood-collecting bhikkhu, friends, when he walks for almsfood, is respected, revered, honoured, venerated, and given homage. Come, friends, let us all be almsfood-collectors, and we too from time to time will get to see agreeable forms with the eye ... to touch agreeable tangible objects with the body. And we too will be respected, revered, honoured, venerated, and given homage when we walk for almsfood." And this conversation of those bhikkhus continued without coming to an end.

Then the Lord, emerging from seclusion in the evening, went to the kareri-tree pavilion and sat down on the seat prepared for him. Sitting there, the Lord asked the bhikkhus: "What were you talking about just now, bhikkhus, while gathered here together? What was the topic of discussion that you had left unfinished?"

"After the meal, revered sir, on returning from collecting almsfood, we had gathered here in the kareri-tree pavilion when this topic of conversation arose: 'An almsfood-collecting bhikkhu, friends, while walking for almsfood, from time to time gets to see agreeable forms with the eye ... to touch agreeable tangible objects with the body. And we too will be respected ... when we walk for almsfood.' This, revered sir, was our discussion that was left unfinished when the Lord arrived."

"It is not right, bhikkhus, that you sons of good family who have gone forth out of faith from home to the homeless state should talk on such a topic. When you have gathered together, bhikkhus, you should do one of two things: either engage in talk on Dhamma or maintain noble silence."[13]

Then, on realizing its significance, the Lord uttered on that occasion this inspired utterance:

The devas hold dear such a bhikkhu
Who collects his food on alms round,
Self-sufficient, supporting no other,
But not if he is intent on praise and fame.

3.9 A Craft *(Sippa Sutta)*

Thus have I heard. At one time the Lord was staying near Sāvatthī in the Jeta Wood at Anāthapiṇḍika's monastery. On that occasion ... a number of bhikkhus had gathered together in the kareri-tree pavilion when this topic of conversation arose: "Who, friend, knows a craft? Who is trained in what craft? Which craft is the chief of crafts?" Herein, some said, "Elephant-craft is the chief of crafts"; some said, "Horsemanship is the chief of crafts"; some said, "Chariot-craft ... Archery ... Swordsmanship ... Communicating by gestures[14] ... Accountancy ... Mathematics ... The art of writing ... The art of poetry ... The art of debate[15] ... Political science[16] is the chief of crafts." And this conversation of those bhikkhus continued without coming to an end.

Then the Lord, emerging from seclusion in the evening, went to the kareri-tree pavilion... "It is not right, bhikkhus, that you should talk on such a topic. When you have gathered together, bhikkhus, you should do one of two things: either engage in talk on Dhamma or maintain noble silence."

Then, on realizing its significance, the Lord uttered on that occasion this inspired utterance:

Who lives by no craft, unburdened, desiring the goal,
With restrained faculties, wholly released,
Wandering homeless, unselfish, desireless,
Conceit abandoned, solitary—he is a bhikkhu.

3.10 Examining the World *(Lokavolokana Sutta)*

Thus have I heard. At one time the Lord was staying at Uruvelā, beside the river Nerañjarā at the foot of the Bodhi Tree, having just realized full enlightenment. At that time the Lord sat cross-legged for seven days experiencing the bliss of liberation. Then, at the end of those seven days, the Lord emerged from that concentration and examined the world with the Buddha-eye. While examining the world with the Buddha-eye, the Lord saw beings tormented by various torments and consumed by various feverish longings born of passion, hate, and delusion.[17]

Then, on realizing its significance, the Lord uttered on that occasion this inspired utterance:

This world is subject to torment;
Afflicted by contact, it calls a disease "self":
For however it is conceived
It is ever otherwise than that. [18]

Becoming something other,
The world is held by being,
Is afflicted by being yet delights in being.

But what it delights in brings fear,
And what it fears is suffering.
Now this holy life is lived
In order to abandon being.

Whatever recluses and brahmins have said that freedom from being comes about through some kind of being, none of them, I say, are freed from being. And whatever recluses and brahmins have said that escape from being comes about through non-being, none of them, I say, have escaped from being.[19] *This suffering arises dependent upon clinging. With the ending of all grasping, no suffering is produced.* [20]

Look at the people in the world, afflicted by ignorance,
Come into being, delighting in being, not freed.
Whatever forms of being exist, in any way, anywhere,
All these forms of being are impermanent,
Subject to suffering, of a nature to change.

On seeing this as it actually is with perfect wisdom
The craving for being is abandoned,
Yet one does not delight in non-being.
Nibbāna is total dispassion and cessation
(Attained) with the complete destruction of cravings.

A bhikkhu whose cravings are extinguished
By not grasping has no renewal of being.
Māra is vanquished, the battle is won:
The stable one has passed beyond all forms of being. [21]

CHAPTER 4

MEGHIYA
(Meghiyavagga)

4.1 Meghiya *(Meghiya Sutta)*

Thus have I heard. At one time the Lord was staying at Cālikā on Cālikā Hill. At that time the Venerable Meghiya was the Lord's attendant.[1] Then the Venerable Meghiya approached the Lord, prostrated himself, stood to one side, and said: "I wish to go into Jantu village for almsfood, revered sir."

"Do now, Meghiya, what you think it is time to do."

Then the Venerable Meghiya, having put on his robe in the forenoon and taken his bowl and outer cloak, entered Jantu village for almsfood. Having walked in Jantu village for almsfood, after the meal, on returning from collecting almsfood, he approached the bank of the river Kimikālā. As he was walking and wandering up and down beside the river for exercise, he saw a pleasant and charming mango grove. On seeing it he thought: "This mango grove is very pleasant and charming. It is eminently suitable for the endeavour (in meditation) of a young man of good family who is intent on the endeavour. If the Lord were to give me permission, I would come and endeavour in this mango grove."

Then the Venerable Meghiya approached the Lord, prostrated himself, sat down to one side, and said: "Revered sir, having put on my robe in the forenoon … I approached the bank of the river Kimikālā and saw a pleasant and charming mango grove. On seeing it I thought: 'This mango grove is very pleasant and charming. It is eminently suitable for the endeavour (in meditation) of a young man of good family who is intent on the endeavour. If the Lord were to give me permission, I would come and endeavour in this mango grove.' If, revered sir, the Lord gives me permission, I would go to that mango grove to endeavour (in meditation)."

When this was said the Lord replied to the Venerable Meghiya: "As we are alone, Meghiya, wait a while until some other bhikkhu comes."

A second time the Venerable Meghiya said to the Lord: "Revered sir, the Lord has nothing further that should be done and nothing to add to what has been done. But for me, revered sir, there is something further that should be done and something to add to what has been done. If, revered sir, the Lord gives me permission, I would go to that mango grove to endeavour (in meditation)."

A second time the Lord replied to the Venerable Meghiya: "As we are alone, Meghiya, wait a while until some other bhikkhu comes."

A third time the Venerable Meghiya said to the Lord: "Revered sir, the Lord has nothing further that should be done ... I would go to that mango grove to endeavour (in meditation)."

"As you are talking of endeavouring, Meghiya, what can I say? Do now, Meghiya, what you think it is time to do."

Then the Venerable Meghiya rose from his seat, prostrated himself before the Lord, and keeping his right side towards him, went to that mango grove. On entering that mango grove he sat down at the foot of a certain tree for the rest period during the middle of the day.

Now, while the Venerable Meghiya was staying in that mango grove, there kept occurring to him three bad, unwholesome kinds of thoughts: sensual thought, malevolent thought, and cruel thought. The Venerable Meghiya then reflected: "It is indeed strange! It is indeed remarkable! Although I have gone forth out of faith from home to the homeless state, yet I am overwhelmed by these three bad, unwholesome kinds of thoughts: sensual thought, malevolent thought, and cruel thought."[2]

Then the Venerable Meghiya, on emerging from seclusion in the late afternoon, approached the Lord, prostrated himself, sat down to one side, and said: "Revered sir, while I was staying in that mango grove there kept occurring to me three bad, unwholesome kinds of thoughts ... and I thought: 'It is indeed strange!... I am overwhelmed by these three bad, unwholesome kinds of thoughts: sensual thought, malevolent thought, and cruel thought.'"

"When mind-deliverance is as yet immature, Meghiya, five things lead to its maturity. What five?

"Here, Meghiya, a bhikkhu has good friends, good associates, good companions. When mind-deliverance is as yet immature, Meghiya, this is the first thing that leads to its maturity.

"Furthermore, Meghiya, a bhikkhu is virtuous, he lives restrained by the restraint of the Pātimokkha,[3] endowed with conduct and resort; seeing danger in the smallest faults, he trains in the training rules he has accepted. When mind-deliverance is as yet immature, Meghiya, this is the second thing that leads to its maturity.

"Furthermore, Meghiya, a bhikkhu obtains at will, with no trouble or difficulty, talk that is effacing, a help in opening up the mind, and which conduces to complete turning away, dispassion, cessation, peace, direct knowledge, enlightenment, and Nibbāna—that is, talk about fewness of wishes, talk about contentment, talk about seclusion, talk about being non-gregarious, talk about putting forth energy, talk about virtue, talk about concentration, talk about wisdom, talk about deliverance, talk about the knowledge and vision of deliverance. When mind-deliverance is as yet immature, Meghiya, this is the third thing that leads to its maturity.

"Furthermore, Meghiya, a bhikkhu lives with energy instigated for the abandoning of unwholesome states and the acquiring of wholesome states; he is vigorous, energetic, and persevering with regard to wholesome states. When mind-deliverance is as yet immature, Meghiya, this is the fourth thing that leads to its maturity.

"Furthermore, Meghiya, a bhikkhu is wise, endowed with the noble ones' penetrative understanding of rise and disappearance leading to the complete ending of suffering. When mind-deliverance is as yet immature, Meghiya, this is the fifth thing that leads to its maturity. When mind-deliverance is as yet immature, Meghiya, these five things lead to its maturity.

"It is to be expected of a bhikkhu who has good friends, good associates, good companions, that he will be virtuous, that he will live restrained by the restraint of the Pātimokkha, endowed with conduct and resort, and that seeing danger in the smallest faults, he will train in the training rules he has accepted. It is to be expected of a bhikkhu who has good friends ... that he will obtain at will, with no trouble or difficulty, talk that is effacing, a help in opening up the mind ... talk about the knowledge and vision of deliverance. It is to be expected of a bhikkhu who has good friends ... that he will live with energy instigated ... vigorous, energetic, and persevering with regard to wholesome states. It is to be expected of a bhikkhu who has good friends ... that he will be wise, endowed with the noble ones' penetrative understanding of rise and disappearance leading to the complete ending of suffering.

"A bhikkhu, Meghiya, who is established in these five things should also cultivate four additional things: foulness[4] should be cultivated for overcoming lust; lovingkindness should be cultivated for overcoming malevolence; respiration-mindfulness should be cultivated for cutting off (discursive) thinking; the perception of impermanence should be cultivated for the removal of the conceit 'I am.' For when one perceives impermanence, Meghiya, the perception of not-self is established. When one perceives not-self one reaches the removal of the conceit 'I am,' which is called Nibbāna here and now."

Then, on realizing its significance, the Lord uttered on that occasion this inspired utterance:

Trivial thoughts, subtle thoughts,
Mental jerkings that follow one along:
Not understanding these mental thoughts,
One runs back and forth with wandering mind.

But having known these mental thoughts,
The ardent and mindful one restrains them.
An awakened one has entirely abandoned them,
These mental jerkings that follow one along.

4.2 The Turbulent Ones *(Uddhata Sutta)*

Thus have I heard. At one time the Lord was staying near Kusinārā at Upavattana in the sal-tree grove of the Mallas.

On that occasion a number of bhikkhus were living in forest huts not far from the Lord, and they were turbulent, arrogant, frivolous, garrulous, of loose talk, unmindful, uncomprehending, unconcentrated, with wandering minds and uncontrolled faculties.

The Lord saw those bhikkhus living nearby in forest huts … with wandering minds and uncontrolled faculties.

Then, on realizing its significance, the Lord uttered on that occasion this inspired utterance:

With an unguarded body [5]
And encumbered by wrong view,
Overcome by lethargy and torpor,
One goes along in the power of Māra.

So one should be guarded in mind,
One should make right thought one's domain.
When he has put right view to the forefront
And understood rise and fall,
A bhikkhu who overcomes lethargy and torpor
Will forsake all bad destinations. [6]

4.3 The Cowherd (*Gopāla Sutta*)

Thus have I heard. At one time the Lord was journeying among the people of Kosala together with a large Order of bhikkhus. Then the Lord stepped off the road, and going up to the foot of a tree, he sat down on a seat prepared for him. A certain cowherd approached the Lord, prostrated himself, and sat down to one side. The Lord then instructed, roused, inspired, and gladdened that cowherd with a talk on Dhamma. And that cowherd, being instructed, roused, inspired, and gladdened by the Lord's talk on Dhamma, said to the Lord: "Please consent, revered sir, to my providing a meal tomorrow for the Lord together with the Order of bhikkhus."

The Lord consented by remaining silent. Then, on seeing that the Lord had consented, the cowherd arose from his seat, prostrated himself before the Lord, and keeping his right side toward him, went away. When the night had ended the cowherd prepared in his own dwelling a large quantity of thick rice-gruel boiled in milk and (a quantity) of fresh ghee, and announced to the Lord the time (for the meal, saying), "It is time, revered sir, the meal is ready."

Then the Lord, putting on his robe in the forenoon and taking his bowl and outer cloak, together with the Order of bhikkhus went to the dwelling of that cowherd. On arriving he sat down on the seat prepared for him. Then the cowherd, with his own hand, served and satisfied the Order of bhikkhus headed by the Buddha with the thick rice-gruel and fresh ghee. When the Lord had eaten and removed his hand from the bowl, the cowherd chose a low seat and sat down to one side. The Lord then instructed, roused, inspired, and gladdened that cowherd with a talk on Dhamma, and then arose from his seat and departed.

Now, not long after the Lord had departed a certain man murdered that cowherd along the village boundary.

Then a number of bhikkhus approached the Lord, prostrated themselves, sat down to one side, and said: "Revered sir, that cowherd who today with his own hand served and satisfied the Order of bhikkhus headed by the Buddha with thick rice-gruel and fresh ghee, has been murdered, it is said, by a certain man along the village boundary."

Then, on realizing its significance, the Lord uttered on that occasion this inspired utterance:

Whatever an enemy might do to an enemy,
Or a hater to those he hates,
A wrongly directed mind
Can do even greater harm than that.

4.4 The Moonlit Night *(Juṇha Sutta)*

Thus have I heard. At one time the Lord was staying near Rājagaha in the Bamboo Wood at the Squirrels' Feeding Place. On that occasion the Venerable Sāriputta and the Venerable Mahāmoggallāna were staying in the Pigeons' Glen. It happened that the Venerable Sāriputta, on a moonlit night, was seated in the open air with his head newly shaved and had attained a certain (stage of) concentration.[7]

At that moment two yakkhas who were companions were going from north to south on some business or other when they saw the Venerable Sāriputta, on the moonlit night, seated in the open air with his head newly shaved. On seeing him one yakkha said to the other: "The idea has occurred to me, friend, to give this recluse a blow on the head."

When he said this the other yakkha said: "Take care, friend! Do not strike the recluse! He is a mighty recluse, friend, of great supernormal potency and power."

A second time and a third the first yakkha said to the other: "The idea has occurred to me, friend, to give this recluse a blow on the head."

And a second time and a third time the other yakkha said: "Take care, friend! Do not strike the recluse! He is a mighty recluse, friend, of great supernormal potency and power."

Then the first yakkha, not heeding (the warning of) the other yakkha, gave the Venerable Sāriputta a blow on the head. And so great was the blow that it might have felled an elephant seven or seven-and-a-half cubits high, or split a great mountain peak. Thereupon that yakkha, crying out, "I am burning! I am burning!" instantly fell into the great hell. The Venerable Mahāmoggallāna, with divine vision purified and surpassing that of humans, saw that yakkha giving the Venerable Sāriputta a blow on the head. On seeing this he approached the Venerable Sāriputta and said: "Are you well, friend? Are you bearing up? Have you any pain?"

"I am well, friend Moggallāna. I am bearing up, friend Moggallāna, although I do have a slight headache."

"It is wonderful, friend Sāriputta! It is marvellous, friend Sāriputta! How great is the supernormal potency and power of the Venerable Sāriputta! Just now, friend Sāriputta, a certain yakkha gave you a blow on the head. And so great was the blow it might have felled an elephant seven or seven-and-a-half cubits high or split a great mountain peak. And yet the Venerable Sāriputta just says, 'I am well, friend Moggallāna. I am bearing up, friend Moggallāna, although I do have a slight headache.'"

"It is wonderful, friend Moggallāna! It is marvellous, friend Moggallāna! How great is the supernormal potency and power of the Venerable Mahāmoggallāna in that he can actually see a yakkha. Now, we could not even see a mud sprite."[8]

The Lord, with divine hearing purified and surpassing that of humans, heard this conversation of these two great perfected ones.

Then, on realizing its significance, the Lord uttered on that occasion this inspired utterance:

Whose mind stands like a mountain,
Steady, it is not perturbed,
Unattached to things that arouse attachment,
Unangered by things that provoke anger.
When his mind is cultivated thus
How can suffering come to him?

4.5 The Bull Elephant *(Nāga Sutta)*

Thus have I heard. At one time the Lord was staying near Kosambī at the Ghosita monastery. At that time the Lord was living hemmed in by bhikkhus and bhikkhunīs, by male and female lay followers, by kings and royal ministers, by sectarian teachers and their disciples, and he lived in discomfort and not at ease.[9] Then the Lord thought: "At present I am living hemmed in by bhikkhus and bhikkhunis ... by sectarian teachers and their disciples, and I live in discomfort and not at ease. Suppose I were to live alone, secluded from the crowd?"

Then the Lord, having put on his robe in the forenoon and taken his bowl and outer cloak, entered Kosambī for almsfood. Having walked for almsfood in Kosambī and returned after the meal, he set his lodging in order by himself, took his bowl and cloak, and without informing his attendant or taking leave of the Order of bhikkhus, he set off alone, without a companion, for Pārileyyaka. Walking on tour by stages, he arrived at Pārileyyaka and stayed near Pārileyyaka in a protected forest at the foot of an auspicious sal-tree.

Now, a certain bull elephant was living hemmed in by elephants and she-elephants, by elephant calves and sucklings; he ate grass with the tips pulled off and they ate the branches he had broken down. He drank muddied water and on going down and coming out of the water he was jostled by she-elephants; and he lived in discomfort and not at ease. Then that bull elephant thought: "At present I am living hemmed in by elephants and she-elephants, by elephant calves and sucklings; I eat grass with the tips pulled off and they eat the branches which I break down. I drink muddied water and on going down and coming out of the water I am jostled by she-elephants; and I live in discomfort and not at ease. Suppose I were to live alone, secluded from the crowd?"

So that bull elephant left the herd and went to Pārileyyaka, to the protected forest, and approached the Lord at the foot of the auspicious sal-tree. On reaching the place where the Lord was staying that bull elephant kept the place free of grass and brought water with his trunk for the Lord's use.

Then, while the Lord was in solitude and seclusion, this thought arose in his mind: "Formerly I was living hemmed in by bhikkhus and bhikkhunīs ... and I was living in discomfort and not at ease. But now I live not hemmed in by bhikkhus and bhikkhunīs ... in comfort and at ease." And also this thought arose in that bull elephant's mind: "Formerly I was living hemmed in by elephants and she-elephants ... and I was living in discomfort and not at ease, but now I live not hemmed in by elephants and she-elephants ... I eat unbroken grass and (others) do not eat the branches which I break down. I drink clear water and on going down and coming out of the water I am not jostled by she-elephants, and I live in comfort and at ease."

Then the Lord, on observing his own solitude, understood with his mind the thought in the mind of that bull elephant, and uttered on that occasion this inspired utterance:

This unites mind with mind,
The perfected one and the bull elephant [10]
With tusks as long as chariot-poles:
That each delights in being alone in the forest.

4.6 Piṇḍola *(Piṇḍola Sutta)*

Thus have I heard. At one time the Lord was staying near Sāvatthī in the Jeta Wood at Anāthapiṇḍika's monastery. On that occasion the Venerable Piṇḍola Bhāradvāja was sitting cross-legged not far from the Lord, holding his body erect—a forest-dweller, an almsfood-collector, a rag-robe-wearer, a three-robe-wearer, one of few wishes, contented, secluded, solitary, energetic, an ascetic, devoted to the higher mind.[11]

The Lord saw the Venerable Piṇḍola Bhāradvāja sitting cross-legged not far away ... devoted to the higher mind.

Then, on realizing its significance, the Lord uttered on that occasion this inspired utterance:

Not insulting, not injuring,
Restraint by the Pātimokkha,
Moderation in eating,
Lodging in a secluded place,
Being intent on the higher mind—
This is the instruction of the awakened ones.[12]

4.7 Sāriputta (1) *(Sāriputta Sutta)*

Thus have I heard. At one time the Lord was staying near Sāvatthī in the Jeta Wood at Anāthapiṇḍika's monastery. On that occasion the Venerable Sāriputta was sitting cross-legged not far from the Lord, holding his body erect, being one of few wishes, contented, secluded, solitary, energetic, devoted to the higher mind.

The Lord saw the Venerable Sāriputta sitting cross-legged not far away ... devoted to the higher mind.

Then, on realizing its significance, the Lord uttered on that occasion this inspired utterance:

Diligent, devoted to the higher mind,
A sage trained in wisdom's ways,
There are no sorrows for the stable one
Who is calm and ever mindful.

4.8 Sundarī *(Sundarī Sutta)*

Thus have I heard. At one time the Lord was staying near Sāvatthī in the Jeta Wood at Anāthapiṇḍika's monastery. At that time the Lord was respected, revered, honoured, venerated, and given homage, and was one who obtained the requisites of robes, almsfood, lodgings, and medicines.[12] And the Order of bhikkhus was also respected.... But the wanderers of other sects were not respected, revered, honoured, venerated, and given homage, and they did not obtain the requisites of robes, almsfood, lodgings, and medicines. Then those wanderers of other sects, unable to tolerate the respect shown towards the Lord and the Order of bhikkhus, approached Sundarī the woman wanderer and said, "Sister, will you do something useful for your kinsmen?"

"What can I do, masters? What am I able to do? I would sacrifice even my life for the sake of my kinsmen."

"Then, sister, go often to the Jeta Wood."

"Very well, masters," Sundarī the woman wanderer replied, and she went often to the Jeta Wood. Then, when those wanderers knew that Sundarī the woman wanderer had been seen by many people going often to the Jeta Wood, they murdered her and buried her there, in a hole dug in a ditch of the Jeta Wood. Then they went to King Pasenadi of Kosala and said, "Great king, Sundarī the woman wanderer cannot be found."

"Where do you suspect she is?"

"In the Jeta Wood, great king."

"Then search the Jeta Wood."

On searching the Jeta Wood those wanderers dug up the body from the hole in the ditch where it had been buried, and putting it on a litter had it taken to Sāvatthī. Going from street to street and from crossroad to crossroad, they aroused people's indignation by saying, "See, masters, the work of the followers of the Sakyan son.[13] These recluses, the followers of the Sakyan son, are shameless, immoral, of bad conduct, liars, not livers of the holy life. They claim that they live by Dhamma, that they lead a balanced life, that they live the holy life, that they are speakers of truth, that they are virtuous and of good conduct, but they have no status as recluses, they have no status as brahmins; their recluse status is destroyed, their brahmin status is destroyed. Where is their recluse status? Where is their brahmin status? They have lost their recluse status, they have lost their brahmin status. How can a man, having taken his manly pleasure, murder a woman?"

Because of this, when people saw bhikkhus in Sāvatthī they reviled, abused, provoked, and annoyed them with insults and harsh words, saying: "These recluses, the followers of the Sakyan son, are shameless, immoral, of bad conduct.... How can a man, having taken his manly pleasure, murder a woman?"

Then a number of bhikkhus, having dressed in the forenoon and taken their bowls and outer cloaks, entered Sāvatthī for almsfood. Having walked in Sāvatthī for almsfood and returned after the meal, they approached the Lord, prostrated themselves, sat down to one side, and said: "At present, revered sir, when people see bhikkhus in Sāvatthī, they revile, abuse, provoke, and annoy them with insults and harsh words...."

"This commotion, bhikkhus, will not continue long. It will continue for only seven days, and after seven days it will disappear. So, bhikkhus, when people revile you, abuse, provoke, and annoy you with insults and harsh words, you should respond with this verse:

The false accuser[14] *goes to hell,*
And also one who denies the deed he did.
Both these become equal hereafter,
Persons of base actions in the world beyond.

So those bhikkhus learned this verse in the Lord's presence, and when those people, on seeing bhikkhus, reviled them, they responded with the verse.

Then those people thought: "These recluses, the followers of the Sakyan son, did not do it; it was not done by them. These recluses, the followers of the Sakyan son, are asserting (their innocence)."[15] And the commotion did not continue for long. The commotion continued for only seven days, and after seven days it disappeared.

Then a number of bhikkhus approached the Lord, prostrated themselves, sat down to one side, and said: "It is wonderful, revered sir! It is marvellous, revered sir! How well was this foretold by the Lord: 'This commotion, bhikkhus, will not continue for long. After seven days it will disappear.' Revered sir, that commotion has disappeared."

Then, on realizing its significance, the Lord uttered on that occasion this inspired utterance:

Uncontrolled people pierce one with words
As they pierce a battle-elephant with arrows.
On hearing harsh words being uttered to him
A bhikkhu should endure them without hate.[16]

4.9 Upasena (*Upasena Sutta*)

Thus have I heard. At one time the Lord was staying near Rājagaha in the Bamboo Wood at the Squirrels' Feeding Place. Then, while the Venerable Upasena Vaṅgantaputta[17] was in seclusion, this thought arose in his mind: "It is a gain for me; it is a great gain for me, that my teacher is the Lord, the Arahat, the fully Awakened One; that I have gone forth from home to the homeless state in this well-taught Dhamma and discipline; that my fellows in the holy life are virtuous and of good conduct; that I have fulfilled the moral virtues; that I am concentrated and unified of mind; that I am an arahat who is free from the taints; that I am of great supernormal potency and power. Fortunate has been my life and fortunate will be my death!"

Then the Lord understood with his mind the thought in the mind of the Venerable Upasena Vaṅgantaputta, and uttered on that occasion this inspired utterance:

Whose life causes no remorse
And who sorrows not at death,
The wise one who has seen that state [18]
Sorrows not in the midst of sorrow.

For a bhikkhu whose mind is calmed,
Who has destroyed the craving for being,
The wandering on in births is finished;
There is no further being for him.

4.10 Sāriputta (2) (*Sāriputta Sutta*)

Thus have I heard. At one time the Lord was staying near Sāvatthī in the Jeta Wood at Anāthapiṇḍika's monastery. On that occasion the Venerable Sāriputta was sitting cross-legged not far from the Lord, holding his body erect and reviewing his own state of peace.[19]

The Lord saw the Venerable Sāriputta sitting cross-legged not far away … reviewing his own state of peace.

Then, on realizing its significance, the Lord uttered on that occasion this inspired utterance:

For a bhikkhu whose mind is calm and peaceful,
Who has cut the cord (of craving for being). [20]
The wandering on in births is finished:
He is freed from Māra's bonds.

CHAPTER 5

SOṆA
(Soṇavagga)

5.1 The King *(Rāja Sutta)*

Thus have I heard. At one time the Lord was staying near Sāvatthī in the Jeta Wood at Anāthapiṇḍika's monastery. On that occasion King Pasenadi of Kosala had gone to the upper storey of the royal palace with Queen Mallikā. Then King Pasenadi of Kosala said to Queen Mallikā, "Is there anyone, Mallikā, dearer to you than yourself?"

"There is no one, great king, dearer to me than myself. But is there anyone, great king, dearer to you than yourself?"

"Neither is there anyone, Mallikā, dearer to me than myself."

Then King Pasenadi of Kosala descended from the palace and went to visit the Lord. On approaching the Lord, he prostrated himself, sat down to one side, and reported this conversation.

Then, on realizing its significance, the Lord uttered on that occasion this inspired utterance:

On traversing all directions with the mind
One finds no one anywhere dearer than oneself.
Likewise everyone holds himself most dear,
Hence one who loves himself should not harm another.

5.2 Short-lived *(Appāyuka Sutta)*

Thus have I heard. At one time the Lord was staying near Sāvatthī in the Jeta Wood at Anāthapiṇḍika's monastery. Then the Venerable Ānanda, on emerging from seclusion in the evening, approached the Lord, prostrated himself, sat down to one side, and said: "It is wonderful, revered sir! It is marvellous, revered sir! How short-lived was the Lord's mother. Seven days after the Lord was born, the Lord's mother died and was reborn into the Tusita-group (of devas)."

"So it is, Ānanda. Short-lived are the mothers of bodhisattas. Seven days after bodhisattas are born, their mothers die and are reborn into the Tusita-group (of devas)."[1]

Then, on realizing its significance, the Lord uttered on that occasion this inspired utterance:

Whatever beings are born or will be born,
They will journey on leaving the body.
Knowing that all must be abandoned,
A skilful one, ardent, should lead the holy life.

5.3 Suppabuddha the Leper *(Suppabuddhakuṭṭhi Sutta)*

Thus have I heard. At one time the Lord was staying near Rājagaha in the Bamboo Wood at the Squirrels' Feeding Place. At that time there was in Rājagaha a leper called Suppabuddha, a poor, pitiable, wretched person.

Now, on one occasion the Lord was sitting teaching Dhamma surrounded by a large gathering. Suppabuddha the leper saw in the distance that a large group of people had collected together, and on seeing it he thought: "Surely some food is being distributed. Suppose I were to approach that large group of people: I might well get some food there." So Suppabuddha the leper approached that large group of people and saw the Lord sitting and teaching Dhamma surrounded by that large gathering. On seeing it he thought: "There is no food being distributed here. This is the recluse Gotama teaching Dhamma in the assembly. Suppose I too were to listen to Dhamma." So he sat down to one side (thinking), "I too will listen to Dhamma."

Then the Lord, comprehending the minds of (everyone in) that whole gathering with his own mind, considered: "Who here is capable of understanding Dhamma?" Then the Lord saw Suppabuddha the leper sitting amongst that group of people, and on seeing him he thought: "This one here is capable of understanding Dhamma." For the sake of Suppabuddha the leper he then gave a progressive talk, that is, a talk on generosity, on virtue, on heaven; he made known the disappointment, degradation, and corruption of sensual pleasures and the benefit in renouncing them. When the Lord knew that the mind of Suppabuddha the leper was ready, malleable, free from hindrances, elated, and purified, he then made known that Dhamma-teaching special to the Buddhas: suffering, origination, cessation, and the path. And just as a clean cloth without stains would properly take up dye, so in Suppabuddha the leper, even as he was sitting there, there arose the stainless, undefiled Dhamma-vision that whatever is subject to origination is subject to cessation.[2]

Then Suppabuddha the leper—having seen Dhamma, attained to Dhamma, known Dhamma, plunged into Dhamma, crossed over doubt, become free from uncertainty, attained to complete confidence, become independent of others in the Teacher's teaching—arose from his seat and approached the Lord. He prostrated himself, sat down (again) to one side, and said to the Lord: "It is wonderful, revered sir! It is marvellous, revered sir! Just as if, revered sir, one should set upright what is overturned, or should uncover what is concealed, or should point out the path to one who is lost, or should bring an oil-lamp into the darkness so that those with eyes could see visible objects, even so, by various methods, the Lord has explained Dhamma. I, revered sir, go for refuge to the Lord, to Dhamma, and to the Order of bhikkhus. May the Lord accept me as a lay follower gone for refuge from this day forth for as long as life lasts."

Thereupon Suppabuddha the leper, after being instructed, roused, inspired, and gladdened by the Lord's talk on Dhamma, being pleased and appreciative of what the Lord had said, arose from his seat, prostrated himself before the Lord, and keeping his right side towards him, went away.

Now, it happened that a cow with a young calf attacked Suppabuddha the leper and killed him.[3] Then a number of bhikkhus approached the Lord, prostrated themselves, sat down to one side, and said: "Revered sir, the leper

Suppabuddha, who was instructed, roused, inspired, and gladdened by the Lord's talk on Dhamma, has died. What is his destiny, what is his future birth?"

"Suppabuddha the leper, bhikkhus, was a wise man. He practised according to Dhamma and did not trouble me by disputing about Dhamma. Suppabuddha the leper, bhikkhus, by destroying three fetters, is a stream-enterer, not liable to fall away, assured, bound for enlightenment."

When this was said a certain bhikkhu asked the Lord: "Revered sir, what was the cause, what was the reason, Suppabuddha the leper was a poor, pitiable, wretched person?"

"Formerly, bhikkhus, Suppabuddha the leper was the son of a rich merchant in this very Rājagaha. While being conducted to the pleasure-garden he saw Tagarasikhī, the pacceka-buddha,[4] entering the city for almsfood, and on seeing him he thought, 'Who is that leper wandering about?' And having spat at him and (disrespectfully) turned his left side towards him, he went away. Through the ripening of just that deed he suffered in hell for many years, for many hundreds of years, for many thousands of years, for many hundred thousands of years. And through the residual result of just that deed he became a poor, pitiable, wretched person in this very Rājagaha. But on meeting with the Dhamma and Discipline made known by the Tathāgata, he acquired faith, virtue, learning, relinquishment, and wisdom. Thus upon the dissolution of the body, after death, he re-arose in a happy realm, in a heavenly world, in companionship with the devas of the Tāvatiṃsa heaven. There he surpasses the other devas in beauty and splendour."

Then, on realizing its significance, the Lord uttered on that occasion this inspired utterance:

As a man with good eyesight, on a journey,
Would endeavour to avoid any dangerous place,
So too a wise man in the world of the living
Should avoid demeritorious deeds.

5.4 The Boys (*Kumāraka Sutta*)

Thus have I heard. At one time the Lord was staying near Sāvatthī in the Jeta Wood at Anāthapiṇḍika's monastery. On that occasion a number of boys in between Sāvatthī and the Jeta Wood were tormenting the fish (in a pool).[5] Then the Lord, having put on his robe in the forenoon and taken his bowl and outer cloak, was going to Sāvatthī to collect almsfood when he saw those boys in between Sāvatthī and the Jeta Wood tormenting the fish. On seeing this he went up to them and said:

"Do you boys fear pain? Do you dislike pain?"

"Yes, revered sir, we do fear pain. We dislike pain."

Then, on realizing its significance, the Lord uttered on that occasion this inspired utterance:

If you fear pain, if you dislike pain,
Do not do a bad deed openly or in secret.
If you have done a bad deed or do one now,
You will not escape pain, though you try to flee.

5.5 The Observance Day (*Uposatha Sutta*)

Thus have I heard. At one time the Lord was staying near Sāvatthī in the Eastern Park at Migāra's mother's mansion. On that occasion the Lord was sitting surrounded by the Order of bhikkhus, as it was the day of the Uposatha observance.[6] Then, when the night was far advanced and the first watch had ended, the Venerable Ānanda arose from his seat, arranged his robe over one shoulder, raised his folded hands, and said to the Lord: "The night is far advanced, revered sir, the first watch has ended and the bhikkhus have been sitting for a long time. Revered sir, let the Lord recite the Pātimokkha to the bhikkhus." When this was said the Lord remained silent.

When the night was (still further) advanced and the middle watch had ended, a second time the Venerable Ānanda arose from his seat ... and said to the Lord: "The night is far advanced, revered sir, the middle watch has ended and the bhikkhus have been sitting for a long time. Revered sir, let the Lord recite the Pātimokkha to the bhikkhus." A second time the Lord remained silent.

When the night was (yet further) advanced and the last watch had ended, as dawn was approaching and the night was drawing to a close, a third time the Venerable Ānanda arose from his seat ... and said to the Lord: "The night is far advanced, revered sir, the last watch has ended; dawn is approaching and the night is drawing to a close and the bhikkhus have been sitting for a long time. Revered sir, let the Lord recite the Pātimokka to the bhikkhus."

"The gathering is not pure, Ānanda."

Then the Venerable Mahāmoggallāna thought: "Concerning which person has the Lord said, 'The gathering is not pure, Ānanda'?" And the Venerable Mahāmoggallāna, comprehending the minds of the whole Order of bhikkhus with his own mind, saw that person sitting in the midst of the Order of bhikkhus—immoral, wicked, of impure and suspect behaviour, secretive in his acts, no recluse though pretending to be one, not practising the holy life though pretending to do so, rotten within, lustful and corrupt. On seeing him he arose from his seat, approached that person, and said: "Get up, friend. You are seen by the Lord. You cannot live in communion with the bhikkhus." But that person remained silent.

A second time and a third time the Venerable Mahāmoggallāna told that person to get up, and a second time and a third time that person remained silent. Then the Venerable Mahāmoggllāna took that person by the arm, pulled him outside the gate, and bolted it. Then he approached the Lord and said: "Revered sir, I have ejected that person. The assembly is quite pure. Revered sir, let the Lord recite the Pātimokkha to the bhikkhus."

"It is strange, Moggallāna, it is remarkable, Moggallāna, how that stupid person should have waited until he was taken by the arm."

Then the Lord addressed the bhikkhus: "From now on, bhikkhus, I shall not participate in the Uposatha observance or recite the Pātimokkha. From now on you yourselves should participate in the Uposatha observance and recite the Pātimokkha. It is impossible, bhikkhus, it cannot happen, that the Tathāgata should participate in the Uposatha observance and recite the Pātimokkha with a gathering that is not pure.

"Bhikkhus, there are these eight wonderful and marvellous qualities of the great ocean, seeing which the asuras delight in the great ocean. What are the eight?

(1) "The great ocean, bhikkhus, gradually shelves, slopes, and inclines, and there is no sudden precipice. Since the great ocean gradually shelves ... this is the first wonderful and marvellous quality of the great ocean, seeing which the asuras delight in the great ocean.

(2) "Furthermore, the great ocean is stable and does not exceed the limits of the tide-line. This is the second wonderful and marvellous quality of the great ocean....

(3) "Furthermore, the great ocean does not tolerate a dead body; for when there is a dead body in the great ocean, it soon conveys it to the shore and casts it up on dry land. This is the third wonderful and marvellous quality of the great ocean....

(4) "Furthermore, whatever great rivers there are—the Ganges, the Yamunā, the Aciravatī, the Sarabhū, and the Mahī—on reaching the great ocean lose their former names and identities and are just called 'the great ocean.' This is the fourth wonderful and marvellous quality of the great ocean....

(5) "Furthermore, although the rivers of the world flow into the great ocean and showers of rain fall from the sky, no lessening or filling up of the great ocean is evident. This is the fifth wonderful and marvellous quality of the great ocean....

(6) "Furthermore, the great ocean has one taste, the taste of salt. This is the sixth wonderful and marvellous quality of the great ocean....

(7) "Furthermore, the great ocean contains many precious substances, various precious substances, such as these: pearl, crystal, beryl, conch, quartz, coral, silver, gold, ruby, and cat's

eye. This is the seventh wonderful and marvellous quality of the great ocean....

(8) "Furthermore, the great ocean is the abode of mighty creatures, of such creatures as these: the timi, timiṅgala, timirapiṅgala, asuras, nāgas, and gandhabbas.[7]. There exist in the great ocean beings a hundred yojanas in size, beings two hundred, three hundred, four hundred, and five hundred yojanas in size.[8] This is the eighth wonderful and marvellous quality of the great ocean....

"These, bhikkhus, are the eight wonderful and marvellous qualities of the great ocean, seeing which the asuras delight in the great ocean.

"Similarly, bhikkhus, there are eight wonderful and marvellous qualities in this Dhamma and Discipline, seeing which bhikkhus delight in this Dhamma and Discipline. What are the eight?

(1) "Just as the great ocean gradually shelves, slopes, and inclines, and there is no sudden precipice, so also in this Dhamma and Discipline there is a gradual training, a gradual course, a gradual progression, and there is no sudden penetration to final knowledge.[9] Since, in this Dhamma and Discipline there is a gradual training, ... this is the first wonderful and marvellous quality in this Dhamma and Discipline, seeing which bhikkhus delight in this Dhamma and Discipline.

(2) "Just as the great ocean is stable and does not exceed the limits of the tide-line, so also my disciples do not transgress a training rule laid down by me for disciples even for the sake of their lives. This is the second wonderful and marvellous quality in this Dhamma and Discipline....

(3) "Just as the great ocean does not tolerate a dead body ... and casts it up on dry land, so also whatsoever person is immoral, wicked, of impure and suspect behaviour, secretive in his acts, no recluse though pretending to be one, not practising the holy life though pretending to do so, rotten within, lustful and corrupt, the Order does not associate with him, but when it

has met together soon throws him out. Even though he may be sitting in the midst of the Order of bhikkhus, yet he is far from the Order and the Order is far from him. This is the third wonderful and marvellous quality in this Dhamma and Discipline....

(4) "Just as whatever great rivers there are ... on reaching the great ocean lose their former names and identities and are just called 'the great ocean,' so also (those of) the four castes—nobles, brahmins, merchants, and workers—having gone forth from home to the homeless state in the Dhamma and Discipline made known by the Tathāgata, abandon their former names and identities and are just called 'recluses, the followers of the Sakyan son.' This is the fourth wonderful and marvellous quality in this Dhamma and Discipline....

(5) "Just as, although the rivers of the world flow into the great ocean and showers of rain fall from the sky, no lessening or filling up of the great ocean is evident, so also, although many bhikkhus attain final Nibbāna in the Nibbāna-element with no residue left,[10] no lessening or filling up of the Nibbāna-element is evident. This is the fifth wonderful and marvellous quality in this Dhamma and Discipline....

(6) "Just as the great ocean has one taste, the taste of salt, so also this Dhamma and Discipline has one taste, the taste of liberation. This is the sixth wonderful and marvellous quality in this Dhamma and Discipline....

(7) "Just as the great ocean contains many precious substances, various precious substances ... so also this Dhamma and Discipline contains many precious things, various precious things, such as these: the four foundations of mindfulness, the four right endeavours, the four bases for successful accomplishment, the five faculties, the five powers, the seven enlightenment factors, and the Noble Eightfold Path.[11] This is the seventh wonderful and marvellous quality in this Dhamma and Discipline....

(8) "Just as the great ocean is the abode of mighty creatures ... so also this Dhamma and Discipline is the abode of mighty creatures, such as these: the stream-enterer and the one who is on the way to realizing the fruit of stream-entry, the once-returner and the one who is on the way to realizing the fruit of

once-returning, the non-returner and the one who is on the way to realizing the fruit of non-returning, the arahat and the one who is on the way to arahatship. This is the eighth wonderful and marvellous quality in this Dhamma and Discipline.

"These, bhikkhus, are the eight wonderful and marvellous qualities in this Dhamma and Discipline, seeing which bhikkhus delight in this Dhamma and Discipline."

Then, on realizing its significance, the Lord uttered on that occasion this inspired utterance:

Rain soddens what is covered up,
It does not sodden what is open.
Therefore uncover what is covered
That the rain will not sodden it. [12]

5.6 Soṇa *(Soṇa Sutta)*

Thus have I heard. At one time the Lord was staying near Sāvatthī in the Jeta Wood at Anāthapiṇḍika's monastery. At that time the Venerable Mahākaccāna was staying among the people of Avantī near Kuraraghara on Pavatta Hill with the lay follower Soṇa Koṭikaṇṇa as his supporter.

Now, while the lay follower Soṇa Koṭikaṇṇa was in seclusion, this train of thought arose in his mind: "According to how Master Mahākaccāna teaches Dhamma, it is not easy for one living at home to practise the holy life wholly fulfilled, wholly purified, and polished like a conch shell. Suppose I were to have my hair and beard shaved off, clothe myself in the yellow robes, and go forth from home to the homeless state."

So the lay follower Soṇa Koṭikaṇṇa went to the Venerable Mahākaccāna, prostrated himself, sat down to one side, and said: "Just now, revered sir, while in seclusion (I thought): 'According to how Master Mahākaccāna, teaches Dhamma ... and go forth from home to the homeless state.' Allow me, revered Master Mahākaccāna, to go forth."

When this was said, the Venerable Mahākaccāna replied to the lay follower Soṇa Koṭikaṇṇa: "Soṇa, it is hard to lead the holy life with its one meal a day and sleeping alone for the rest of one's life. Come now, Soṇa, devote yourself to the teaching of the Buddhas while remaining a householder, and try for a limited period to lead the holy life, eating one meal a day and sleeping alone."

Then the lay follower Soṇa Koṭikaṇṇa's idea of going forth subsided.

On a second occasion while the lay follower Soṇa Koṭikaṇṇa was in seclusion again the same thought arose. He went to the Venerable Mahākaccāna and asked to go forth, but again he received the same reply. On the third occasion, however, the Venerable Mahākaccāna allowed the lay follower Soṇa Koṭikaṇṇa to go forth.

At that time there were few bhikkhus in the southern country of Avantī, so (only) after a lapse of three years did the Venerable Mahākaccāna, with trouble and difficulty, manage to assemble together from here and there a group of ten (bhikkhus to form) an Order of bhikkhus[13] and give the higher ordination to the Venerable Soṇa.

Then, on emerging from seclusion after the rains retreat, the following thought occurred to the Venerable Soṇa: "I have not seen the Lord face to face. I have only heard that he is like this and like that. If my preceptor would give me permission, I would go to see the Lord, the Arahat, the Fully Enlightened One."

So the Venerable Soṇa, on emerging from seclusion in the evening, approached the Venerable Mahākaccāna, prostrated himself, sat down to one side, and said: "Just now, revered sir, while in seclusion (I thought): 'I have not seen the Lord.... If my preceptor would give me permission, I would go to see the Lord, the Arahat, the Fully Enlightened One.'"

"Good, good, Soṇa! Go, Soṇa, and see the Lord, the Arahat, the Fully Enlightened One. Soṇa, you should see that Lord who inspires trust and confidence, who has calmed senses and tranquil mind, who has attained perfect poise and calm, who is controlled, a perfected one, watchful with restrained senses. When you see him, pay homage in my name with your head at the Lord's feet and ask whether he is free from sickness and ailment and is healthy, strong, and living in comfort, saying: 'My preceptor, revered sir, Mahākaccāna, pays homage with his head at the Lord's feet and asks whether he is free from sickness ... and living in comfort.'"

"Very well, revered sir," said the Venerable Soṇa. And pleased and appreciative of the words of the Venerable Mahākaccāna, he arose from his seat, prostrated himself before the Venerable Mahākaccāna, (and left) keeping his right side towards him. Having set his lodging in order and taken his bowl and outer cloak, he departed on tour for Sāvatthī. Walking on tour by stages, he reached Sāvatthī, the Jeta Wood and Anāthapiṇḍika's monastery, and went to the Lord. Having approached the Lord, he prostrated himself, sat down to one side, and said to the Lord: "My preceptor, revered sir, the Venerable Mahākaccāna ... asks whether the Lord is ... living in comfort."

"Are you well, bhikkhu? Are you in good health? Are you but little fatigued by the journey coming here and been having no difficulty obtaining almsfood?"

"I am well, Lord. I am in good health, Lord. I am not fatigued by the journey coming here, revered sir, and have been having no difficulty obtaining almsfood."

Then the Lord said to the Venerable Ānanda, "Arrange a lodging, Ānanda, for this newly arrived bhikkhu."

Then the Venerable Ānanda thought: "When the Lord orders me, saying, 'Arrange a lodging, Ānanda, for this newly arrived bhikkhu,' it is because he wishes to be alone with this bhikkhu; the Lord wishes to be alone with the Venerable Soṇa." So in the dwelling where the Lord was living he arranged a lodging for the Venerable Soṇa.

Then the Lord, having spent much of the night seated in the open air, washed his feet and entered the dwelling. And the Venerable Soṇa did likewise. Then towards dawn the Lord got up from his seat and requested the Venerable Soṇa, "I would like you, bhikkhu, to recite Dhamma."

"Very well, revered sir," the Venerable Soṇa replied to the Lord, and he chanted the whole of the sixteen sections of the

Aṭṭhakavagga.[14] At the conclusion of the Venerable Soṇa's chanting, the Lord was highly pleased and said: "Good, good, bhikkhu! You have learnt the sixteen sections of the Aṭṭhakavagga well, bhikkhu; you have considered and remembered them well. You possess a fine voice, incisive and distinct, that makes the meaning clear. How many years (seniority)[15] do you have, bhikkhu?"

"I have one year, Lord."

"Why, bhikkhu, did you delay so long?"

"For a long time, revered sir, I had seen the danger in sensual pleasures, but the household life, with its many activities and things to be done, held me back."

Then, on realizing its significance, the Lord uttered on that occasion this inspired utterance:

Having seen the danger in the world,
Having known the state without clinging,
A noble one does not delight in evil;
In evil a pure one finds no delight. [16]

5.7 **Revata** *(Revata Sutta)*

Thus have I heard. At one time the Lord was staying near Sāvatthī in the Jeta Wood at Anāthapiṇḍika's monastery. On that occasion the Venerable Revata the Doubter was sitting cross-legged not far from the Lord, holding his body erect and reviewing his own purification by overcoming doubt.[17]

The Lord saw the Venerable Revata the Doubter sitting cross-legged not far away, holding his body erect and reviewing his own purification by overcoming doubt.

Then, on realizing its significance, the Lord uttered on that occasion this inspired utterance:

Whatever doubts as to here or beyond
In one's own or another's experience,
The meditators abandon all these,
The ardent ones leading the holy life.

5.8 Ānanda *(Ānanda Sutta)*

Thus have I heard. At one time the Lord was staying near Rājagaha in the Bamboo Wood at the Squirrels' Feeding Place. At that time, on the day of the Uposatha observance, the Venerable Ānanda dressed in the forenoon, took his bowl and outer cloak, and entered Rājagaha for almsfood. Devadatta[18] saw the Venerable Ānanda walking for almsfood in Rājagaha, and on seeing him he approached the Venerable Ānanda and said: "From today, friend Ānanda, I shall keep the Uposatha observance and enact the business of the Order apart from the Lord and apart from the Order of bhikkhus."

Then the Venerable Ānanda, having walked in Rājagaha for almsfood and returned after the meal, approached the Lord, prostrated himself, sat down to one side, and said to the Lord: "Revered sir, I had dressed in the forenoon, taken my bowl and outer cloak, and entered Rājagaha for almsfood. Devadatta saw me ... and said to me: 'From today I shall keep the Uposatha observance ... apart from the Order of bhikkhus.' Today, revered sir, Devadatta will divide the Order,[19] he will keep the Uposatha observance and enact the business of the Order (separately)."

Then, on realizing its significance, the Lord uttered on that occasion this inspired utterance:

For the good to do what is good is easy,
For the bad to do what is good is difficult;
For the bad to do what is bad is easy,
For the noble to do what is bad is difficult. [20]

5.9 Abusing *(Sadhāyamāna Sutta)*

Thus have I heard. At one time the Lord was journeying among the people of Kosala together with a large Order of bhikkhus. On that occasion a number of youths passed by in a mocking manner[21] not far from the Lord.

The Lord saw those youths passing by in a mocking manner....

Then, on realizing its significance, the Lord uttered on that occasion this inspired utterance:

The dullards who appear as wise men
Recite with speech alone as their range.
As much as they wish they stretch their mouths;
What leads them on they do not know. [22]

5.10 (Cūḷa) Panthaka *(Cūḷapanthaka Sutta)*

Thus have I heard. At one time the Lord was staying near Sāvatthī in the Jeta Wood at Anāthapiṇḍika's monastery. On that occasion the Venerable Cūḷapanthaka[23] was sitting cross-legged not far from the Lord, holding his body erect, having set up mindfulness before him.

The Lord saw the Venerable Cūḷapanthaka sitting cross-legged not far away, holding his body erect, having set up mindfulness before him.

Then, on realizing its significance, the Lord uttered on that occasion this inspired utterance:

With body steady and mind steady
Whether standing, sitting, or lying down,
A bhikkhu making this mindfulness firm
Shall obtain successive distinctions. [24]
On obtaining distinctions in succession
He goes beyond sight of the King of Death. [25]

CHAPTER 6

BORN BLIND
(Jaccandhavagga)

6.1 Relinquishing the Life-force *(Āyusaṅkhāravossajana Sutta)*

Thus have I heard. At one time the Lord was staying near Vesālī in the Great Wood in the Hall of the Gabled House. Then in the forenoon the Lord, having put on his robe and taken his bowl and outer cloak, entered Vesālī for almsfood. Having walked in Vesālī for almsfood and returned after the meal, he addressed the Venerable Ānanda:[1] "Take a mat, Ānanda. I will go to the Cāpāla Shrine[2] for the midday period."

"Very well, revered sir," the Venerable Ānanda replied, and taking a mat he followed close behind the Lord.

Then the Lord approached the Cāpāla Shrine and on reaching it sat down on a prepared seat. Sitting there the Lord addressed the Venerable Ānanda: "Pleasant, Ānanda, is Vesālī. Pleasant is the Udena Shrine, the Gotamaka Shrine, the Sattamba Shrine, the Bahuputta Shrine, the Sārandada Shrine, and the Cāpāla Shrine.[3] When anyone, Ānanda, has developed and cultivated the four bases of successful accomplishment,[4] made them the vehicle, made them the basis, established, consolidated, and properly practised them, he could if he so wishes live out the aeon or what remains of the aeon.[5] The Tathāgata, Ānanda, has developed and cultivated the four bases of successful accomplishment ... and properly practised them, and if he so wishes, the Tathāgata could live out the aeon or what remains of the aeon."

But even though such a broad hint was made by the Lord, such an evident indication, the Venerable Ānanda was unable to comprehend it. And he did not entreat the Lord (by saying): "Revered sir, let the Lord live out the aeon, let the Sugata live out the aeon, for the welfare of the many, for the happiness of the many, out of compassion for the world, for the good, welfare, and happiness of devas and men," as his mind was possessed by Māra.[6]

A second time and a third time the Lord addressed the Venerable Ānanda, saying: "Pleasant, Ānanda, is Vesālī.... The Tathāgata could live out the aeon or what remains of the aeon."

But a second time and a third time the Venerable Ānanda was unable to comprehend it ... as his mind was possessed by Māra.

Then the Lord addressed the Venerable Ānanda: "Go, Ānanda. Do now what you think it is time to do."

"Very well, revered sir," the Venerable Ānanda replied, and rising from his seat, he prostrated himself before the Lord, and keeping his right side towards him, he went and sat down at the foot of a certain tree not far away.

Then, not long after the departure of the Venerable Ānanda, Māra the Evil One approached the Lord. Standing to one side, Māra the Evil One said to the Lord: "Let the Lord, revered sir, now attain final Nibbāna, let the Sugata attain final Nibbāna. It is now time, revered sir, for the Lord's final Nibbāna. These words, revered sir, were spoken by the Lord:[7] 'I will not attain final Nibbāna, Evil One, until my bhikkhu disciples are wise, disciplined, confident, attained to security from bondage,[8] learned, experts in Dhamma, practising according to Dhamma, practising the proper way, living by following Dhamma; nor until, after learning (it) from their own teachers, they will (be able to) announce, teach, declare, establish, reveal, expound, and explain (it to others); nor until, refuting with Dhamma the arisen theories of others (outsiders), they will (be able to) teach Dhamma that is convincing.' But now, revered sir, the Lord's bhikkhu disciples are wise ... and (are able to) teach Dhamma that is convincing. Let the Lord, revered sir, now attain final Nibbāna, let the Sugata attain final Nibbāna. It is now time, revered sir, for the Lord's final Nibbāna.

"These words, revered sir, were spoken by the Lord: 'I will not attain final Nibbāna, Evil One, until my bhikkhunī disciples are wise ... and (are able to) teach Dhamma that is convincing. I will not attain final Nibbāna until the men lay followers ... the women lay followers who are my disciples are wise … and (are able to) teach Dhamma that is convincing.' But now, revered sir, the Lord's bhikkhunī disciples … the men and women lay followers who are the Lord's disciples are wise … and (are able to) teach Dhamma that is convincing. Let the Lord now attain final Nibbāna, let the Sugata attain final Nibbāna. It is now time, revered sir, for the Lord's final Nibbāna.

"These words were spoken by the Lord: 'I will not attain final Nibbāna, Evil One, until this holy life of mine has become successful and prosperous, widely spread and disseminated among many, until it is well expounded among devas and men.' But now, revered sir, the Lord's holy life is successful and prosperous, widely spread and disseminated among many, it is well expounded among devas and men. It is now time, revered sir, for the Lord's final Nibbāna."

When this had been said, the Lord addressed Māra the Evil One: "You may rest content, Evil One. It will not be long before the Tathāgata's final Nibbāna. Three months from now the Tathāgata will attain final Nibbāna."

It was then, at the Cāpāla Shrine, that the Lord, mindful and clearly comprehending, relinquished the life-force. And when the Lord had relinquished the life-force, a great earthquake occurred and a fearful hair-raising peal of thunder rent the air.

Then, on realizing its significance, the Lord uttered on that occasion this inspired utterance:

The sage relinquished the force of being
Which originates the measurable and immeasurable, [9]
Inwardly happy and composed, he sundered
Personal existence like a coat of mail.

6.2 The Jaṭila Ascetics *(Jaṭila Sutta)*

Thus have I heard. At one time the Lord was staying near Sāvatthī in the Eastern Park in Migāra's mother's mansion. On that occasion the Lord had emerged from seclusion in the evening and was sitting outside the gate. Then King Pasenadi of Kosala approached the Lord, prostrated himself, and sat down to one side.

At that moment, not far from the Lord, there passed by seven Jāṭila ascetics, seven Nigaṇṭhas (Jains), seven naked ascetics, seven single-garment ascetics, and seven wanderers, all with hairy bodies and long nails and carrying (their requisites in) a bundle on a shoulder pole.[10] King Pasenadi of Kosala saw those (groups of) seven passing by not far from the Lord. On seeing them he arose from his seat, arranged his robe over one shoulder, knelt down with his right knee on the ground, and raising his folded hands towards those (groups of) seven, he announced his name three times thus: "Revered sirs, I am King Pasenadi of Kosala!" Then, soon after the departure of those (groups of) seven, King Pasenadi of Kosala approached the Lord (again), prostrated himself, sat down to one side, and said to the Lord: "Revered sir, could any one of these be among those in the world who are arahats or who have entered the path to arahatship?"

"Great king, being a layman enjoying the pleasures of the senses, living at home with the encumbrance of children, making use of sandalwood (perfume) from Kāsī,[11] wearing garlands, scents and unguents, and handling gold and silver, it is difficult for you to know whether or not these are arahats or whether they have entered the path to arahatship. It is by living with a person that his virtue is to be known, great king, and then only after a long time, not after a short period; and only by considering it, not without consideration; and only by one who is wise, not by a fool. It is by associating with a person that his purity[12] is to be known.... It is in adversity that a person's fortitude is to be known.... It is by discussion with a person that his wisdom is to be known, great king, and then only after a long time, not after a short period; and only by considering it, not without consideration; and only by one who is wise, not by a fool."

"It is wonderful, revered sir! It is marvellous, revered sir! How well this has been said by the Lord. These, revered sir, are my men in disguise,[13] informers who are returning after spying on the country. First information is gathered by them and afterwards I will make them disclose it. Now, revered sir, when they have washed off the dust and mud, are well bathed and perfumed, and have trimmed their hair and beards and dressed themselves in white garments,[14] they will go about given to and provided with the five kinds of sensual pleasure."

Then, on realizing its significance, the Lord uttered on that occasion this inspired utterance:

One should not strive everywhere,[15]
One should not be another's man.
One should not live depending on another,
One should not make a business of Dhamma.

6.3 Reviewing *(Paccavekkhana Sutta)*

Thus have I heard. At one time the Lord was staying near Sāvatthī in the Jeta Wood at Anāthapiṇḍika's monastery. On that occasion the Lord was sitting reviewing the various unwholesome states that had been abandoned by him and the various wholesome states brought to completion through (meditational) development.

Then, on realizing that the various unwholesome states had been abandoned by him and the various wholesome states had been brought to completion through (meditational) development, the Lord uttered on that occasion this inspired utterance:

What formerly was, later was not;
What formerly was not, later was;
It was not and will not be
And does not now exist. [16]

6.4 Various Sectarians (1) *(Paṭhamanānātitthiya Sutta)*

Thus have I heard. At one time the Lord was staying near Sāvatthī in the Jeta Wood at Anāthapiṇḍika's monastery. At that time there were a number of recluses and brahmins, wanderers of various sects, living around Sāvatthī. And they were of various views, of various beliefs, of various opinions, and they relied for their support on their various views. There were some recluses and brahmins who asserted and held this view: "The world is eternal; only this is true, any other (view) is false." There were some recluses and brahmins who asserted: "The world is not eternal; only this is true, any other (view) is false." There were some who asserted: "The world is finite... The world is infinite... The life-principle and the body are the same ... The life-principle and the body are different... The Tathāgata exists beyond death... The Tathāgata does not exist beyond death... The Tathāgata both exists and does not exist beyond death; The Tathāgata neither exists nor does not exist beyond death; only this is true, any other (view) is false."[17] And they lived quarrelsome, disputatious, and wrangling, wounding each other with verbal darts, saying: "Dhamma is like this, Dhamma is not like that! Dhamma is not like this, Dhamma is like that!"

Then a number of bhikkhus, having put on their robes in the forenoon and taken their bowls and outer cloaks, entered Sāvatthī for almsfood. Having walked in Sāvatthī for almsfood and returned after the meal, they approached the Lord, prostrated themselves, sat down to one side, and said to the Lord: "At present, revered sir, there are a number of recluses and brahmins, wanderers of various sects, living around Sāvatthī. And they are of various views... saying: 'Dhamma is like this!... Dhamma is like that!'"

"The wanderers of other sects, bhikkhus, are blind, unseeing. They do not know what is beneficial, they do not know what is harmful. They do not know what is Dhamma, they do not know what is not Dhamma. Not knowing what is beneficial and what is harmful, not knowing what is Dhamma and what is not Dhamma, they are quarrelsome ... saying: 'Dhamma is like this!... Dhamma is like that!'

"Formerly, bhikkhus, there was a certain king in this very Sāvatthī. And that king addressed a man: 'Come now, my good man, bring together all those persons in Sāvatthī who have been blind from birth.'

"'Yes, your majesty,' that man replied, and after detaining all the blind people in Sāvatthī, he approached the king and said, 'All the blind people in Sāvatthī have been brought together, your majesty.'

"'Now, my man, show the blind people an elephant.'

"'Very well, your majesty,' the man replied to the king, and he presented an elephant to the blind people, saying, 'This, blind people, is an elephant.'

"To some of the blind people he presented the head of the elephant, saying, 'This is an elephant.' To some he presented an ear of the elephant, saying, 'This is an elephant.' To some he presented a tusk ... the trunk ... the body ... the foot ... the hindquarters ... the tail ... the tuft at the end of the tail, saying, 'This is an elephant.'

"Then, bhikkhus, the man, having shown the elephant to the blind people, went to the king and said, 'The blind people have been shown the elephant, your majesty. Do now what you think is suitable.' Then the king approached those blind people and said, 'Have you been shown the elephant?'

"'Yes, your majesty, we have been shown the elephant.'

"'Tell me, blind people, what is an elephant like? '

"Those blind people who had been shown the head of the elephant replied, 'An elephant, your majesty, is just like a water jar.' Those blind people who had been shown the ear of the elephant replied. "An elephant, your majesty, is just like a winnowing basket.' Those blind people who had been shown the tusk of the elephant replied, 'An elephant, your majesty, is just like a ploughshare.' Those blind people who had been shown the trunk replied, 'An elephant, your majesty, is just like a plough pole.' Those blind people who had been shown the body replied, 'An elephant, your majesty, is just like a storeroom.' Those blind people who had been shown the foot replied, 'An elephant, your majesty, is just like a post.' Those blind people who had been shown the hindquarters replied, 'An elephant, your majesty, is just like a mortar.' Those blind people who had been shown the tail replied, 'An elephant, your majesty, is just like a pestle.' Those blind people who had been shown the tuft at the end of the tail replied, 'An elephant, your majesty, is just like a broom.'

"Saying 'An elephant is like this, an elephant is not like that! An elephant is not like this, an elephant is like that!' they fought each other with their fists. And the king was delighted (with the spectacle).

"Even so, bhikkhus, are those wanderers of various sects blind, unseeing... saying, "Dhamma is like this!... Dhamma is like that!'"

Then, on realizing its significance, the Lord uttered on that occasion this inspired utterance:

Some recluses and brahmins, so called,
Are deeply attached to their own views;
People who see only one side of things
Engage in quarrels and disputes.

6.5 Various Sectarians (2) *(Dutiyanānātitthiya Sutta)*

Thus have I heard. At one time the Lord was staying near Sāvatthī in the Jeta Wood at Anāthapiṇḍika's monastery. At that time there were a number of recluses and brahmins, wanderers of various sects, living around Sāvatthī. And they were of various views, of various beliefs, of various opinions, and they relied for support on their various views. There were some recluses and brahmins who asserted and held this view: "The self and the world are eternal; only this is true, any other (view) is false." There were some who asserted: "The self and the world are not eternal ... The self and the world are both eternal and not eternal ... The self and the world are neither eternal nor not eternal...."

"The self and the world are self-produced ... produced by another ... both self-produced and produced by another ... neither self-produced nor produced by another, but have arisen without a cause...."

"Pleasure and pain, the self and the world, are self-produced ... produced by another ... both self-produced and produced by another ... neither self-produced nor produced by another, but have arisen without a cause; only this is true, any other (view) is false."

And they lived quarrelsome, disputatious, and wrangling, wounding each other with verbal darts, saying: "Dhamma is like this, Dhamma is not like that! Dhamma is not like this, Dhamma is like that!"

Then a number of bhikkhus, having put on their robes in the forenoon and taken their bowls and outer cloaks, entered Sāvatthī for almsfood. Having walked in Sāvatthī for almsfood and returned after the meal, they approached the Lord, prostrated themselves, sat down to one side, and said to the Lord: "At present, revered sir, there are a number of recluses and brahmins, wanderers of various sects, living around Sāvatthī. And they are of various views … saying: 'Dhamma is like this!… Dhamma is like that!'"

"The wanderers of other sects, bhikkhus, are blind, unseeing. They do not know what is beneficial, they do not know what is harmful. They do not know what is Dhamma, they do not know what is not Dhamma. Not knowing what is beneficial and what is harmful, not knowing what is Dhamma and what is not Dhamma, they are quarrelsome … saying: 'Dhamma is like this!… Dhamma is like that!'"

Then, on realizing its significance, the Lord uttered on that occasion this inspired utterance:

Some recluses and brahmins, so called,
Are deeply attached to their own views;
Not finding a firm foothold
They sink in the middle of the stream.

6.6 Various Sectarians (3) *(Tatiyanānātitthiya Sutta)*

Thus have I heard…. (as in 6.5) And they lived quarrelsome, disputatious, and wrangling, wounding each other with verbal darts, saying: "Dhamma is like this, Dhamma is not like that! Dhamma is not like this, Dhamma is like that!"

Then, on realizing its significance, the Lord uttered on that occasion this inspired utterance:

This humankind is attached to self-production
Or holds to production by another.
Those who have not understood this
Have not seen it as a dart.

But one who sees (this as it is),
Having drawn out the dart,
Does not think, "I am the agent,"
Nor does he think, "Another is the agent."

This humankind is possessed by conceit,
Fettered by conceit, bound by conceit.
Speaking vindictively because of their views,
They do not go beyond saṃsāra. [18]

6.7 Subhūti *(Subhūti Sutta)*

Thus have I heard. At one time the Lord was staying near Sāvatthī in the Jeta Wood at Anāthapiṇḍika's monastery. On that occasion the Venerable Subhūti was sitting cross-legged not far from the Lord, holding his body erect, having attained a non-discursive concentration.[19]

The Lord saw the Venerable Subhūti sitting cross-legged not far away, holding his body erect, having attained a non-discursive concentration. Then, on realizing its significance, the Lord uttered on that occasion this inspired utterance:

In whom discursive thoughts have been burnt up,
Entirely cut off within himself,
Having overcome that tie, perceiving the formless,
Surmounting the four bonds, he never comes back. [20]

6.8 The Courtesan *(Gaṇikā Sutta)*

Thus have I heard. At one time the Lord was staying near Rājagaha in the Bamboo Wood at the Squirrels' Feeding Place.

At that time there were two factions enamoured of and infatuated with a certain courtesan. They were quarrelsome, disputatious, and wrangling, and attacked each other with their fists, with clods of earth, with staves, and with weapons, so that they went to their death or suffered near to death.

Then a number of bhikkhus, having put on their robes in the forenoon and taken their bowls and outer cloaks, entered Rājagaha for almsfood. Having walked in Rājagaha for almsfood and returned after the meal, they approached the Lord, prostrated themselves, sat down to one side, and said to the Lord: "At present, revered sir, there are two factions ... or suffered near to death."

Then, on realizing its significance, the Lord uttered on that occasion this inspired utterance:

> *What has been attained and what is still to be attained—both these are littered with dust for a frail person who trains after (one with wrong view). Those who hold training as the essence, or who hold virtue-and-vow, pure livelihood, celibacy, and service as the essence—this is one extreme. And those with such theories and such views as "There is no fault in sensual desires"—this is the second extreme. Both these extremes cause the cemeteries to grow, and the cemeteries cause wrong views to grow. By not penetrating these two extremes some hold back and some go too far. But for those who penetrated them, and were no more found among them, and who did not conceive on this account, there is no round for the manifestation of them.* [21]

6.9 Insects *(Upāti Sutta)*

Thus have I heard. At one time the Lord was staying near Sāvatthī in the Jeta Wood at Anāthapiṇḍika's monastery. On that occasion on a very dark night the Lord was sitting in the open air and oil-lamps were burning. Now, at that time many flying insects[22] were coming to misfortune and destruction by falling into those oil-lamps. The Lord saw those flying insects coming to misfortune and destruction by falling into those oil-lamps.

Then, on realizing its significance, the Lord uttered on that occasion this inspired utterance:

Rushing headlong and missing the essence,
They bring about renewed bondage.
Like insects falling into the flame
Some are intent only on what is seen and heard. [23]

6.10 The Appearance of Tathāgatas *(Tathāgatuppāda Sutta)*

Thus have I heard. At one time the Lord was staying near Sāvatthī in the Jeta Wood at Anāthapiṇḍika's monastery. Then the Venerable Ānanda approached the Lord, prostrated himself, sat down to one side, and said to the Lord: "Revered sir, as long as Tathāgatas do not appear in the world, Arahats, Fully Awakened Ones, so long are wanderers of other sects respected, revered, honoured, venerated, and given homage, and they obtain the requisites of robes, almsfood, lodgings, and medicines. But when Tathāgatas appear in the world, Arahats, Fully Awakened Ones, then the wanderers of other sects are not respected, revered, honoured, venerated, and given homage, and they do not obtain the requisites of robes, almsfood, lodgings, and medicines. Now, revered sir, only the Lord is respected, revered, honoured, venerated, and given homage ... and also the Order of bhikkhus."

"So it is, Ānanda. As long as Tathāgatas do not appear in the world ... so long are wanderers of other sects respected.... Now only the Tathāgata is respected ... and also the Order of bhikkhus."

Then, on realizing its significance, the Lord uttered on that occasion this inspired utterance:

The glow worm shines as long as the sun has not risen, but when that illuminant arises, the glow worm's light is quenched and shines no more. Even so, the wanderers shine only as long as Fully Awakened Ones do not appear in the world. These thinkers [24] *are not purified nor yet their disciples, for those of perverse views are not released from suffering.*

CHAPTER 7

THE MINOR SECTION
(Cūḷavagga)

7.1 Bhaddiya (1) *(Paṭhamalakuṇṭakabhaddiya Sutta)*

Thus have I heard. At one time the Lord was staying near Sāvatthī in the Jeta Wood at Anāthapiṇḍika's monastery. On that occasion the Venerable Sāriputta, by a variety of means, was instructing, rousing, inspiring, and gladdening the Venerable Bhaddiya the dwarf[1] with talk on Dhamma. Then, while the Venerable Bhaddiya the dwarf was being instructed by the Venerable Sāriputta ... with talk on Dhamma, his mind was freed from the taints without grasping.

The Lord saw that while the Venerable Bhaddiya the dwarf was being instructed by the Venerable Sāriputta ... with talk on Dhamma, his mind was freed from the taints without grasping.

Then, on realizing its significance, the Lord uttered on that occasion this inspired utterance:

Above, below, and everywhere released,
One not observing "I am this" [2]
Has crossed the flood not crossed before,
Freed thus with no renewal of being.

7.2 Bhaddiya (2) *(Dutiyalakuṇṭakabhaddiya Sutta)*

Thus have I heard. At one time the Lord was staying near Sāvatthī in the Jeta Wood at Anāthapiṇḍika's monastery. On that occasion the Venerable Sāriputta, by a variety of means, was instructing, rousing, inspiring, and gladdening the Venerable Bhaddiya the dwarf with talk on Dhamma, much more so since he considered him to be (still) a learner.[3]

The Lord saw the Venerable Sāriputta ... instructing, rousing, inspiring, and gladdening the Venerable Bhaddiya the dwarf with talk on Dhamma....

Then, on realizing its significance, the Lord uttered on that occasion this inspired utterance:

He has cut the round, won the desireless,
The dried up river flows no more;
The severed round does not revolve—
Just this is the end of suffering. [4]

7.3 Clinging (1) *(Paṭhamasatta Sutta)*

Thus have I heard. At one time the Lord was staying near Sāvatthī in the Jeta Wood at Anāthapiṇḍika's monastery. At that time most people in Sāvatthī clung excessively to sensual pleasures. They lived greedy for, longing for, bound by, infatuated with, addicted to, and intoxicated by sensual pleasures.

Now, a number of bhikkhus, having put on their robes in the forenoon and taken their bowls and outer cloaks, entered Sāvatthī for almsfood. Having walked in Sāvatthī for almsfood and returned after the meal, they approached the Lord, prostrated themselves, sat down to one side, and said: "Here in Sāvatthī, revered sir, most people cling excessively to sensual pleasures. They live greedy for, longing for, bound by, infatuated with, addicted to, and intoxicated by sensual pleasures."

Then, on realizing its significance, the Lord uttered on that occasion this inspired utterance:

Clinging to sense pleasures, to sensual ties,
Seeing in fetters nothing to be blamed,
Never will those tied down by fetters
Cross the flood so wide and great.

7.4 Clinging (2) *(Dutiyasatta Sutta)*

Thus have I heard. At one time the Lord was staying near Sāvatthī in the Jeta Wood at Anāthapiṇḍika's monastery. On that occasion most people in Sāvatthī clung[5] to sensual pleasures. They lived greedy for, longing for, bound by, infatuated with, addicted to, and intoxicated by sensual pleasures.

Now the Lord, having robed himself in the forenoon and taken his bowl and outer cloak, entered Sāvatthī for almsfood. The Lord saw how most people in Sāvatthī were clinging to sensual pleasures and were greedy for ... sensual pleasures.

Then, on realizing its significance, the Lord uttered on that occasion this inspired utterance:

Blinded by sense pleasures,
Enmeshed in the net,
Covered by the cloak of craving,
Bound in the bondage of negligence
Like fish in a fisherman's trap,
They go to decay and death,
As a suckling calf to its mother.

7.5 Bhaddiya (3) *(Aparalakuṇṭakabhaddiya Sutta)*

Thus have I heard. At one time the Lord was staying near Sāvatthī in the Jeta Wood at Anāthapiṇḍika's monastery. On that occasion the Venerable Bhaddiya the dwarf, following behind a number of bhikkhus, was approaching the Lord.

The Lord saw from afar the Venerable Bhaddiya the dwarf coming, following behind a number of bhikkhus—ugly, unsightly, deformed,[6] and generally despised by the bhikkhus. On seeing him he said to the bhikkhus: "Bhikkhus, do you see that bhikkhu coming, following behind a number of bhikkhus—ugly, unsightly, deformed, and generally despised by the bhikkhus?"

"Yes, revered sir."

"Bhikkhus, that bhikkhu is of great supernormal potency and power. It is not easy to find any attainment which that bhikkhu has not already attained. He has realized here and now through his own direct knowledge that unequalled goal of the holy life, for the sake of which sons of good family rightly go forth from home to the homeless state, and entering into it he abides in it."

Then, on realizing its significance, the Lord uttered on that occasion this inspired utterance:

Faultless, with its white awning,
The one-spoked chariot rolls;
See him coming, trouble-free,
The stream cut, no more in bondage. [7]

7.6 The Destruction of Craving *(Taṇhāsaṅkhaya Sutta)*

Thus have I heard. At one time the Lord was staying near Sāvatthī in the Jeta Wood at Anāthapiṇḍika's monastery. On that occasion the Venerable Aññāta Koṇḍañña was sitting cross-legged not far from the Lord, holding his body erect and reviewing his deliverance by the destruction of craving.[8]

The Lord saw the venerable Aññāta Koṇḍañña sitting cross-legged not far away, holding his body erect and reviewing his deliverance by the destruction of craving.

Then, on realizing its significance, the Lord uttered on that occasion this inspired utterance:

For whom there is no root and soil
There are no leaves, how then creepers? [9]
Who can blame that heroic sage
Free from every form of bondage?
Even the devas praise such a one,
By Brahmā too he is praised.

7.7 The Destruction of Proliferation *(Papañcakkhaya Sutta)*

Thus have I heard. At one time the Lord was staying near Sāvatthī in the Jeta Wood at Anāthapiṇḍika's monastery. On that occasion the Lord was sitting reviewing his own abandonment of perceptions and concepts born of proliferation.[10]

Then the Lord, on realizing his own abandonment of perceptions and concepts born of proliferation, uttered on that occasion this inspired utterance:

The world with its devas does not despise
That cravingless sage as he fares along,
For whom there are no proliferations and stagnation,
Who has overcome the tether and bar. [11]

7.8 Kaccāna *(Kaccāna Sutta)*

Thus have I heard. At one time the Lord was staying near Sāvatthī in the Jeta Wood at Anāthapiṇḍika's monastery. On that occasion the Venerable Mahākaccāna was sitting cross-legged not far from the Lord, holding his body erect, having mindfulness with regard to the body set up and well established within him.[12]

The Lord saw the Venerable Mahākaccāna sitting cross-legged not far away, holding his body erect, having mindfulness with regard to the body set up and well established within him.

Then, on realizing its significance, the Lord uttered on that occasion this inspired utterance:

He for whom mindfulness of the body
Is always constantly established thus:
"If there had not been, there would not be for me;
There will not be, and there will not be for me," [13]
If he dwells upon that in graded steps
In time he will pass beyond attachment.

7.9 The Well *(Udapāna Sutta)*

Thus have I heard. At one time the Lord was journeying among the Mallas[14] together with a large Order of bhikkhus and came to the brahmin village of the Mallas called Thūna. The brahmin householders who lived in Thūna heard: "The recluse Gotama, the Sakyan son who went forth from the Sakya clan, has been journeying among the Mallas together with a large Order of bhikkhus and has arrived at Thūna." They then filled the well to the brim with grass and chaff, thinking, "Don't let those shaven-headed recluses[15] get water to drink."

Then the Lord stepped off the road, and going up to the foot of a certain tree, sat down on a seat prepared for him. Sitting there the Lord addressed the Venerable Ānanda: "Come, Ānanda, fetch me some water from that well."

Thereupon the Venerable Ānanda said to the Lord: "Just now, revered sir, the brahmin householders living in Thūna filled the well to the brim with grass and chaff, thinking, 'Don't let those shaven-headed recluses get water to drink.'"

Then a second time the Lord addressed the Venerable Ānanda: "Come, Ānanda, fetch me some water...." And a second time the Venerable Ānanda said to the Lord: "Just now, revered sir, the brahmin householders filled the well to the brim with grass and chaff...."

Then for a third time the Lord addressed the Venerable Ānanda: "Come, Ānanda, fetch me some water from that well."

"Yes, revered sir," the Venerable Ānanda replied, and taking a bowl he went to the well. Now, as the Venerable Ānanda was approaching it, the well threw up all its grass and chaff from its mouth and stood filled to the brim with pure, clean, clear water, as if it were overflowing. Then the Venerable Ānanda thought: "It is indeed wonderful, it is indeed marvellous, the great supernormal potency and power of the Tathāgata! As I was approaching this well, it threw up all that grass and chaff from its mouth and now stands filled to the brim with pure, clean, clear water, as if it were overflowing." And taking some water in the bowl he approached the Lord and said: "It is indeed wonderful, it is indeed marvellous, the great supernormal potency and power of the Tathāgata! This well ... now stands filled to the brim with pure, clean, clear water, as if it were overflowing. Drink the water, Lord. Drink the water, Sugata."

Then, on realizing its significance, the Lord uttered on that occasion this inspired utterance:

What use is there for a well
If there is water everywhere?
When craving's root is severed
What should one go about seeking?

7.10 Udena (*Udena Sutta*)

Thus have I heard. At one time the Lord was staying near Kosambī in the Ghosita monastery. At that time the women's quarters in the royal park of King Udena had burnt down and five hundred women headed by Sāmāvatī had died.[16]

Then a number of bhikkhus, having put on their robes in the forenoon and taken their bowls and outer cloaks, entered Kosambī for almsfood. Having walked in Kosambī for almsfood and returned after the meal, they approached the Lord, prostrated themselves, sat down to one side, and said to the Lord: "Revered sir, the women's quarters in the royal park of King Udena have burnt down and five hundred women headed by Sāmāvatī have died. What is the destiny, what is the future birth, of those women lay followers?"

"Bhikkhus, some of these women lay followers were stream-enterers, some once-returners, some never-returners.[17] Not fruitless was the death of any of those women lay followers."

Then, on realizing its significance, the Lord uttered on that occasion this inspired utterance:

The world is held in bondage by delusion
And only appears to be capable. [18]
To a fool, held in bondage by clinging
And wrapped up in darkness,
It appears to be eternal,
But for one who sees there is nothing.

Chapter 8

Pāṭali Village
(Pāṭaligāmiyavagga)

8.1 Parinibbāna (1) *(Paṭhamaparinibbāna Sutta)*

Thus have I heard. At one time the Lord was staying near Sāvatthī in the Jeta Wood at Anāthapiṇḍika's monastery. On that occasion the Lord was instructing, rousing, inspiring, and gladdening the bhikkhus with a Dhamma talk connected with Nibbāna, and those bhikkhus, being receptive and attentive and concentrating the whole mind, were intent on listening to Dhamma.

Then, on realizing its significance, the Lord uttered on that occasion this inspired utterance:

> *There is, bhikkhus, that base*[1] *where there is no earth, no water, no fire, no air; no base consisting of the infinity of space, no base consisting of the infinity of consciousness, no base consisting of nothingness, no base consisting of neither-perception-nor-non-perception; neither this world nor another world nor both; neither sun nor moon.*[2] *Here, bhikkhus, I say there is no coming, no going, no staying, no deceasing, no uprising. Not fixed, not movable, it has no support.*[3] *Just this is the end of suffering.*

8.2 Parinibbāna (2) *(Dutiyaparinibbāna Sutta)*

Thus have I heard. At one time the Lord was staying near Sāvatthī in the Jeta Wood at Anāthapiṇḍika's monastery. On that occasion the Lord was instructing … the bhikkhus with a Dhamma talk connected with Nibbāna, and those bhikkhus … were intent on listening to Dhamma.[4]

Then, on realizing its significance, the Lord uttered on that occasion this inspired utterance:

The uninclined[5] is hard to see,
The truth is not easy to see;
Craving is penetrated by one who knows,
For one who sees there is nothing.

8.3 Parinibbāna (3) *(Tatiyaparinibbāna Sutta)*

Thus have I heard. At one time the Lord was staying near Sāvatthī in the Jeta Wood at Anāthapiṇḍika's monastery. On that occasion the Lord was instructing … the bhikkhus with a Dhamma talk connected with Nibbāna, and those bhikkhus … were intent on listening to Dhamma.

Then, on realizing its significance, the Lord uttered on that occasion this inspired utterance:

There is, bhikkhus, a not-born, a not-brought-to-being, a not-made, a not-conditioned. If, bhikkhus, there were no not-born, not-brought-to-being, not-made, not-conditioned, no escape would be discerned from what is born, brought-to-being, made, conditioned. But since there is a not-born, a not-brought-to-being, a not-made, a not-conditioned, therefore an escape is discerned from what is born, brought-to-being, made, conditioned.

8.4 Parinibbāna (4) *(Catutthaparinibbāna Sutta)*

Thus have I heard. At one time the Lord was staying near Sāvatthī in the Jeta Wood at Anāthapiṇḍika's monastery. On that occasion the Lord was instructing … the bhikkhus with a Dhamma talk connected with Nibbāna, and those bhikkhus … were intent on listening to Dhamma.[4]

Then, on realizing its significance, the Lord uttered on that occasion this inspired utterance:

For the supported[6] there is instability, for the unsupported there is no instability; when there is no instability there is serenity; when there is serenity there is no inclination:[7] when there is no inclination there is no coming-and-going; when there is no coming-and-going there is no decease-and-uprising; when there is no decease-and-uprising there is neither "here" nor "beyond" nor "in between the two."[8] Just this is the end of suffering.

8.5 Cunda *(Cunda Sutta)*

Thus have I heard. At one time the Lord, while walking on tour among the Mallas together with a large Order of bhikkhus, arrived at Pāvā. And the Lord stayed at Pāvā in the mango grove of Cunda the smith.[9] Now, Cunda the smith heard: "It is said that the Lord, while walking on tour among the Mallas together with a large Order of bhikkhus, has arrived at Pāvā and is staying at Pāvā in my mango grove." Then Cunda the smith approached the Lord, prostrated himself, and sat down to one side, and the Lord instructed, roused, inspired, and gladdened him with a talk on Dhamma. Then Cunda the smith, being instructed, roused, inspired, and gladdened by the Lord's talk on Dhamma, said to the Lord: "Please consent, revered sir, to my providing a meal tomorrow for the Lord together with the Order of bhikkhus."

The Lord consented by remaining silent. Then, on seeing that the Lord had consented, Cunda the smith rose from his seat, prostrated himself before the Lord, and keeping his right side towards him, went away.

When the night had ended Cunda the smith prepared in his own dwelling choice solid and soft food including a quantity of *sūkaramaddava*,[10] and announced to the Lord the time (for the meal, saying), "It is time, revered sir, the meal is ready."

Then the Lord, putting on his robe in the forenoon and taking his bowl and outer cloak, together with the Order of bhikkhus went to the dwelling of Cunda the smith. On arriving he sat down on the seat prepared for him and said to Cunda the smith: "Serve me, Cunda, with that *sūkaramaddava* you have prepared and serve the Order of bhikkhus with the other food."

"Very well, revered sir," Cunda the smith replied, and he served the Lord with the *sūkaramaddava* and the Order of bhikkhus with the other prepared food. Then the Lord said to Cunda the smith: "Bury in a pit what is left over of the *sūkaramaddava*, Cunda, for I do not see in this world with its devas, māras, and brahmās, among humankind with its recluses and brahmins, its princes and ordinary people anyone here who could eat and fully digest it other than the Tathāgata."

"Very well, revered sir," Cunda the smith replied, and he buried what was left over of the *sūkaramaddava* in a pit. Then he returned to the Lord, prostrated himself, and sat down to one side. As he sat there the Lord instructed, roused, inspired, and gladdened him with a talk on Dhamma. Then he rose from his seat and departed.

Then, after the Lord had eaten the food of Cunda the smith, a severe sickness arose in him, dysentery accompanied by the passing of blood and dire and deadly pains. These pains the Lord endured, mindful and clearly comprehending, without complaint.

Then the Lord said to the Venerable Ānanda, "Come, Ānanda, we will go to Kusinārā."

On eating the smith Cunda's food,
So I heard,
The Wise One felt a sickness
Dire, as to end in death.

When he ate the sūkaramaddava,
A dire sickness arose in the Teacher.
Then, being purged of it, the Lord announced:
"I will go to the city of Kusinārā."[11]

Then the Lord stepped off the road, went up to the foot of a tree, and said to the Venerable Ānanda: "Come, Ānanda, fold my robe in four and prepare a seat. I am tired and wish to sit down."

"Yes, revered sir," the Venerable Ānanda replied to the Lord, and folding the robe in four, he prepared a seat and the Lord sat down. Sitting there the Lord addressed the Venerable Ānanda: "Come, Ānanda, fetch me some water. I am thirsty, Ānanda, and wish to drink." Thereupon the Venerable Ānanda said to the Lord: "Just now, revered sir, as many as five hundred wagons have crossed over and the shallow water stirred up by the wheels flows muddied. But there is the river Kukuṭṭhā close by, with clear, pleasant, cool, pure water easily approachable and delightfully situated. Here the Lord can drink the water and refresh his body."

Then a second time and a third time the Lord said: "Come, Ānanda, fetch me some water...."

"Very well, revered sir," the Venerable Ānanda replied to the Lord, and taking a bowl, he went to the stream. Then, as the Venerable Ānanda approached, that shallow water, stirred up by the wheels and flowing muddied, flowed pure, clear, and unmuddied. Then the Venerable Ānanda thought: "It is indeed wonderful, it is indeed marvellous, the great supernormal potency and power of the Tathāgata! This stream ... now flows pure, clear, and unmuddied." And taking some water in the bowl he approached the Lord and said: "It is indeed wonderful, it is indeed marvellous, the great supernormal potency and power of the Tathāgata!... Drink the water, Lord. Drink the water, Sugata." And the Lord drank the water.

Then the Lord, together with a large Order of bhikkhus, went to the river Kukuṭṭhā, and entering into the water, he bathed and drank. Having come out of the water, he went to a mango grove and said to the Venerable Cundaka: "Come, Cundaka, fold my robe in four and prepare a couch. I am tired and wish to lie down."

"Yes, revered sir," the Venerable Cundaka replied, and folding the robe in four, he prepared a couch. And the Lord lay down on his right side in the lion's resting posture, placing one foot on the other, mindful and clearly comprehending, determining the time of arising.[12] And the Venerable Cundaka sat down in front of the Lord.

The Buddha came to the Kukuṭṭhā River,
With pure, pleasant, clear waters.
The Teacher immersed his weary frame,
The Tathāgata, incomparable in the world.

Having bathed, drank, and come back out,
The honoured Teacher amid the group of bhikkhus,
The foremost Teacher, the Lord here now,[13]
The great sage, went to the mango grove.

To the bhikkhu called Cundaka he said:
"Prepare my robe folded into four."
Ordered by the Composed One,
Cunda quickly laid out the four-folded robe.
The Teacher lay down his weary frame
And Cunda sat down there in front.

Then the Lord said to the Venerable Ānanda: "It may be, Ānanda, that someone will cause remorse in Cunda the smith by saying: 'It is a loss for you, friend Cunda, it is an ill gain for you, that the Tathāgata attained final Nibbāna after he received his last meal from you.' That remorse of Cunda the smith should be dispelled in this way: 'It is a gain for you, friend Cunda, it is a great gain for you, that the Tathāgata attained final Nibbāna after he received his last meal from you. Face to face I heard it from the Lord, friend Cunda, face to face I learnt it: These two offerings of almsfood are of equal fruit, of equal result, of very much greater fruit and profit than any other offering of almsfood. What two? That offering of almsfood which the Tathāgata ate just before he realized supreme enlightenment[14] and that offering of almsfood which the Tathāgata ate just before he attained final Nibbāna in the Nibbāna-element with no residue left. These two offerings of almsfood are of equal fruit, of equal result, of very much greater fruit and profit than any other offering of almsfood. A deed has been performed by the worthy Cunda the smith conducive to long life, beauty, happiness, heaven, fame, and supremacy.' In this way the remorse of Cunda the smith should be dispelled."

Then, on realizing its significance, the Lord uttered on that occasion this inspired utterance:

Merit grows for one who gives;
No enmity builds up for one restrained;
One skilled abandons evil deeds;
With passion, hate, and delusion exhausted,
One attains release, final Nibbāna.

8.6 Pāṭali Village (*Pāṭaligāmiya Sutta*)

Thus have I heard. At one time the Lord, while walking on tour among the people of Magadha together with a large Order of bhikkhus, arrived at the village of Pāṭali and stayed there. The lay followers of Pāṭali village heard: "It is said that the Lord, while walking on tour among the people of Magadha together with a large Order of bhikkhus, has arrived at Pāṭali village."

Then the lay followers of Pāṭali village approached the Lord, prostrated themselves, sat down to one side, and said to the Lord, "Revered sir, let the Lord consent to lodge in our rest house." The Lord consented by remaining silent. Then, on seeing that the Lord had consented, the lay followers of Pāṭali village rose from their seats, prostrated themselves before the Lord, and keeping their right sides towards him, went to the resthouse. On arriving they spread coverings over the whole floor of the rest house, prepared seats, placed a water jar there, and set up an oil-lamp. Then they went to the Lord, prostrated themselves, and standing there they said to the Lord: "The whole floor of the rest house has been spread with coverings, seats are prepared, a water jar has been placed there, and an oil-lamp set up. Let the Lord do now what he thinks it time to do."

Then the Lord, robing himself in the forenoon and taking his bowl and outer cloak, went to the rest house together with the Order of bhikkhus. On arriving he washed his feet, entered the rest house, and sat down by the middle pillar facing east. The

Order of bhikkhus ... sat down near the western wall facing east with the Lord before them. And the lay followers of Pāṭali village, having washed their feet, entered the rest house and sat down near the eastern wall facing west with the Lord in front of them. Then the Lord addressed the lay followers of Pāṭali village:

"There are, householders, these five disadvantages for the immoral person through his failing in virtue. What are the five?

"Here, householders, the immoral unvirtuous person through negligence suffers great loss of wealth; this is the first disadvantage for the immoral person through his failing in virtue. Furthermore, householders, an evil repute is spread about concerning an immoral unvirtuous person; this is the second disadvantage........ Again, householders, whatever assembly an immoral unvirtuous person approaches—whether an assembly of nobles, of brahmins, of householders, or of recluses—he approaches lacking confidence and assurance: this is the third disadvantage.... Again, householders, an immoral unvirtuous person dies confused; this is the fourth disadvantage.... Finally, householders, upon the breakup of the body, after death, an immoral unvirtuous person re-arises in a realm of misery, an unhappy state, the place of downfall, hell; this is the fifth disadvantage....

"These, householders, are the five disadvantages for the immoral person through his failing in virtue.

"There are, householders, these five benefits for a moral person through his achievement in virtue. What are the five?

"Here, householders, the moral virtuous person through diligence obtains a great mass of wealth; this is the first benefit for the moral person through his achievement in virtue. Furthermore, householders, a good repute is spread about concerning a moral virtuous person; this is the second benefit.... Again, householders, whatever assembly a moral virtuous person approaches ... he approaches confident and assured: this is the third benefit.... Again, householders, a moral virtuous person dies unconfused; this is the fourth benefit.... Finally, householders, upon the breakup of the body, after death, a moral virtuous person re-arises in a happy state, in a heavenly world; this is the fifth benefit....

"These, householders, are the five benefits for the moral person through his achievement in virtue."

Then the Lord, having instructed, roused, inspired, and gladdened the lay followers of Pāṭali village with talk on Dhamma for much of the night, sent them away, saying: "The night is far spent, householders. Do now what you think it is time to do."

Then the lay followers of Pāṭali village, being pleased with and appreciative of what the Lord had said, rose from their seats, prostrated themselves before the Lord, and keeping their right sides towards him, departed. Soon after the lay followers of Pāṭali village had departed the Lord retired to an empty room.

At that time Sunīdha and Vassakāra, government ministers of Magadha, were building a city at Pāṭali village to ward off the Vajjīs.[15] And large numbers of devatās, counted in thousands, occupied sites around Pāṭali village. Wherever powerful devatās occupy sites, powerful kings and royal ministers are inclined to build settlements. And wherever middling and minor devatās occupy sites, middling and minor kings and royal ministers are inclined to build settlements. Now, with the divine eye purified and surpassing that of humans the Lord saw those devatās, counted in thousands, occupying sites around Pāṭali village. Then the Lord, at the end of the night when dawn was approaching, got up and said to the Venerable Ānanda, "Ānanda, who is building a city at Pāṭali village?"

"Sunīdha and Vassakāra, the government ministers of Magadha, revered sir, are building a city at Pāṭali village to ward off the Vajjīs."

"It is as if Sunīdha and Vassakāra had consulted the devas of the Tāvatiṃsa heaven, Ānanda, (before deciding) on building a city at Pāṭali village to ward off the Vajjīs. I have seen, Ānanda, with the divine eye ... large numbers of devatās, counted in thousands, occupying sites around Pāṭali village. Wherever powerful devatās occupy sites ... kings and royal ministers are inclined to build settlements. As far as the sphere of influence of the Noble One extends,[16] Ānanda, as far as the trade routes spread, this will be the chief city where bales of merchandise will be opened up. But Pāṭaliputta, Ānanda, will suffer three disasters: from fire, from water, or from the breaking of an alliance." [17]

Then Sunīdha and Vassakāra, the government ministers of Magadha, approached the Lord, exchanged friendly greetings with him, stood to one side, and said, "Please consent, good Gotama, to our providing a meal tomorrow for you together with the Order of bhikkhus." The Lord consented by remaining silent. Then, on seeing that the Lord had consented, Sunīdha and Vassakāra went to their own dwelling. Having prepared there choice solid and soft food, they announced to the Lord the time (for the meal, saying), "It is time, good Gotama, the meal is ready."

Then the Lord, putting on his robe in the forenoon and taking his bowl and outer cloak, together with the Order of bhikkhus went to the dwelling of Sunīdha and Vassakāra. On arriving he sat down on the seat prepared for him. Then Sunīdha and Vassakāra, the government ministers of Magadha, served and satisfied with their own hands the Order of bhikkhus headed by the Buddha with choice food, both solid and soft. Then, when the Lord had eaten and washed his hand and bowl, Sunīdha and Vassakāra, choosing a low seat, sat down to one side. And the Lord thanked Sunīdha and Vassakāra with these verses:

"In whatever place a wise man
Sets up his home,
Here he should feed the virtuous,
The controlled who lead the holy life.

To those devatās there
He should make offerings;
Revered, they will revere him,
Honoured, they will honour him.

They will show compassion for him
As a mother shows for her own child.
A man for whom devatās have compassion
Always has good fortune."

Having thanked Sunīdha and Vassakāra with these verses, the Lord rose from his seat and departed.

On that occasion Sunīdha and Vassakāra followed in the footsteps of the Lord, thinking: "Whichever gate the recluse Gotama leaves by today will be called the Gotama Gate, and the ford by which he will cross the river Ganges will be called the Gotama Ford." And the gate by which the Lord departed came to be called the Gotama Gate.

Then the Lord approached the river Ganges, but at that time the river was so full that a crow (standing on the bank) could drink from it. Some people there, wishing to cross to the other shore, were searching for a boat, some were searching for a floating log, and some were constructing a raft. Then, just as a strong man might extend his flexed arm or flex his extended arm, so did the Lord vanish from the hither bank of the river Ganges and re-appear on the far bank together with the Order of bhikkhus. And the Lord saw those people ... constructing a raft.

Then, on realizing its significance, the Lord uttered on that occasion this inspired utterance:

Those who have made a bridge
Cross over the river flood,
Leaving the swampy pools behind.
While people are binding a raft
The wise are already across.[18]

8.7 The Two Ways *(Dvidhāpatha Sutta)*

Thus have I heard. At one time the Lord was journeying along a road among the people of Kosala with the Venerable Nāgasamāla as his attendant.[19] As they went along the Venerable Nāgasamāla saw that the road divided, and on perceiving this, said to the Lord: "Revered sir, that is the way;

let us go that way." Whereupon the Lord said to the Venerable Nāgasamāla, "This is the way, Nāgasamāla; let us go this way."

A second time and a third time the Venerable Nāgasamāla said to the Lord: "Revered sir, that is the way; let us go that way." And a second time and a third time the Lord said: "This is the way, Nāgasamāla; let us go this way."

Then the Venerable Nāgasamāla put the Lord's bowl and cloak down on the ground and went off, saying, "Here, revered sir, is the Lord's bowl and cloak." As the Venerable Nāgasamāla was going along that road, robbers came upon him, knocked him down and kicked him, and broke his bowl and tore his robe. Then the Venerable Nāgasamāla, with broken bowl and torn robe, went back to the Lord. Having prostrated himself before the Lord, he sat down to one side and said: "Just now, revered sir, as I was going along that road, robbers came upon me, knocked me down and kicked me, and broke my bowl and tore my robe."

Then, on realizing its significance, the Lord uttered on that occasion this inspired utterance:

Travelling together, dwelling as one,
A wise man must mix with foolish people.
But having known a bad one he leaves him behind
As the milk-drinking heron leaves the water. [20]

8.8 Visākhā *(Visākhā Sutta)*

Thus have I heard. At one time the Lord was staying near Sāvatthī in the Eastern Park at Migāra's mother's mansion. On that occasion the dearly beloved grandchild of Visākhā, Migāra's mother, had died. Then Visākhā, Migāra's mother, with wet clothes and hair,[21] approached the Lord in the middle of the day. Having prostrated herself, she sat down to one side, and the Lord said to her: "Where have you come from, Visākhā, arriving here in the middle of the day with wet clothes and hair?"

"Revered sir, my dearly beloved grandchild has died. That is why I have arrived here in the middle of the day with wet clothes and hair."

"Visākhā, would you like to have as many children and grandchildren as there are people in Sāvatthī?"

"I would, Lord, like to have as many children and grandchildren as there are people in Sāvatthī."

"But how many people, Visākhā, die daily in Sāvatthī?"

"Perhaps ten people, revered sir, die daily in Sāvatthī. Or perhaps nine people die ... or eight, seven, six, five, four, three, two people die ... or perhaps one person dies daily in Sāvatthī. Revered sir, Sāvatthī is never without people dying."

"What do you think, Visākhā, would you ever be without wet clothes or wet hair?"

"No, revered sir. Enough with my having so many children and grandchildren!"

"Visākhā, those who have a hundred dear ones have a hundred sufferings. Those who have ninety dear ones have ninety sufferings. Those who have eighty ... seventy ... sixty ... fifty ... forty ... thirty ... twenty ... ten ... five ... four ... three ... two dear ones have two sufferings. Those who have one dear one have one suffering. Those who have no dear ones have no suffering. They are sorrowless, stainless, without despair, I say."

Then, on realizing its significance, the Lord uttered on that occasion this inspired utterance:

Whatever sorrows or lamentations there are,
The various kinds of suffering in the world,
It is because of something dear that these exist;
Without something dear these do not exist.

So they are happy and free from sorrow
Who have nothing dear anywhere in the world.
So aspiring to be sorrowless and stainless
Do not hold dear anything anywhere in the world.

8.9 Dabba (1) *(Paṭhamadabba Sutta)*

Thus have I heard. At one time the Lord was staying near Rājagaha in the Bamboo Wood at the Squirrels' Feeding Place. Then the Venerable Dabba Mallaputta approached the Lord, prostrated himself, sat down to one side, and said to the Lord, "Now, Sugata, is the time for my final Nibbāna."

"Do now, Dabba, what you think it time to do."

Then the Venerable Dabba Mallaputta arose from his seat, prostrated himself before the Lord, and keeping his right side towards him, rose up in the air; and in the sky, while sitting cross-legged in space, he entered into the fire element, emerged, and attained final Nibbāna.[22]

Now, when the Venerable Dabba Mallaputta ... entered into the fire element, emerged, and attained final Nibbāna, his body was burnt up and utterly consumed so that neither ashes nor soot remained behind. Just as, when ghee or oil is burnt and consumed, neither ashes nor soot remain behind, even so it was when the Venerable Dabba Mallaputta attained final Nibbāna.

Then, on realizing its significance, the Lord uttered on that occasion this inspired utterance:

The body disintegrated, perception ceased,
All feelings became cool,
Mental activities were calmed,
And consciousness came to an end. [23]

8.10 Dabba (2) *(Dutiyadabba Sutta)*

Thus have I heard. At one time the Lord was staying near Sāvatthī in the Jeta Wood at Anāthapiṇḍika's monastery. There the Lord addressed the bhikkhus, saying, "Bhikkhus!"

"Yes, most revered sir," those bhikkhus responded to the Lord.

The Lord said: "When Dabba Mallaputta rose up in the air, and in the sky, while sitting cross-legged in space, entered into the fire element, emerged, and attained final Nibbāna, his body was burnt up and utterly consumed, so that neither ashes nor soot remained. Just as, when ghee or oil is burnt … so his body was burnt up and utterly consumed."

Then, on realizing its significance, the Lord uttered on that occasion this inspired utterance:

Just as the bourn is not known
Of the gradual fading glow
Given off by the furnace-heated iron
As it is struck with the smith's hammer, [24]
So there is no pointing to the bourn
Of those perfectly released,
Who have crossed the flood
Of bondage to sense desires
And attained unshakeable bliss.

The Book of the Inspired Utterances is finished.

Part II

The Itivuttaka

The Buddha's Sayings

INTRODUCTION

The present work offers a translation of the Itivuttaka, a collection of 112 short discourses of the Buddha in both prose and verse. The text belongs to the Pali Canon of the Theravāda school, being placed between the Udāna and the Sutta Nipāta. It was previously translated by F.L. Woodward and published together with his translation of the Udāna in *Minor Anthologies of the Pali Canon*, Vol. II (London, 1935).

According to the commentarial tradition, the suttas or discourses of the Itivuttaka were collected by the woman lay-disciple Khujjuttarā from sermons given by the Buddha while he was staying at Kosambī. Khujjuttarā was a servant of Sāmāvatī, the consort of King Udena. She had become a stream-enterer after meeting the Buddha and subsequently converted the women of the palace headed by Sāmāvatī to the teaching. She used to go regularly to listen to the Buddha and then later repeated what she had heard to the other women. The collection of these sayings became the Itivuttaka. It is said that the emphatic statements at the beginning and end of each of the suttas, reproduced here only in the first and last, were made by Khujjuttarā to stress that they were the Buddha's words and not her own.

Whether or not this story is true, the Itivuttaka is the only book in the Pali Canon that introduces and concludes its suttas in this fashion, and it is from the opening statement that the title is derived: "This was said (*vuttaṃ*) by the Lord ... so (*iti*) I heard"—hence *Itivuttaka*, "The So-was-said" or "Sayings."

These "Sayings" are grouped into four unequal sections arranged, like the Aṅguttara Nikāya, according to the number of items they contain, from one to four. Besides these four sections—The Ones, The Twos, The Threes, and The Fours—the text is further subdivided into *vaggas*, groups of roughly ten suttas. But to simplify the presentation, in this translation these sub-groupings have been ignored. Only the four main sections have been retained and the suttas numbered from 1 to 112, as in the PTS edition. A number of the suttas and verses are also found in other parts of the Sutta Piṭaka, especially the Aṅguttara Nikāya, but many are unique to this collection.

In translating the Itivuttaka I have attempted to follow the text as closely as possible and to produce an exact and literal rendition. With the verses, however, while remaining faithful to the meaning, I occasionally found it necessary to depart from the syntax of the Pali. Although I did not attempt to produce a metrical translation, by transposing lines and words and controlling the number of syllables in the line, I aimed at producing a readable and rhythmic English rendering of the original Pali verse.

In this translation of the Itivuttaka, as in my rendering of the Udāna, a few words have been left untranslated. *Dhamma* is the "real truth," the "essential idea" and the "ideal" of the Buddha's teaching. When this Dhamma is revealed to others, the person who understands it is able to attain the final aim of the teaching: to overcome suffering and realize Nibbāna, the ultimate goal.

The word *bhikkhu* is often translated as "monk," but at the time of the Buddha it was not used in such a general sense. A bhikkhu can be defined as "one who is dependent upon another's gifts of alms as his means of subsistence" (see Suttas 91 and 107), but "almsman" or "beggar," the literal meaning, would be quite misleading as it does not imply the honoured status accorded to the bhikkhu. The feminine is *bhikkhunī*, a Buddhist nun, mentioned only occasionally in the present work. Ordinary people called the Buddha's followers "recluses" (*samaṇa*), which approximates more to what we understand as a "monk" or celibate. A *samaṇa* was one who had actually forsaken the confined and circumscribed family life of a householder. But in later times this general term tended to be used less often when the Sangha, the monastic community, had become well established, identifiable and settled. In the earliest period the Buddha usually used the word "bhikkhu" when addressing his following of samaṇas, and the same word was used by the monks amongst themselves and by the inner circle of faithful layfollowers who were established in the Dhamma. And it is to these that the Itivuttaka and the other suttas of the Pali Canon were originally directed.

Mention is also made in the Itivuttaka of the *devas*. These are gods, inhabitants of the heavenly worlds, but they are also mortal beings subject to fall when the good kamma that brought them to that realm is exhausted (see Sutta 83). Above the devas are the *brahmās*, high divinities still more powerful than the devas but likewise transient. Their chief is Mahā Brahmā, "the Great Brahmā," who sometimes deludedly fancies himself to be an omnipotent creator.

This translation was made from the PTS edition of the Itivuttaka, but other editions of the text, especially the Burmese Chaṭṭhasaṅgāyana edition, were also consulted for alternative readings of doubtful passages and for clearing up mistakes and omissions in the text, fortunately few in number. This is in marked contrast to the PTS edition of the Udāna, which is full of errors. In compiling the notes frequent use was made of the commentary, the *Paramatthadīpanī* of Ācariya Dhammapāla. To understand a text, in the places where the use of a word or phrase is ambiguous, the commentary is essential for deciding the traditional meaning and significance of these passages.

The titles of the suttas are taken from the Burmese edition of the text. The PTS edition does not include them, though they can be deduced from the summaries found at the end of each *vagga*. Woodward also does not give them in his translation. The use of initial titles is actually a modern innovation of the printed book. The tradition in Pali literature is either the end-name—often several alternatives are given for important works—or else the summary at the end of the *vagga*, making use of one or more key words from each of the suttas. The summaries originally served as a device to aid memory in an oral tradition which lacked the benefit of the printed word.

JOHN D. IRELAND

Namo tassa bhagavato arahato sammāsambuddhassa

CHAPTER 1

THE SECTION OF THE ONES
(Ekanipāta)

1–13 Greed *(Lobha Sutta)*

This was said by the Lord, said by the Arahant, so I heard:[1]

"Abandon one thing, bhikkhus, and I guarantee you non-returning. What is that one thing? Greed is that one thing, bhikkhus. Abandon that and I guarantee you non-returning."[2]

Beings coveting with greed
Go to rebirth in a bad bourn.[3]
But having rightly understood greed,
Those with insight abandon it.
By abandoning it they never come
Back to this world again.

This too is the meaning of what was said by the Lord, so I heard.[1]

2–13 Hate *(Dosa Sutta)*

This was said by the Lord....

"... Hate is that one thing, bhikkhus.[4] Abandon that and I guarantee you non-returning."

Beings corrupted by hate
Go to rebirth in a bad bourn.
But having rightly understood hate,
Those with insight abandon it.
By abandoning it they never come
Back to this world again.

3–13 Delusion *(Moha Sutta)*

This was said by the Lord....

"... Delusion is that one thing, bhikkhus. Abandon that and I guarantee you non-returning."

Beings confused by delusion
Go to rebirth in a bad bourn.
But having rightly understood delusion,
Those with insight abandon it.
By abandoning it they never come
Back to this world again.

4–13 Anger *(Kodha Sutta)*

This was said by the Lord....

"... Anger is that one thing, bhikkhus. Abandon that and I guarantee you non-returning."

Beings enraged with anger
Go to rebirth in a bad bourn.
But having rightly understood anger,
Those with insight abandon it.
By abandoning it they never come
Back to this world again.

5–13 Contempt *(Makkha Sutta)*

This was said by the Lord....

"... Contempt is that one thing, bhikkhus. Abandon that and I guarantee you non-returning."

Beings despising others with contempt
Go to rebirth in a bad bourn.
But having rightly understood contempt,
Those with insight abandon it.
By abandoning it they never come
Back to this world again.

6–13 Conceit *(Māna Sutta)*

This was said by the Lord....

"... Conceit is that one thing, bhikkhus. Abandon that and I guarantee you non-returning."

Beings puffed up with conceit
Go to rebirth in a bad bourn.
But having rightly understood conceit,
Those with insight abandon it.
By abandoning it they never come
Back to this world again.

7–13 Understanding the All *(Sabbapariññā Sutta)*

This was said by the Lord....

"Bhikkhus, one who has not directly known and fully understood the 'All,'[5] who has not detached his mind from it and abandoned it, is incapable of destroying suffering. But one who has directly known and fully understood the 'All,' and who has detached his mind from it and abandoned it, is capable of destroying suffering."

One who knows the "All" in every way,
Who is not attached to anything,
Having fully understood the "All,"
Has overcome all suffering.

8–13 Understanding Conceit *(Mānapariññā Sutta)*

This was said by the Lord....

"Bhikkhus, one who has not directly known and fully understood conceit, who has not detached his mind from it and abandoned it, is incapable of destroying suffering. But one who has directly known and fully understood conceit, and who has detached his mind from it and abandoned it, is capable of destroying suffering."

Humankind is possessed by conceit,
Bound by conceit and delighted with being;
Not fully understanding conceit,
They come again to renewal of being.[6]

But those who have abandoned conceit,
And who by destroying conceit are freed,
Have conquered the bondage of conceit
And overcome all suffering.

9–13 Understanding Greed, etc.
(Lobha-, Dosa-, Moha-, Kodha-, Makkhapariññā Sutta)

This was said by the Lord….

"… One who has directly known and fully understood greed, hate, delusion, anger, contempt … is capable of destroying suffering."[7]

10–13 Ignorance *(Avijjānīvaraṇa Sutta)*

This was said by the Lord….

"Bhikkhus, I do not perceive any single hindrance other than the hindrance of ignorance by which humankind is so obstructed and for so long a time runs on and wanders in saṃsāra.[8] It is indeed through the hindrance of ignorance that humankind is obstructed and for a long time runs on and wanders in saṃsāra."

No other single thing exists
Like the hindrance of delusion,
Which so obstructs humankind
And makes it wander on forever.

Those who have abandoned delusion,
Cleaving through this mass of darkness,
No longer roam and wander on;
In them the cause is found no more.

11–13 Craving (*Taṇhāsaṃyojana Sutta*)

This was said by the Lord....

"Bhikkhus, I do not perceive any single fetter other than the fetter of craving by which beings are so tied and for so long a time run on and wander in saṃsāra. It is indeed through the fetter of craving that beings are tied and for a long time run on and wander in saṃsāra."

A man companioned by craving
Wanders on this long journey;
He cannot go beyond saṃsāra
In this state of being or another.

Having understood the danger thus—
That craving is the origin of suffering—
A bhikkhu should wander mindfully,
Free from craving, without grasping.

12–13 The Learner (*Paṭhama-sekha Sutta*)

This was said by the Lord....

"Bhikkhus, in regard to internal factors, I do not perceive another single factor so helpful as wise attention[9] for a bhikkhu who is a learner, who has not attained perfection but lives aspiring for the supreme security from bondage.[10] Bhikkhus, a bhikkhu who wisely attends abandons what is unwholesome and develops what is wholesome."

For a bhikkhu who is a learner
There is no other thing so helpful
For reaching the highest goal
As the factor wise attention.
Wisely striving a bhikkhu may attain
The destruction of all suffering.

13–13 The Good Friend *(Dutiya-sekha Sutta)*

This was said by the Lord....

"Bhikkhus, in regard to external factors, I do not perceive another single factor so helpful as good friendship for a bhikkhu who is a learner, who has not attained perfection but lives aspiring for the supreme security from bondage.[11] Bhikkhus, a bhikkhu who has a good friend abandons what is unwholesome and develops what is wholesome."

When a bhikkhu has good friends,
And is reverential and respectful,
Doing what his friends advise,
Clearly comprehending and mindful,
He may progressively attain
The destruction of all fetters.[12]

14–13 Disunity in the Sangha *(Saṅghabheda Sutta)*

This was said by the Lord....

"There is one thing, bhikkhus, which, when it appears in the world, appears for the detriment of many people, for the misery of many people, for the loss, detriment, and suffering of devas and humans. What is that one thing? It is disunity in the Sangha.[13] When the Sangha is divided there are mutual quarrels, mutual recriminations, mutual denigrations, and mutual expulsions. In this situation those who are unsympathetic are not converted and some who are sympathetic change their minds."[14]

One who divides the Sangha
Abides in a state of misery, in hell,
For the aeon's full duration.
Delighting in dissent, unrighteous,
He is deprived of security from bondage;
By dividing a unified Sangha
He suffers in hell for an aeon.[15]

15–13 Unity in the Sangha *(Saṅghasāmaggi Sutta)*

This was said by the Lord....

"There is one thing, bhikkhus, which, when it appears in the world, appears for the welfare of many people, for the happiness of many people, for the good, welfare, and happiness of devas and humans. What is that one thing? It is unity in the Sangha. When the Sangha is united there are no mutual quarrels, mutual recriminations, mutual denigrations, and mutual expulsions. In this situation those who are unsympathetic are converted and those who are sympathetic increase in faith."

Pleasant is unity in the Sangha.
One who helps those in unity,
Who delights in unity and is righteous,
Is not deprived of security from bondage.[16]
By making the Sangha united
He rejoices in heaven for an aeon.

16–13 A Corrupt Mind *(Paduṭṭhacitta Sutta)*

This was said by the Lord....

"Here, bhikkhus, some person has a corrupt mind. Having examined his mind with my mind, I know that if this person were to die at this time, as if carried there he would be placed in hell.[17] What is the reason for that? It is because his mind is corrupt. It is because of the mind's corruption that some beings here, when the body perishes, are reborn after death in a state of misery, a bad bourn, a state of ruin, hell."

Understanding the corrupt mind
Of some person dwelling here,
The Buddha explained its meaning
In the presence of the bhikkhus.

If that person were to die
At this very moment now,
He would be reborn in hell
Because of his corrupt mind.

As if they were carried off
And placed there, thus
Beings go to a bad bourn
Because of mind's corruption.[18]

17–13 A Confident Mind *(Pasannacitta Sutta)*

This was said by the Lord....

"Here, bhikkhus, some person has a confident mind.[19] Having examined his mind with my mind, I know that if this person were to die at this time, as if carried there he would be placed in heaven. What is the reason for that? It is because his mind is confident. It is because of the mind's confidence that some beings here, when the body perishes, are reborn after death in a good bourn, in a heavenly world."

Understanding the confident mind
Of some person dwelling here,
The Buddha explained its meaning
In the presence of the bhikkhus.

If that person were to die
At this very moment now,
He would arise in a good bourn
Because of his confident mind.

As if they were carried off
And placed there, thus
Beings go to a good bourn
Because of mind's confidence.

18–13 Meritorious Deeds *(Mettā Sutta)*

This was said by the Lord....

"Bhikkhus, do not fear meritorious deeds. This is an expression denoting happiness, what is desirable, wished for, dear and agreeable, that is, 'meritorious deeds.' For I know full well,[20] bhikkhus, that for a long time I experienced desirable, wished for, dear and agreeable results from often performing meritorious deeds.

"Having cultivated for seven years a mind of loving-kindness,[21] for seven aeons of contraction and expansion I did not return to this world. Whenever the aeon contracted I reached the plane of Streaming Radiance, and when the aeon expanded I arose in an empty Brahma-mansion. And there I was a Brahmā, the Great Brahmā, the Unvanquished Victor, the All-seeing, the All-powerful.[22] Thirty-six times I was Sakka, the ruler of the devas.[23] And many hundreds of times I was a Wheel-turning Monarch, righteous, a king of righteousness, conqueror of the four quarters of the earth, maintaining stability in the land, in possession of the seven jewels.[24] What need is there to speak of mere local kingship?

"It occurred to me, bhikkhus, to wonder: 'Of what kind of deed of mine is this the fruit? Of what deed's ripening is it that I am now of such great accomplishment and power?' And then it occurred to me: 'It is the fruit of three kinds of deeds of mine, the ripening of three kinds of deeds that I am now of such great accomplishment and power: deeds of giving, of self-mastery, and of refraining.'"[25]

One should train in deeds of merit
That yield long-lasting happiness:
Generosity, a balanced life,
Developing a loving mind.

By cultivating these three things,
Deeds yielding happiness,
The wise person is reborn in bliss
In an untroubled happy world.

19–13 Diligence *(Ubhayattha Sutta)*

This was said by the Lord....

"There is one thing, bhikkhus, developed and continually practised, by which both kinds of welfare are acquired and maintained: welfare here and now, and that pertaining to the future. What is that one thing? It is diligence in wholesome states.[26] This is that one thing...."

The wise praise diligence
In doing deeds of merit;
For one who is wise and diligent
Obtains a twofold benefit:

Welfare in the here and now
And welfare in a future life.
And because one has realized the good,
The wise person is called a sage.

20–13 A Heap of Bones *(Aṭṭhipuñja Sutta)*

This was said by the Lord....

"Bhikkhus, the skeletons of a single person, running on and wandering in saṃsāra for an aeon, would make a heap of bones, a quantity of bones as large as this Mount Vepulla, if there were someone to collect them and if the collection were not destroyed."

The bones of a single person
Accumulated in a single aeon
Would make a heap like a mountain—
So said the Great Sage.

He declared it to be
As great as Mount Vepulla
To the north of Vulture's Peak
In the hill-fort of Magadha.

But when one sees with perfect wisdom
The four noble truths as they are—
Suffering, the origin of suffering,
The overcoming of suffering,
And the noble eightfold path
Leading to relief from suffering—

Having merely run on
Seven times at the most,
By destroying all fetters
One makes an end of suffering.[27]

21–13 Lying *(Musāvāda Sutta)*

This was said by the Lord….

"Bhikkhus, I say that for an individual who transgresses in one thing, there is no evil deed whatsoever he would not do. What is that one thing? It is this, bhikkhus: deliberately telling a lie."

There is no evil that cannot be done
By a person who deliberately lies,
Who transgresses in one thing,
Taking no account of the next world.

22–13 Giving *(Dāna Sutta)*

This was said by the Lord….

"Bhikkhus, if beings knew, as I know, the result of giving and sharing,[28] they would not eat without having given, nor would they allow the stain of meanness to obsess them and take root in their minds. Even if it were their last morsel, their last mouthful, they would not eat[29] without having shared it, if there were someone to share it with. But, bhikkhus, as beings do not know, as I know, the result of giving and sharing, they eat without having given, and the stain of meanness obsesses them and takes root in their minds."

If beings only knew—
So said the Great Sage—
How the result of sharing
Is of such great fruit,
With a gladdened mind,
Rid of the stain of meanness,
They would duly give to noble ones
Who make what is given fruitful.

Having given much food as offerings
To those most worthy of offerings,
The donors go to heaven
On departing the human state.

Having gone to heaven they rejoice,
And enjoying pleasures there,
The unselfish experience the result
Of generously sharing with others.

23–13 The Development of Loving-kindness
(Mettābhāvanā Sutta)

This was said by the Lord....

"Bhikkhus, whatever grounds there are for making merit productive of a future birth,[30] all these do not equal a sixteenth part of the mind-release of loving-kindness.[31] The mind-release of loving-kindness surpasses them and shines forth, bright and brilliant.

"Just as the radiance of all the stars does not equal a sixteenth part of the moon's radiance, but the moon's radiance surpasses them and shines forth, bright and brilliant, even so, whatever grounds there are for making merit productive of a future birth, all these do not equal a sixteenth part of the mind-release of loving-kindness....

"Just as in the last month of the rainy season, in the autumn, when the sky is clear and free of clouds, the sun, on ascending, dispels the darkness of space and shines forth, bright and brilliant, even so, whatever grounds there are for making merit productive of a future birth, all these do not equal a sixteenth part of the mind-release of loving-kindness....

"And just as in the night, at the moment of dawn, the morning star shines forth, bright and brilliant, even so, whatever grounds there are for making merit productive of a future birth, all these do not equal a sixteenth part of the mind-release of loving-kindness. The mind-release of loving-kindness surpasses them and shines forth, bright and brilliant."

For one who mindfully develops
Boundless loving-kindness
Seeing the destruction of clinging,
The fetters are worn away.

If with an uncorrupted mind
He pervades just one being
With loving kindly thoughts,
He makes some merit thereby.

But a noble one produces
An abundance of merit
By having a compassionate mind
Towards all living beings.[32]

Those royal seers who conquered
The earth crowded with beings
Went about performing sacrifices:
The horse sacrifice, the man sacrifice,
The water rites, the soma sacrifice,
And that called "the Unobstructed." [33]

But these do not share even a sixteenth part
Of a well cultivated mind of love,
Just as the entire starry host
Is dimmed by the moon's radiance.

One who does not kill
Nor cause others to kill,
Who does not conquer
Nor cause others to conquer,
Kindly towards all beings—
He has enmity for none.

This too is the meaning of what was said by the Lord, so I heard.

CHAPTER 2

THE SECTION OF THE TWOS
(Dukanipāta)

1–13 Living in Discomfort *(Dukkhavihāra Sutta)*

This was said by the Lord....

"Bhikkhus, possessed of two things, a bhikkhu lives in discomfort here and now, bringing upon himself vexation, trouble, and distress, and when the body perishes after death a bad bourn is to be expected. What are the two? Being unguarded regarding the doors of the senses and being immoderate in eating.[1] These are the two things possessed of which a bhikkhu lives in discomfort...."

The eye, ear, nose, tongue,
Body and likewise the mind—
A bhikkhu who leaves these doors
Unguarded here,

Immoderate in eating,
Of uncontrolled senses,
Experiences suffering
Both bodily and mental.

Being tormented by body,
And tormented by mind,
Such a one lives in discomfort
Both by day and by night.

2–13 Living in Comfort *(Sukhavihāra Sutta)*

This was said by the Lord....

"Bhikkhus, possessed of two things a bhikkhu lives in comfort here and now, not bringing upon himself vexation, trouble, and distress, and when the body perishes after death a good bourn is to be expected. What are the two? Being guarded regarding the doors of the senses and being moderate in eating. These are the two...."

The eye, ear, nose, tongue,
Body and likewise the mind—
A bhikkhu who has these doors
Well guarded here,

Moderate in eating,
Of controlled senses,
Experiences happiness
Both bodily and mental.

Not tormented by body,
Nor tormented by mind,
Such a one lives in comfort
Both by day and by night.

3–13 Remorse *(Tapanīya Sutta)*

This was said by the Lord....

"There are two things, bhikkhus, causing remorse. What are the two? Here someone has not done what is good, not done what is wholesome, not done what is beneficial,[2] but has done evil, callous, wrongful deeds. He is remorseful on thinking, 'I have not done good,' and is remorseful on thinking, 'I have done evil.' These, bhikkhus, are the two things causing remorse."

Having performed misconduct
By body, misconduct by speech,
Misconduct by mind, and whatever else
Is reckoned a fault—

Not having done a good deed
And done much that is bad—
When his body perishes
That foolish one is reborn in hell.

4–13 Non-remorse *(Atapanīya Sutta)*

This was said by the Lord....

"There are two things, bhikkhus, causing no remorse. What are the two? Here someone has done what is good, done what is wholesome, done what is beneficial, and has not done evil, callous, wrongful deeds. He is not remorseful on thinking, 'I have done good,' and is not remorseful on thinking, 'I have done no evil.' These, bhikkhus, are the two things causing no remorse."

Having abandoned misconduct
By body, misconduct by speech,
Misconduct by mind, and whatever else
Is reckoned a fault—

Not having done a bad deed
And done much that is good—
When his body perishes
That wise one is reborn in heaven.

5–13 Behaviour (1) *(Paṭhama-sīla Sutta)*

This was said by the Lord....

"Possessing two things, bhikkhus, a person is placed in hell as if carried there. What are the two things? Bad behaviour and a bad view.[3] These, bhikkhus, are the two things...."

If a person possesses these two things—
Bad behaviour and a bad view—
When his body perishes
That foolish one is reborn in hell.

6–13 Behaviour (2) *(Dutiya-sīla Sutta)*

This was said by the Lord....

"Possessing two things, bhikkhus, a person is placed in heaven as if carried there. What are the two things? Good behaviour and a good view. These are the two things...."

If a person possesses these two things—
Good behaviour and a good view—
When his body perishes
That wise one is reborn in heaven.

7–13 Ardour *(Ātāpi Sutta)*

This was said by the Lord....

"Bhikkhus, a bhikkhu who is without ardour and without fear of wrongdoing is incapable of attaining enlightenment, incapable of attaining Nibbāna, incapable of attaining the supreme security from bondage. But a bhikkhu who has ardour and fear of wrongdoing is capable of doing so."

One who is not ardent, reckless,
Lazy, and of little vigour,
Full of lethargy and torpor,
Shameless and without respect—
Such a bhikkhu cannot attain
Enlightenment which is supreme.

But a mindful and discerning meditator,
Ardent, scrupulous, and diligent,
Having severed the fetters of birth and decay,
Can attain for himself right here and now
Enlightenment which is supreme.

8–13 Not Deceiving (1) *(Paṭhama-nakuhana Sutta)*

This was said by the Lord....

"Bhikkhus, this holy life is not lived for the sake of deceiving people, for the sake of cajoling people, for the sake of profiting in gain, honour, and fame, nor with the idea, 'Let people know me thus.' This holy life, bhikkhus, is lived for the sake of restraint and abandoning."[4]

The Lord taught a holy life
Not based on tradition,[5]
For restraint and abandoning,
Leading to and merging in Nibbāna.

This is the path followed by the great,
Pursued by the lofty sages.
Those who enter that course
As taught by the Enlightened One,
Heeding the Teacher's instruction,
Will make an end of suffering.

9–13 Not Deceiving (2) *(Dutiya-nakuhana Sutta)*

This was said by the Lord....

"Bhikkhus, this holy life is not lived for the sake of deceiving people, for the sake of cajoling people, for the sake of profiting in gain, honour, and fame, nor with the idea, 'Let people know me thus.' This holy life, bhikkhus, is lived for the sake of direct knowledge and full understanding."[6]

The Lord taught a holy life
Not based on tradition,
For knowledge and understanding,
Leading to and merging in Nibbāna.

This is the path followed by the great,
Pursued by the lofty sages.
Those who enter that course
As taught by the Enlightened One,
Heeding the Teacher's instruction,
Will make an end of suffering.[7]

10–13 Happiness *(Somanassa Sutta)*

This was said by the Lord....

"Bhikkhus, possessing two things a bhikkhu lives here and now with much pleasure and happiness and is properly motivated for the destruction of the taints.[8] What are the two things? Being moved by a sense of urgency on occasions for urgency, and, being moved, making a proper endeavour. These, bhikkhus, are the two things...."[9]

A wise person should be urgently moved
On occasions that make for urgency;
As an ardent discerning bhikkhu
He should investigate with wisdom.

One living ardent thus,
Of peaceful conduct, not proud,
Practising tranquillity of mind,
May attain the destruction of suffering.

11–13 Often Occurring Thoughts *(Vitakka Sutta)*

This was said by the Lord....

"Bhikkhus, two thoughts often occur to the Tathāgata,[10] the Arahant, the Fully Enlightened One: the thought of security (for beings) and the thought of solitude.[11]

"The Tathāgata, bhikkhus, is one who delights in and enjoys non-ill will.[12] As the Tathāgata delights in and enjoys non-ill will, this thought often occurs to him: 'By this behaviour I do not oppress anyone either frail or firm.'[13] The Tathāgata, bhikkhus, is one who delights in and enjoys solitude. As the Tathāgata delights in and enjoys solitude, this thought often occurs to him: 'What is unwholesome has been abandoned.'[14]

"Therefore, bhikkhus, I say, you too must live delighting in and enjoying non-ill will. As you so live this thought will often occur to you: 'By this behaviour we do not oppress anyone either frail or firm.'

"Bhikkhus, you too must live delighting in and enjoying solitude. As you so live this thought will often occur to you: 'What is unwholesome? What has not been abandoned? What have we abandoned?'"

Two thoughts occur to him,
The Tathāgata, the Awakened One
Who endured what is beyond endurance:[15]
Security (for beings) was the first thought spoken of,
Solitude was the second announced.

The dispeller of darkness, gone beyond,
The great sage who has reached attainment,
Become a master, freed from taints,
Who has crossed over entirely,[16]
Released by the destruction of craving—
That sage bears his final body,
And having left behind Māra, I say,[17]
He has gone beyond decay.

As one standing on a mountain peak
Might see all round the people down below,
So having ascended the Dhamma-palace,
The vastly wise one, all-seeing,
Views the people of the world.
The sorrowless one views below
Those still immersed in sorrow,
Overwhelmed by birth and decay.[18]

12–13 Dhamma-teachings *(Desanā Sutta)*

This was said by the Lord....

"There are, bhikkhus, two successive Dhamma-teachings of the Tathāgata, the Arahant, the Fully Enlightened One. What are the two? 'See evil as evil'— this is the first Dhamma-teaching. 'Having seen evil as evil, be rid of it, be detached from it, be freed from it'—this is the second Dhamma-teaching. These, bhikkhus, are the two successive Dhamma-teachings of the Tathāgata...."

Regard the ordered words he spoke,
The Tathāgata, the Awakened One,
Compassionate for all beings,
And the two things he proclaimed:

"See what is evil" is one,
The other "Be detached from it."
With a mind become detached from evil
You will make an end of suffering.

13–13 Knowledge *(Vijjā Sutta)*

This was said by the Lord....

"Ignorance, bhikkhus, precedes and leads to unwholesome states, and shamelessness and lack of fear of wrongdoing follow after. Knowledge, bhikkhus, precedes and leads to wholesome states, and shame and fear of wrongdoing follow after." [19]

Whatever bad bourns there are
In this world and hereafter,
All are rooted in ignorance,
Constructed by desire and greed.

Since one of evil desires
Is shameless and disrespectful,
From that evil flows forth
And he goes to a state of misery.

Thus by discarding desire and greed,
Along with ignorance as well,
A bhikkhu arouses knowledge
And abandons all bad bourns.

14–13 Deprived of Wisdom *(Paññāparihīna Sutta)*

This was said by the Lord....

"Bhikkhus, those beings are thoroughly deprived who are deprived of noble wisdom. They live in discomfort even here and now, with vexation, trouble, and distress, and when the body perishes at death a bad bourn is to be expected.

"Those beings are not deprived who are not deprived of noble wisdom. They live in comfort here and now, without vexation, trouble, or distress, and when the body perishes at death a good bourn is to be expected."

See the world with its devas,
Destitute of wisdom,
Established in name-and-form,
Conceiving this to be the truth.[20]

Wisdom which leads to penetration[21]
Is the best thing in the world;
By this one completely understands
The ending of both birth and being.

Devas and human beings hold dear
Those awakened ones ever mindful,
Possessing joyous wisdom,
Bearing their final bodies.

15–13 The Bright Protectors *(Sukkadhamma Sutta)*

This was said by the Lord....

"Bhikkhus, these two bright principles protect the world. What are the two? Shame and fear of wrongdoing.[22] If, bhikkhus, these two bright principles did not protect the world, there would not be discerned respect for mother or maternal aunt or maternal uncle's wife or a teacher's wife or the wives of other honoured persons, and the world would have fallen into promiscuity, as with goats, sheep, chickens, pigs, dogs, and jackals. But as these two bright principles protect the world, there is discerned respect for mother ... and the wives of other honoured persons."

Those in whom shame and fear of wrong
Are not consistently found
Have deviated from the bright root
And are led back to birth and death.

But those in whom shame and fear of wrong
Are consistently ever present,
Peaceful, mature in the holy life,
They put an end to renewal of being.

16–13 The Not-born (*Ajāta Sutta*)

This was said by the Lord....

"There is, bhikkhus, a not-born, a not-brought-to-being, a not-made, a not-conditioned.[23] If, bhikkhus, there were no not-born, not-brought-to-being, not-made, not-conditioned, no escape would be discerned from what is born, brought-to-being, made, conditioned. But since there is a not-born, a not-brought-to-being, a not-made, a not-conditioned, therefore an escape is discerned from what is born, brought-to-being, made, conditioned."

The born, come-to-be, produced,
The made, the conditioned, the transient,
Conjoined with decay and death,
A nest of disease, perishable,
Sprung from nutriment and craving's cord—[24]
That is not fit to take delight in.

The escape from that, the peaceful,
Beyond reasoning, everlasting,
The not-born, the unproduced,
The sorrowless state that is void of stain,
The cessation of states linked to suffering,
The stilling of the conditioned—bliss.

17–13 The Nibbāna-element (*Nibbānadhātu Sutta*)

This was said by the Lord....

"Bhikkhus, there are these two Nibbāna-elements. What are the two? The Nibbāna-element with residue left and the Nibbāna-element with no residue left.

"What, bhikkhus, is the Nibbāna-element with residue left? Here a bhikkhu is an arahant, one whose taints are destroyed,[25] the holy life fulfilled, who has done what had to be done, laid down the burden, attained the goal, destroyed the fetters of being, completely released through final knowledge. However, his five sense faculties remain unimpaired, by which he still experiences what is agreeable and disagreeable and feels pleasure and pain. It is the extinction of attachment, hate, and delusion in him that is called the Nibbāna-element with residue left.[26]

"Now what, bhikkhus, is the Nibbāna-element with no residue left? Here a bhikkhu is an arahant ... completely released through final knowledge. For him, here in this very life, all that is experienced, not being delighted in, will be extinguished. That, bhikkhus, is called the Nibbāna-element with no residue left.[27]

"These, bhikkhus, are the two Nibbāna-elements."

These two Nibbāna-elements were made known
By the Seeing One, stable[28] and unattached:
One is the element seen here and now
With residue, but with the cord of being destroyed;[29]
The other, having no residue for the future,
Is that wherein all modes of being utterly cease.

Having understood the unconditioned state,
Released in mind with the cord of being destroyed,
They have attained to the Dhamma-essence.
Delighting in the destruction (of craving),
Those stable ones have abandoned all being.

18–13 Living in Seclusion *(Paṭisallāna Sutta)*

This was said by the Lord....

"Live enjoying seclusion,[30] bhikkhus; live delighting in seclusion, engage in practising inner mental tranquillity, not neglecting meditation, possessing insight,[31] and frequenting empty places. If you live enjoying seclusion, bhikkhus, ... and frequenting empty places, one of two fruits is to be expected: final knowledge here and now or, there being some residual defilement, the state of non-returning."

Those of peaceful mind, discerning,
Mindful, given to meditation,
Clearly see things rightly[32]
And long not for sensual pleasures.

Those peaceful ones, delighting in diligence,
Who see fear in negligence,
Are incapable of falling away
And are close to Nibbāna.

19–13 The Benefits of the Training *(Sikkhānisaṃsa Sutta)*

This was said by the Lord....

"Bhikkhus, live so as to realize the benefits of the training, the attainment of higher wisdom, the essence of release, and the control of mindfulness. Bhikkhus, if you live to realize the benefits of the training ... one of two fruits is to be expected: final knowledge here and now or, there being some residual defilement, the state of non-returning."

One who has completed the training,
Incapable of falling away,
Attained to the higher wisdom,
A seer of the end of birth—
That sage bears his final body,
And having left behind conceit,
He has gone beyond decay, I say.

Therefore ever delighting in meditation,
Concentrated, with ardent energy,
Seeing the end of birth, O bhikkhus,
Conquer Māra and his host,[33]
And go beyond all birth and death.

20–13 Vigilance *(Jāgariya Sutta)*

This was said by the Lord....

"Bhikkhus, a bhikkhu should be vigilant; he should live mindful, clearly comprehending, concentrated, happy and calm, and should know when it is suitable to cultivate those things that are wholesome.[34] Bhikkhus, for a bhikkhu who is vigilant and living thus, one of two fruits is to be expected: final knowledge here and now or, there being some residual defilement, the state of non-returning."

You vigilant ones hear this:
Wake up, you who are asleep!
Vigilance is better than sleep:
There is no fear for the vigilant.

One who is vigilant and mindful,
Comprehending and concentrated,
Joyful and calm in his thoughts,

By rightly investigating the Dhamma
With unified mind, will in time
Destroy the darkness of ignorance.

Therefore be devoted to vigilance,
An ardent, discerning, meditative bhikkhu.
Having severed the fetter of birth and decay,
One may here and now attain
Enlightenment which is supreme.

21–13 A State of Misery *(Āpāyika Sutta)*

This was said by the Lord....

"Bhikkhus, these two will go to a state of misery, to hell, by not giving up such conduct as this. What two? One who while no liver of the holy life pretends to be one who lives the holy life, and one who falsely accuses another who lives the holy life in complete purity of not living it. These two will go to a state of misery, to hell, by not giving up such conduct as this."

The false-accuser goes to hell
And also one who denies the deed he did;
Both these become equal hereafter,
Persons of base actions in the world beyond.

Many imposters wear the yellow robe
Though evil-natured and uncontrolled.
Because of their evil deeds,
Those evil ones are born in hell.

Far better for him to swallow
A fiery hot iron ball
Than that immoral and uncontrolled
He should eat the country's alms.[35]

22–13 Held by Views *(Diṭṭhigata Sutta)*

This was said by the Lord....

"Bhikkhus, held by two kinds of views, some devas and human beings hold back and some overreach; only those with vision see.

"And how, bhikkhus, do some hold back? Devas and humans enjoy being, delight in being, are satisfied with being. When Dhamma is taught to them for the cessation of being,[36] their minds do not enter into it or acquire confidence in it or settle upon it or become resolved upon it. Thus, bhikkhus, do some hold back.[37]

"How, bhikkhus, do some overreach? Now, some are troubled, ashamed, and disgusted by this very same being and they rejoice in (the idea of) non-being, asserting: 'In as much as this self, good sirs, when the body perishes at death, is annihilated and destroyed and does not exist after death—this is peaceful, this is excellent, this is reality!' Thus, bhikkhus, do some overreach.[38]

"How, bhikkhus, do those with vision see? Herein a bhikkhu sees what has come to be as having come to be. Having seen it thus, he practises the course for turning away, for dispassion, for the cessation of what has come to be. Thus, bhikkhus, do those with vision see."[39]

Having seen what has come to be
As having come to be,
Passing beyond what has come to be,
They are released in accordance with truth
By exhausting the craving for being.

When a bhikkhu has fully understood
That which has come to be as such,
Free from craving to be this or that,
By the extinction of what has come to be
He comes no more to renewal of being.

This too is the meaning of what was said by the Lord, so I heard.

CHAPTER 3

THE SECTION OF THE THREES
(Tikanipāta)

1–13 Roots *(Mūla Sutta)*

This was said by the Lord….

"Bhikkhus, there are these three unwholesome roots. What three? The unwholesome root greed, the unwholesome root hate, and the unwholesome root delusion. These are the three."

Greed and hate and delusion,
Arisen from within himself,
Harm an evil-minded person
As its own fruit destroys the bamboo tree.[1]

2–13 Elements *(Dhātu Sutta)*

This was said by the Lord….

"Bhikkhus, there are these three elements. What three? The form element, the formless element, and the element of cessation.[2] These are the three."

By fully understanding the form element
Without getting stuck in the formless,
They are released into cessation
And leave Death far behind them.[3]

Having touched with his own person[4]
The deathless element free from clinging,
Having realized the relinquishment of clinging
His taints all gone,
The Fully Enlightened One proclaims
The sorrowless state that is void of stain.

3–13 Feelings (1) *(Paṭhama-vedanā Sutta)*

This was said by the Lord....

"Bhikkhus, there are these three feelings. What three? Pleasant feeling, painful feeling, and neither-pleasant-nor-painful feeling. These are the three."

A disciple of the Buddha,
Concentrated, clearly comprehending
And mindful, knows feelings
And the origin of feelings,
Where they cease and the path
That leads to their full destruction.[5]
With the destruction of feelings a bhikkhu,
Without longing, has attained Nibbāna.

4–13 Feelings (2) *(Dutiya-vedanā Sutta)*

This was said by the Lord....

"Bhikkhus, there are these three feelings. What three? Pleasant feeling, painful feeling, and neither-pleasant-nor-painful feeling. Pleasant feeling, bhikkhus, should be seen as suffering,[6] painful feeling should be seen as a dart, neither-pleasant-nor-painful feeling should be seen as impermanent.

"When a bhikkhu has seen these three feelings thus, he is said to be a noble one who sees rightly. He has cut off craving, destroyed the fetters, and by thoroughly understanding conceit, he has made an end of suffering."

One sees pleasure as suffering
And sees pain as a dart.
One sees as impermanent the peaceful feeling
That is neither pleasant nor painful.

Such a bhikkhu who sees rightly
Is thereby well released.
Accomplished in knowledge, at peace,
That sage has overcome all bonds.

5–13 Search (1) *(Paṭhama-esanā Sutta)*

This was said by the Lord....

"Bhikkhus, there are these three kinds of search.[7] What three? The search for sensual gratification, the search for being, and the search for a holy life.[8] These are the three."

A disciple of the Buddha,
Concentrated, clearly comprehending
And mindful, knows searches
And the origin of searches,
Where they cease and the path
That leads to their full destruction.
With the destruction of searches a bhikkhu,
Without longing, has attained Nibbāna.

6–13 Search (2) *(Dutiya-esanā Sutta)*

This was said by the Lord....

"Bhikkhus, there are these three kinds of search..."

Sensual search, the search for being,
The search for a holy life of one
Who takes his stand upon a view
And holds it tightly as the truth—
These are heapings of defilements.

For a bhikkhu wholly dispassionate
And freed by the destruction of craving,
Searches have been relinquished
And uprooted the standpoint of views.
With the destruction of searches a bhikkhu
Is free from desire and doubt.

7–13 Taints (1) *(Paṭhama-āsava Sutta)*

This was said by the Lord....

"Bhikkhus, there are these three taints. What three? The taint of sensual desire, the taint of being, and the taint of ignorance. These are the three."

A disciple of the Buddha,
Concentrated, clearly comprehending
And mindful, knows the taints
And the origin of taints,
Where they cease and the path
That leads to their full destruction.
With the destruction of the taints a bhikkhu,
Without longing, has attained Nibbāna.

8–13 Taints (2) *(Dutiya-āsava Sutta)*

This was said by the Lord....

"Bhikkhus, there are these three taints...."

One for whom the taint of desire
For sensual pleasures has been destroyed,
Who has eliminated ignorance
And exhausted the taint of being—
Such a one is released without clinging.
Having conquered Māra and his mount,[9]
He bears his final body.

9–13 Craving *(Taṇhā Sutta)*

This was said by the Lord....

"Bhikkhus, there are these three cravings. What three? The craving for sensual pleasures, the craving for being, and the craving for non-being. These are the three."

Those fettered by the bond of craving,
Whose minds delight in being this or that,
Are people in the bondage of Māra
Who enjoy no security from bondage.
Such beings continue in saṃsāra,
Going on from birth to death.

But those who have abandoned craving,
Free from craving for being this or that,
Having attained the taints' destruction,
Though in the world, have gone beyond.

10–13 Māra's Domain (*Māradheyya Sutta*)

This was said by the Lord....

"Bhikkhus, being in possession of three things, a bhikkhu has passed beyond the domain of Māra[10] and shines like the sun. What are the three? Herein a bhikkhu is in possession of the non-learner's[11] aggregate of virtue, the non-learner's aggregate of concentration, and the non-learner's aggregate of wisdom.[12] These are the three things in possession of which a bhikkhu has passed beyond the domain of Māra and shines like the sun."

Virtue, concentration, and wisdom—
One in whom these are fully developed,
On passing beyond Māra's domain,
Shines forth like the sun.

11–13 Grounds for Making Merit (*Puññakiriyavatthu Sutta*)

This was said by the Lord....

"Bhikkhus, there are these three grounds for making merit. What three? The ground for making merit consisting in giving, the ground for making merit consisting in virtue, and the ground for making merit consisting in mind-development. These are the three."

One should train in deeds of merit
That yield long-lasting happiness:
Generosity, a balanced life,
Developing a loving mind.
By cultivating these three things,
Deeds yielding happiness,
The wise person is reborn in bliss
In an untroubled happy world.[13]

12–13 Eyes (*Cakkhu Sutta*)

This was said by the Lord....

"Bhikkhus, there are these three eyes. What three? The fleshly eye, the divine eye, and the wisdom eye.[14] These, bhikkhus, are the three eyes."

The fleshly eye, the divine eye,
And the unsurpassed wisdom eye—
These three eyes were described
By the Buddha, supreme among men.

The arising of the fleshly eye
Is the path to the divine eye,[15]
But the unsurpassed wisdom eye
Is that from which knowledge arises.
By obtaining such an eye
One is released from all suffering.[16]

13–13 Faculties *(Indriya Sutta)*

This was said by the Lord....

"Bhikkhus, there are these three faculties.[17] What three? The faculty of the assurance: 'I shall come to finally know what is as yet not finally known'; the faculty of final knowledge; and the faculty of one who has finally known.[18] These, bhikkhus, are the three faculties."

For a learner who is training
In conformity with the direct path,[19]
The knowledge of destruction arises first,
And final knowledge immediately follows.[20]

Freed by that final knowledge,
By destroying the fetters of being
The serene one has the certainty:
"Unshakeable is my release."

Endowed with this faculty
The peaceful one delights in the peaceful state.[21]
Having conquered Māra and his mount,
He bears his final body.

14–13 Time (*Addhā Sutta*)

This was said by the Lord....

"Bhikkhus, these are the three times. What three? Past time, future time, and present time. These, bhikkhus, are the three times."

Perceiving what can be expressed through concepts,
Beings take their stand on what is expressed.[22]
Not fully understanding the expressed,
They come under the bondage of Death.

But by fully understanding what is expressed
One does not misconceive the speaker.[23]
His mind has attained to freedom,
The unsurpassed state of peace.

Understanding what is expressed,
The peaceful one delights in the peaceful state.
Standing on Dhamma,[24] *perfect in knowledge,*
He freely makes use of concepts
But no more enters into concept's range.[25]

15–13 Misconduct (*Duccarita Sutta*)

This was said by the Lord....

"Bhikkhus, there are these three kinds of misconduct. What are the three? Misconduct by body, misconduct by speech, and misconduct by mind. These are the three."

Having performed misconduct
By body, misconduct by speech,
Misconduct by mind, and whatever else
Is reckoned a fault—

Not having done a good deed
And done much that is bad—
When his body perishes
That foolish one is reborn in hell.[26]

16–13 Good Conduct *(Sucarita Sutta)*

This was said by the Lord....

"Bhikkhus, there are these three kinds of good conduct. What are the three? Good conduct by body, good conduct by speech, and good conduct by mind. These are the three."

Having abandoned misconduct
By body, misconduct by speech,
Misconduct by mind, and whatever else
Is reckoned a fault—

Not having done a bad deed
And done much that is good—
When his body perishes
That wise one is reborn in heaven.

17–13 Purity *(Soceyya Sutta)*

This was said by the Lord....

"Bhikkhus, there are these three kinds of purity. What are the three? Purity of body, purity of speech, and purity of mind. These are the three."

Bodily pure, pure of speech,
Mentally pure and taintless—
A pure one possessing such purity
Is called one who has abandoned all.

18–13 Perfection *(Moneyya Sutta)*

This was said by the Lord....

"Bhikkhus, there are these three kinds of perfection. What are the three? Perfection of body, perfection of speech, and perfection of mind. These are the three."

Bodily perfect, perfect of speech,
Mentally perfect and taintless;
A sage possessing such perfection[27]
Is called one cleansed of evil.

19–13 Attachment (1) *(Paṭhama-rāga Sutta)*

This was said by the Lord....

"Bhikkhus, one in whom attachment is not abandoned, hate is not abandoned, and delusion is not abandoned, is said to be in the bondage of Māra; he is caught in Māra's noose and at the mercy of the Evil One.

"Bhikkhus, one in whom attachment is abandoned, hate is abandoned, and delusion is abandoned, is said to be free from the bondage of Māra; he has cast off Māra's noose and is not at the mercy of the Evil One."

One who has destroyed attachment
Along with hate and ignorance
Is called one inwardly developed,[28]
A Tathāgata become supreme,[29]
Awakened, past enmity and fear,
One who has abandoned all.

20–13 Attachment (2) *(Dutiya-rāga Sutta)*

This was said by the Lord....

"Bhikkhus, any bhikkhu or bhikkhunī in whom attachment is not abandoned, hate is not abandoned, and delusion is not abandoned, is said to be one who has not crossed the ocean with its waves, breakers, and eddies, with its sharks and demons.[30] But any bhikkhu or bhikkhunī in whom attachment is abandoned, hate is abandoned, and delusion is abandoned, is said to be one who has crossed the ocean with its waves, breakers, and eddies, its sharks and demons—one of whom it is said: 'Crossed over, gone beyond, the brahmin stands on dry ground.'"[31]

One who has destroyed attachment
Along with hate and ignorance
Has crossed this ocean
With its sharks and demons,
Its fearful waves so hard to cross.

He has surmounted every tie,
Left Death behind,
Become free from clinging,
Forsaken suffering and renewal of being.
Vanished, he cannot be defined, I say—
He has bewildered the King of Death.[32]

21–13 Wrong View (*Micchādiṭṭhika Sutta*)

This was said by the Lord....

"Bhikkhus, I have seen beings who practise misconduct by body, speech, and mind, who vilify the noble ones, who hold wrong view and perform various deeds because of their wrong view. When the body perishes, those beings are reborn after death in a state of misery, a bad bourn, a state of ruin, in hell. I say this, bhikkhus, without having learnt it from another recluse or brahmin.[33] It is just because I myself have known it, seen it, and observed it that I say: 'Bhikkhus, I have seen beings who practise misconduct by body, speech, and mind ... reborn after death in a state of misery ... in hell.'"

An individual here with
A wrongly directed mind
Who utters wrong speech
And performs wrong deeds,
One of little learning,
Who does demerit in this short life—
Upon the perishing of the body
That foolish one is reborn in hell.

22–13 Right View (*Sammādiṭṭhika Sutta*)

This was said by the Lord....

"Bhikkhus, I have seen beings who practise good conduct by body, speech, and mind, who do not vilify the noble ones, who hold right view and perform various deeds because of their right view. When the body perishes, those beings are reborn after death in a good bourn, a heavenly world. I say this, bhikkhus, without having learnt it from another recluse or brahmin. It is just because I myself have known it, seen it, and observed it that I say: 'Bhikkhus, I have seen beings who practise good conduct by body, speech, and mind ... reborn after death in a good bourn, a heavenly world.'"

An individual here with
A rightly directed mind
Who utters right speech
And performs right deeds,
One of much learning,
Who does much merit in this short life—
Upon the perishing of the body
That wise one is reborn in heaven.

23–13 Escape *(Nissaraṇiya Sutta)*

This was said by the Lord....

"Bhikkhus, there are these three elements of escape. What three? The escape from sensual desires, that is, renunciation; the escape from form, that is, the formless; and the escape from whatever has come to be, from whatever is conditioned and dependently arisen, that is, cessation.[34] These, bhikkhus, are the three elements of escape."

Having known the escape from sensual desires
And the overcoming of forms,
One whose energy is always ardent
Reaches the stilling of all formations.[35]

Such a bhikkhu who sees rightly
Is thereby well released.
Accomplished in knowledge, at peace,
That sage has overcome all bonds.[36]

24–13 More Peaceful *(Santatara Sutta)*

This was said by the Lord....

"Bhikkhus, the formless is more peaceful than the form realm, and cessation is more peaceful than the formless."

Those beings who reach the form realm
And those established in the formless,
If they do not know cessation,
Come back to renewal of being.

Those who fully understand forms
Without getting stuck in the formless,
Are released into cessation
And leave Death far behind them.

Having touched with his own person
The deathless element free from clinging,
Having realized the relinquishment of clinging,
His taints all gone,
The Fully Enlightened One proclaims
The sorrowless state that is void of stain.[37]

25–13 Sons *(Putta Sutta)*

This was said by the Lord....

"Bhikkhus, these three kinds of sons are found existing in the world. What three? The superior kind, the similar kind, and the inferior kind.

"Now what, bhikkhus, is the superior kind of son? In this instance a son has a mother and father who have not gone for refuge to the Buddha, to the Dhamma, and to the Sangha; who do not abstain from taking life, from taking what has not been given, from wrong conduct in sensual desires, from false speech, and from intoxicating drink leading to negligence;[38] who are unvirtuous and of bad conduct. But the son is one who has gone for refuge to the Buddha, to the Dhamma, and to the Sangha; who abstains from taking life, from taking what has not been given, from wrong conduct in sensual desires, from false speech, and from intoxicating drink leading to negligence; who is virtuous and of good conduct. This, bhikkhus, is the superior kind of son.

"Now what, bhikkhus, is the similar kind of son? In this instance a son has a mother and father who have gone for refuge to the Buddha ... who abstain from taking life ... who are virtuous and of good conduct. And the son also is one who has gone for refuge to the Buddha ... who abstains from taking life ... who is virtuous and of good conduct. This, bhikkhus, is the similar kind of son.

"Now what, bhikkhus, is the inferior kind of son? In this instance a son has a mother and father who have gone for refuge to the Buddha ... who abstain from taking life ... who are virtuous and of good conduct. But the son is one who has not gone for refuge to the Buddha ... who does not abstain from taking life ... who is unvirtuous and of bad conduct. This, bhikkhus, is the inferior kind of son.

"These, bhikkhus, are the three kinds of sons found existing in the world."

The wise wish for a son
Who is superior or similar.
They do not wish for an inferior son,
One who disgraces the family.

But such sons in the world
Who are devoted lay followers,
Excelling in faith and virtue,
Liberal, without selfishness,
Shine forth in assemblies
Like the moon freed from clouds.

26–13 A Rainless Cloud *(Avuṭṭhika Sutta)*

This was said by the Lord....

"Bhikkhus, these three kinds of persons are found existing in the world. What three? One who is like a rainless cloud, one who rains locally, and one who rains everywhere.

"Now what kind of person, bhikkhus, is like a rainless cloud? Here, a certain person is not a giver to anyone; he does not give food, drink, clothing, vehicles, garlands, scents, ointments, beds, lodging, and lamps to recluses and brahmins, to the poor, destitute, and needy. This kind of person is like a rainless cloud.

"Now what, bhikkhus, is the kind of person who rains locally? Here, a certain person is a giver to some but not a giver to others. Food, drink, clothing, vehicles, garlands, scents, ointments, beds, lodging, and lamps he gives only to some recluses and brahmins, to some of the poor, destitute, and needy, but not to others. This is the kind of person who rains locally.

"Now what, bhikkhus, is the kind of person who rains everywhere? Here, a certain person gives to all. He gives food, drink, clothing, vehicles, garlands, scents, ointments, beds, lodging, and lamps to all recluses and brahmins, to the poor, destitute, and needy. This is the kind of person who rains everywhere.

"These, bhikkhus, are the three kinds of persons found existing in the world."

Neither to recluses nor brahmins
Nor to the poor and destitute
Does he distribute his store
Of food and drink and goods;
That base person is called
"One like a rainless cloud."

To some he does not give,
To some he offers alms;
That one wise people call
"One who rains only locally."

A person renowned for his bounty,
Compassionate towards all beings,
Distributes alms gladly.
"Give! Give!" he says.[39]

Like a great storm cloud
That thunders and rains down
Filling the levels and hollows,
Saturating the earth with water,
Even so is such a person.

Having righteously gathered wealth
Which he obtains by his own effort,
He fully satisfies with food and drink
Whatever beings live in need.

27–13 Aspiring for Happiness *(Sukhapatthanā Sutta)*

This was said by the Lord....

"Bhikkhus, aspiring for these three kinds of happiness, a wise person should guard virtuous conduct. What are the three?

Aspiring 'May praise come to me,' a wise person should guard virtuous conduct. Aspiring 'May I become wealthy,' a wise person should guard virtuous conduct. Aspiring 'Upon the perishing of the body at death may I be reborn in a good bourn, in a heavenly world,' a wise person should guard virtuous conduct. These are the three kinds of happiness aspiring for which a wise person should guard virtuous conduct."

Aspiring for three kinds of happiness
The wise person should guard virtue:
Praise, the obtaining of property,
Rejoicing in heaven hereafter.

If one who does no evil
Associates with an evil-doer,
He is suspected of evil
And his disrepute grows.

Whatever person one befriends,
Whomever one associates with,
One becomes of like quality,
One becomes like one's companion.

The follower and the followed,
One who contacts and one contacted,
Are like an arrow coated with poison
That contaminates its quiver.
Fearing contamination the wise person
Should not have evil friends.

A man who ties up putrid fish
With some blades of kusa-grass
Makes the kusa-grass smell putrid;
So it is with those who follow fools.

But a man who wraps tagara powder[40]
In the broad leaf of a tree
Makes the leaf smell fragrant;
So it is with those who follow sages.

Therefore as with the leaf-container,
Understanding the outcome for oneself,
The unvirtuous should not be followed,
A wise person should follow the virtuous.
The unvirtuous lead one to hell,
The virtuous help one reach heaven.

28–13 Perishable *(Bhindanā Sutta)*

This was said by the Lord....

"This body, bhikkhus, is perishable, consciousness is of a nature to dissolve, and all objects of clinging are impermanent, suffering, and subject to change."

Having known the body as perishable
And consciousness as bound to dissolve,
Having seen fear in objects of clinging,
He has gone beyond birth and death;
Having attained supreme peace,
With composed mind he bides his time.

29–13 Like Elements *(Dhātusosaṃsandana Sutta)*

This was said by the Lord....

"Bhikkhus, it is according to like elements that beings associate with each other and come together.[41] Beings of low disposition associate and come together with beings of low disposition. Beings of good disposition associate and come together with beings of good disposition. It was so in the past, it will be so in the future, and it is so in the present."

Desire born of association
Is severed by non-association.
As one riding on a wooden plank
Would sink in the mighty ocean,
Even so one of virtuous life
Sinks by consorting with an idler.

Therefore shun an idle person,
One who makes little effort.
Live with those who dwell secluded,
The noble ones resolved and meditative,
Who are ever strenuous and wise.

30–13 Falling Away *(Parihāna Sutta)*

This was said by the Lord....

"Three things, bhikkhus, lead to the falling away of a learner bhikkhu. What are the three? Here, a learner bhikkhu enjoys activity,[42] is fond of activity, enjoys indulging in activity. He enjoys gossip, is fond of gossip, enjoys indulging in gossip. He enjoys sleep, is fond of sleep, enjoys indulging in sleep. These are the three things that lead to the falling away of a learner bhikkhu.

"Three things, bhikkhus, protect a learner bhikkhu from falling away. What are the three? Here, a learner bhikkhu does not enjoy activity, is not fond of activity, does not enjoy indulging in activity. He does not enjoy gossip, is not fond of gossip, does not enjoy indulging in gossip. He does not enjoy sleep, is not fond of sleep, does not enjoy indulging in sleep. These are the three things that protect a learner bhikkhu from falling away."

A bhikkhu who enjoys activity,
Restless, fond of gossip and sleep,
Will never be able to attain
Enlightenment which is supreme.

Thus let him restrict his duties,
Give up sloth and restlessness;
Such a bhikkhu can attain
Enlightenment which is supreme.

31–13 Unwholesome Thoughts *(Vitakka Sutta)*

This was said by the Lord....

"Bhikkhus, there are these three kinds of unwholesome thoughts. What three? A thought concerned with not being despised;[43] a thought concerned with gain, honour, and fame; a thought concerned with involvement in the affairs of others.[44] These, bhikkhus, are the three kinds of unwholesome thoughts."

One concerned with not being despised,
With gain, honour, and esteem,
And who delights in companionship
Is far from the destruction of fetters.

But having abandoned sons and herds
Family life and possessions,
Such a bhikkhu can attain
Enlightenment which is supreme.

32–13 Homage *(Sakkāra Sutta)*

This was said by the Lord....

"Bhikkhus, I have seen beings, overwhelmed and with minds obsessed by receiving homage, upon the perishing of the body after death take rebirth in a state of misery, a bad bourn, a state of ruin, hell. I have seen beings, overwhelmed and with minds obsessed by not receiving homage … by both receiving homage and (later) not receiving homage, upon the perishing of the body after death take rebirth in a state of misery, a bad bourn, a state of ruin, hell.

"I say this, bhikkhus, without having learnt it from another recluse or brahmin…. It is just because I myself have known it, seen it, and observed it, that I say: I have seen beings, overwhelmed and with minds obsessed by receiving homage … after death take rebirth in … hell."

He is one who lives diligently
With concentration undisturbed,
Both when homage is paid to him
And when he receives no homage.

Meditating continuously, gifted
With subtle view and insight,
Enjoying the destruction of grasping—
They call such a one a "true man."

33–13 Joyous Utterances *(Devasadda Sutta)*

This was said by the Lord….

"Bhikkhus, among the devas these three joyous utterances are proclaimed from time to time upon certain occasions. What three?

"At the time when a noble disciple, having had his hair and beard shaved off and having clothed himself in the yellow robe, intends going forth from home into homelessness, at that time among the devas the joyous utterance is proclaimed: 'A noble disciple intends to do battle with Māra.' This is the first joyous utterance proclaimed among the devas from time to time upon a certain occasion.

"Again, bhikkhus, at the time when a noble disciple lives engaged in cultivating the seven groups of the requisites of enlightenment,[45] at that time among the devas the joyous utterance is proclaimed: 'A noble disciple is doing battle with Māra.' This is the second joyous utterance proclaimed among the devas from time to time upon a certain occasion.

"And again, bhikkhus, at the time when a noble disciple, through realization by his own direct knowledge, here and now enters and abides in the mind-release and wisdom-release that is taintless by the destruction of the taints,[46] at that time among the devas the joyous utterance is proclaimed: 'A noble disciple has won the battle. He was in the forefront of the fight and he now dwells victorious.' This, bhikkhus, is the third joyous utterance proclaimed among the devas from time-to-time upon a certain occasion.

"These, bhikkhus, are the three joyous utterances...."

On seeing that he has won the battle,
Even the devas honour him,
The Fully Enlightened One's disciple,
A great one free from diffidence:

"We salute you, O thoroughbred man,
You who have won a difficult conquest.
Having routed the army of Death,
You are unhindered in liberation."

Thus do the devas extol him,
The one who has attained the goal,
For they do not perceive in him
Ground for subjection to Death's control.[47]

34–13 The Five Prognostic Signs *(Pañcapubbanimitta Sutta)*

This was said by the Lord....

"Bhikkhus, when a deva is due to pass away from a company of devas, five prognostic signs appear: his flower-garlands wither, his clothes become soiled, sweat is released from his armpits, his bodily radiance fades, and the deva takes no delight in his heavenly throne. The devas, observing the prognostic signs that this deva is due to pass away, encourage him in three things with the words: 'Go from here, friend, to a good bourn. Having gone to a good bourn, gain that which is good to gain. Having gained that which is good to gain, become firmly established in it.'"

When this was said, a certain bhikkhu asked the Lord: "Venerable sir, what is reckoned by the devas to be a good bourn? What is reckoned by the devas to be a gain that is good to gain? What is reckoned by the devas to be firmly established?"

"It is human existence, bhikkhus, that is reckoned by the devas to be a good bourn. When a human being acquires faith in the Dhamma-and-Discipline taught by the Tathāgata, this is reckoned by the devas to be a gain that is good to gain. When faith is steadfast in him, firmly rooted, established and strong, not to be destroyed[48] by any recluse or brahmin or deva or Māra or Brahmā or by anyone else in the world, this is reckoned by the devas to be firmly established."

When a deva whose life is exhausted
Passes away from a deva-company,
The devas encourage him
In three ways with the words:

"Go, friend, to a good bourn,
To the fellowship of humans.
On becoming human acquire faith
Unsurpassed in the true Dhamma.

That faith made steadfast,
Become rooted and standing firm,
Will be unshakeable for life
In the true Dhamma well proclaimed.

Having abandoned misconduct by body,
Misconduct by speech as well,
Misconduct by mind, and whatever else
Is reckoned as a fault,

Having done much that is good
Both by body and by speech,
And done good with a mind
That is boundless and free from clinging,

With that merit as a basis[49]
Made abundant by generosity,
You should establish other people
In the true Dhamma and the holy life."

When the devas know that a deva
Is about to pass from their midst,
Out of compassion they encourage him:
"Return here, deva, again and again."

35–13 For the Welfare of Many *(Bahujanahita Sutta)*

This was said by the Lord....

"Bhikkhus, these three persons appearing in the world appear for the welfare of many people, for the happiness of many people, out of compassion for the world, for the good, welfare, and happiness of devas and humans. What three?

"Here, bhikkhus, a Tathāgata appears in the world, an Arahant, a Fully Enlightened One, possessing perfect knowledge and conduct, a sublime one, a world-knower, an unsurpassed leader of persons to be tamed, a teacher of devas and humans, an enlightened one, a Lord. He teaches Dhamma that is good at the outset, good in the middle, and good at the end, with its correct meaning and wording, and he proclaims the holy life in its fulfilment and complete purity. This, bhikkhus, is the first person appearing in the world who appears for the welfare of many people, for the happiness of many people, out of compassion for the world, for the good, welfare, and happiness of devas and humans.

"Next, bhikkhus, there is a disciple of that teacher, an arahant, one whose taints are destroyed, the holy life fulfilled, who has done what had to be done, laid down the burden, attained the goal, destroyed the fetters of being, and is completely released through final knowledge. He teaches Dhamma ... and he proclaims the holy life in its fulfilment and complete purity. This, bhikkhus, is the second person appearing in the world ... for the good, welfare, and happiness of devas and humans.

"And next, bhikkhus, there is a disciple of that teacher, a learner who is following the path, who has learnt much and is of virtuous conduct. He teaches Dhamma ... and he proclaims the holy life in its fulfilment and complete purity. This, bhikkhus, is the third person appearing in the world ... for the good, welfare, and happiness of devas and humans.

"These, bhikkhus, are the three persons appearing in the world who appear for the welfare of many people, for the happiness of many people, out of compassion for the world, for the good, welfare, and happiness of devas and humans."

The teacher, the great sage,
Is the first in the world;
Following him is the disciple
Whose composure is perfected;
And then the learner training on the path,
One who has learnt much and is virtuous.

These three are chief amongst devas and humans:
Illuminators, preaching Dhamma,
Opening the door to the Deathless,
They free many people from bondage.

Those who follow the path
Well taught by the unsurpassed
Caravan-leader, who are diligent
In the Sublime One's dispensation,
Make an end of suffering
Within this very life itself.

36–13 Contemplating Foulness *(Asubhānupassī Sutta)*

This was said by the Lord....

"Bhikkhus, live contemplating the foulness of the body.[50] Let mindfulness of breathing be inwardly well established before you. Live contemplating the impermanence of all formations.

"For those who live contemplating foulness in the body, the tendency to lust with regard to the element of beauty is abandoned. When mindfulness of breathing is inwardly well established before one, the tendencies of extraneous thoughts to produce vexation of mind remain no more.[51] For those who live contemplating the impermanence of all formations, ignorance is abandoned and knowledge arises."

Contemplating foulness in the body,
Being mindful of in-and-out breathing,
Ever ardent and seeing clearly
The calming down of all formations:

Such a bhikkhu who sees rightly
Is thereby well released.
Accomplished in knowledge, at peace,
That sage has overcome all bonds.

37–13 Practice According to Dhamma
(Dhammānudhammapaṭipanna Sutta)

This was said by the Lord....

"When referring to a bhikkhu who practises according to Dhamma, this is the proper way of defining 'practice according to Dhamma.' When speaking he speaks only Dhamma, not non-Dhamma. When thinking he thinks only thoughts of Dhamma, not thoughts of non-Dhamma. By avoiding these two[52] he lives with equanimity, mindful and clearly comprehending."

A bhikkhu enjoying the Dhamma
And delighting in the Dhamma,
Reflecting upon the Dhamma,
Does not fall from the true Dhamma.

Whether walking or standing,
Sitting or lying down,
With mind inwardly restrained,
He attains to lasting peace.

38–13 Producing Blindness *(Andhakaraṇa Sutta)*

This was said by the Lord….

"Bhikkhus, these three kinds of unwholesome thoughts produce blindness, lack of vision, and absence of knowledge; they obstruct wisdom, lead to vexation, and are not conducive to Nibbāna. What are the three? A sensual thought, a thought of ill will, and an aggressive thought. These, bhikkhus, are the three kinds of unwholesome thoughts that produce blindness … and are not conducive to Nibbāna.

"Bhikkhus, these three kinds of wholesome thoughts remove blindness and produce vision, knowledge, and the growth of wisdom; they do not lead to vexation and are conducive to Nibbāna. What are the three? A thought of renunciation, a thought of friendliness,[53] and a thought of harmlessness. These, bhikkhus, are the three kinds of wholesome thoughts that remove blindness … and are conducive to Nibbāna."

Three wholesome thoughts should be entertained,
Three unwholesome thoughts rejected.
One who stops such trains of thought
As a shower settles a cloud of dust,
With a mind that has quelled such thoughts
Attains in this life the state of peace.

39–13 Inner Stains *(Antarāmala Sutta)*

This was said by the Lord….

"Bhikkhus, these three are inner stains, inner enemies, inner foes, inner murderers, inner adversaries. What three? Greed, bhikkhus, is an inner stain … an inner adversary. Hate is an inner stain … an inner adversary. Delusion is an inner stain … an inner adversary. These are the three."[54]

Greed is a cause of misfortune,
Greed agitates the mind;
People do not understand this
As a danger produced within.

A greedy person does not know the good,
A greedy person does not see the Dhamma;
Blinding darkness then prevails
When greed overwhelms a person.

But one who has abandoned greed
Longs not for what invites cupidity.
Greed slips away from him
As a water drop from a lotus leaf.

Hate is a cause of misfortune,
Hate agitates the mind;
People do not understand this
As a danger produced within.

A hater does not know the good,
A hater does not see the Dhamma;
Blinding darkness then prevails
When hate overwhelms a person.

But one who has abandoned hate
Is not angered by what incites to anger.
Hate drops away from him
As a palmyra fruit from its stalk.

Delusion is a cause of misfortune,
Delusion agitates the mind;
People do not understand this
As a danger produced within.

One deluded does not know the good,
One deluded does not see the Dhamma;
Blinding darkness then prevails
When delusion overwhelms a person.

But one who has abandoned delusion
Is not bewildered by confusing things.
He puts an end to all delusion
As the sunrise dispels the dark.

40–13 Devadatta *(Devadatta Sutta)*

This was said by the Lord…

"Bhikkhus, overcome with his mind obsessed by three kinds of wickedness, Devadatta will inevitably go to a state of misery, to hell, for the duration of the aeon.[55] What are the three? Overcome with his mind obsessed by evil desires …; overcome with his mind obsessed by evil friends …; and although there was more that should have been done, he stopped halfway through gaining a trifling attainment of distinction.[56] These, bhikkhus, are the three."

Surely no one of evil desires
Is born again into this world.
Know that he goes to the bourn of those
Who live in the grip of evil desires.

I heard how Devadatta was
Regarded as a wise man,
One developed in meditation
Who shone as it were with fame.

Having thought himself his equal,[57]
He assaulted the Tathāgata
And went to the four-doored frightful place,
Avīci the Unremitting Hell.[58]

When one plots against an innocent
Who has done no evil deed,
That evil merely affects the one
Corrupt of mind and disrespectful.

One who thinks he could pollute
The ocean with a pot of poison
Would not be able to pollute it—
Awesome is that mass of water.

It is similar in attacking with abuse
The Tathāgata who has reached perfection
And ever dwells with peaceful mind—
Abuse has no effect on him.

A wise man should befriend such a one
And constantly follow after him.
A bhikkhu who goes along his path
Can reach the end of suffering.

41–13 Foremost Faith *(Aggappasāda Sutta)*

This was said by the Lord....

"Bhikkhus, there are these three foremost kinds of faith.[59] What are the three?

"Whatever beings there are, whether footless or two-footed or four-footed, with form or without form, percipient or non-percipient or neither-percipient-nor-non-percipient, of these the Tathāgata is reckoned foremost, the Arahant, the Fully Enlightened One. Those who have faith in the Buddha have faith in the foremost, and for those with faith in the foremost the result will be foremost.[60]

"Whatever states[61] there are, whether conditioned or unconditioned, of these detachment is reckoned foremost, that is, the subduing of vanity, the elimination of thirst, the removal of reliance, the termination of the round (of rebirths), the destruction of craving, detachment, cessation, Nibbāna. Those who have faith in the Dhamma of detachment have faith in the foremost, and for those with faith in the foremost the result will be foremost.

"Whatever communities or groups there are, bhikkhus, of these the Sangha of the Tathāgata's disciples is reckoned foremost, that is, the four pairs of persons, the eight individuals.[62] This Sangha of the Lord's disciples is worthy of gifts, worthy of hospitality, worthy of offerings, worthy of reverential salutation, the unsurpassable field of merit for the world. Those who have faith in the Sangha have faith in the foremost, and for those with faith in the foremost the result will be foremost.

"These, bhikkhus, are the three foremost kinds of faith."

This is foremost for those with faith,
For those who know the foremost Dhamma:
Having faith in the Buddha as foremost,
Worthy of offerings, unsurpassed;

Having faith in the Dhamma as foremost,
The peace of detachment, bliss;
Having faith in the Sangha as foremost,
A field of merit unsurpassed.

Distributing gifts among the foremost,
Foremost is the merit that accrues;
Foremost their life and beauty,
Fame, reputation, happiness, and strength.

The wise one who gives to the foremost,
Concentrated on the foremost Dhamma,
Whether he becomes a deva or a human,
Rejoices in his foremost attainment.

42–13 A Means of Subsistence *(Jīvika Sutta)*

This was said by the Lord....

"Bhikkhus, this is a contemptible means of subsistence, this gathering of alms.[63] In the world, bhikkhus, it is a form of abuse to say, 'You alms-gatherer! Wandering about clutching a bowl!' Yet this means of subsistence has been taken up by young men of good family for a reason, for a purpose. They have not been reduced to it by kings nor by robbers nor because of debt nor through fear nor from loss of an alternative means of livelihood, but with the thought: 'We are beset by birth, ageing and death, by sorrow, lamentation, pain, grief, and despair; overcome by suffering, afflicted by suffering. Perhaps an end can be discerned of this whole mass of suffering!'

"So this young man of good family has gone forth (into homelessness), but he may be covetous for objects of desire, strongly passionate, malevolent, corrupt in thought, unmindful, uncomprehending, unconcentrated, of wandering mind and uncontrolled faculties. Just as a brand from a funeral pyre, burnt at both ends and in the middle smeared with excrement, can be used as timber neither in the village nor in the forest, so by such a simile do I speak about this person: he has missed out on the enjoyments of a householder, yet he does not fulfil the purpose of recluseship."

He has missed both a layman's pleasure
And his recluseship, too, the luckless man!
Ruining it, he throws it away
And perishes like a funerary brand.

Far better for him to swallow
A fiery hot iron ball
Than that immoral and uncontrolled
He should eat the country's alms.[64]

43–13 The Hem of the Robe *(Saṅghāṭikaṇṇa Sutta)*

This was said by the Lord....

"Bhikkhus, even though a bhikkhu might hold on to the hem of my robe and follow close behind me step by step, if he is covetous for objects of desire, strongly passionate, malevolent, corrupt in thought, unmindful, uncomprehending, unconcentrated, of wandering mind and uncontrolled faculties, he is far from me and I am far from him. What is the reason? That bhikkhu does not see Dhamma. Not seeing Dhamma, he does not see me.

"Bhikkhus, even though a bhikkhu might live a hundred leagues away, if he is not covetous for objects of desire, not strongly passionate, not malevolent, uncorrupt in thought, with mindfulness established, clearly comprehending, concentrated, of unified mind and controlled faculties, he is close to me and I am close to him. What is the reason? That bhikkhu sees Dhamma. Seeing Dhamma, he sees me."

Though closely following behind,
Full of longings and resentment,
See how far away he is—
The desirous one from the desireless,
One unquenched from the quenched,[65]
A greedy one from the one without greed.

But a wise person who by direct knowledge
Has fully understood the Dhamma,
Becomes desireless and tranquil
Like a calm unruffled lake.

See how close he is to him—
A desireless one to the desireless,
One quenched to the quenched,
The greedless one to the one without greed.

44–13 The Fires *(Aggi Sutta)*

This was said by the Lord....

"Bhikkhus, there are these three fires. What three? The fire of lust, the fire of hate, and the fire of delusion. These, bhikkhus, are the three fires."

The fire of lust burns mortals[66]
Infatuated by sensual pleasures;
The fire of hate burns malevolent people
Who kill other living beings;

The fire of delusion burns the bewildered,
Ignorant of the Noble One's Dhamma.
Being unaware of these three fires,
Humankind delights in personal existence.[67]

Unfree from the bonds of Māra
They swell the ranks of hell,
Existence in the animal realm,
Asura-demons and the sphere of ghosts.[68]

But those engaged in practising
The Buddha's teaching day and night
Ever perceiving the body's foulness,[69]
Extinguish the fire of lust.

Those best of humans by loving-kindness
Extinguish the fire of hate,
And they extinguish the fire of delusion
By wisdom that leads to penetration.[70]

Having extinguished these fires,
Unwearied night and day,
Those discerning ones attain Nibbāna
And overcome all suffering.

The noble seers, masters of knowledge,
Wise ones with perfect understanding,
By directly knowing the end of birth
Come no more to renewal of being.

45–13 Investigating (*Upaparikkha Sutta*)

This was said by the Lord....

"Bhikkhus, a bhikkhu should so investigate that as he investigates, his consciousness is not distracted and diffused externally, and internally is not fixed, and by not grasping anything he should remain undisturbed. If his consciousness is not distracted and diffused externally, and internally is not fixed, and if by not grasping anything he remains undisturbed, then there is no coming into existence of birth, ageing, death, and suffering in the future."[71]

When a bhikkhu has abandoned
The seven ties and cut the cord,[72]
His wandering on in births is finished:
There is no renewal of being for him.

46–13 Sensual Desire (*Kāmuppatti Sutta*)

This was said by the Lord....

"Bhikkhus, there are these three ways of obtaining the objects of sensual desire. What three? There are those objects of sensual desire already existent; there is the way of those who delight in creating them; and there is the way of those who gain control over objects created by others.[73] These are the three ways...."

Those who enjoy what exists,
Those devas exercising control,
Those who delight in creating,
And others who enjoy sense-objects—
Being in this state or another
They cannot pass beyond saṃsāra.[74]

Understanding this danger
In objects of sensual enjoyment,
Let the wise person abandon all sense pleasures,
Those both heavenly and human.[75]

By severing the flow of craving,
The flow so difficult to overcome
Of greed for pleasing, enticing forms,
They attain to final Nibbāna
And overcome all suffering.

The noble seers, masters of knowledge,
Wise ones with perfect understanding,
By directly knowing the end of birth
Come no more to renewal of being.

47–13 The Bonds *(Kāmayoga Sutta)*

This was said by the Lord….

"Bhikkhus, one bound by the bond of sensual desire and by the bond of being is a returner, one who comes back to this state. One freed from the bond of sensual desire but still bound by the bond of being is a non-returner, one who does not come back to this state. One freed from the bond of sensual desire and freed from the bond of being is an arahant, one in whom the taints are destroyed."[76]

Fettered by both these bonds—
The sensual bond and the bond of being—
Living beings continue in saṃsāra,
Journeying on to birth and death.

Those who abandon sensual desires
But have not reached the taints' destruction,
Fettered by the bondage of being,
Are declared to be non-returners.

But those who have cut off doubts,
Destroyed conceit and renewal of being,
Who reach the taints' full destruction,
Though in the world, have gone beyond.

48–13 Lovely Behaviour *(Kalyāṇasīla Sutta)*

This was said by the Lord....

"Bhikkhus, a bhikkhu who is of lovely behaviour, lovely nature, and lovely wisdom is called in this Dhamma-and-Discipline one who is fully accomplished, who has reached fulfilment, the supreme among humans.

"And how is a bhikkhu of lovely behaviour? Here, a bhikkhu is virtuous, he lives restrained by the restraint of the rules of discipline,[77] endowed with perfect conduct and resort; seeing danger in the slightest faults, he undertakes the rules of training and trains in them. In this way a bhikkhu is one who is of lovely behaviour. Thus he is of lovely behaviour.

"And how is he of lovely nature? Here, a bhikkhu lives engaged in cultivating the seven groups of the requisites of enlightenment.[78] In this way a bhikkhu is one who is of lovely nature. Thus he is of lovely behaviour and lovely nature.

"And how is he of lovely wisdom? Here, through realization by his own direct knowledge, a bhikkhu here and now enters and abides in the mind-release and wisdom-release that is taintless by the destruction of the taints. In this way a bhikkhu is one who is of lovely wisdom.

"Thus he is of lovely behaviour, lovely nature, and lovely wisdom. In this Dhamma-and-Discipline he is called one who is fully accomplished, who has reached fulfilment and is supreme among humans."

A conscientious bhikkhu
Who never does wrong in any way,
Neither by body, speech, or mind,
Is called "one of lovely behaviour."

An unassuming bhikkhu
Who has cultivated well the states
That lead to enlightenment
Is called "one of lovely nature."

A taintless bhikkhu
Who understands for himself
The end of suffering here
Is called "one of lovely wisdom."

He who excels in these three things,
Untroubled, with doubt destroyed,
Unattached in all the world,
Is called "one who has abandoned all."[79]

49–13 Giving *(Dāna Sutta)*

This was said by the Lord....

"Bhikkhus, there are these two kinds of giving: the giving of material things and the giving of the Dhamma. Of these two kinds of giving, this is the foremost, namely, the giving of the Dhamma. There are these two kinds of sharing: the sharing of material things and the sharing of the Dhamma. Of these two kinds of sharing, this is the foremost, namely, the sharing of the Dhamma. There are these two kinds of help: help with material things and help with the Dhamma. Of these two kinds of help, this is the foremost, namely, help with the Dhamma."

When they say that giving
Is supreme and unsurpassed,
And the Lord himself has extolled sharing,
Who, wise and knowing,
Confident in that foremost field of merit,
Would not give at the appropriate time?

Both for those who proclaim it
And for those who listen to it,[80]
Confident in the Sublime One's teaching,
The supreme good is fully purified
As they live diligently in the teaching.

50–13 The Threefold Knowledge *(Tevijja Sutta)*

This was said by the Lord….

"Bhikkhus, I declare that it is through the Dhamma that one becomes a brahmin possessing the threefold knowledge: (I do not say this) of another merely because he can talk persuasively and recite.[81] And how do I declare that it is through the Dhamma that one becomes a brahmin possessing the threefold knowledge?

"Here, bhikkhus, a bhikkhu recollects a variety of former lives, that is, one birth, two births, three births, four births, five births, ten births, twenty births, thirty births, forty births, fifty births, a hundred births, a thousand births, a hundred thousand births; many aeons of world-contraction, many aeons of world-expansion, many aeons of both world-contraction and expansion. He recollects in a particular life being such a one by name, of such a clan, of such an appearance, having this kind of nutriment, experiencing these kinds of pleasure and pain, having this lifespan; and deceasing from there he arose here. Thus with all their details and particulars he recollects a variety of former lives. This is the first knowledge attained by him. Ignorance is dispelled, knowledge has arisen; darkness is dispelled, light has arisen, as happens in one who lives diligent, ardent, and resolute.

"Then again, bhikkhus, with the divine eye, purified and surpassing the human, a bhikkhu sees beings passing away and reappearing, inferior and superior, fair and ugly, fortunate and unfortunate, and he understands how beings pass on according to their deeds thus: 'Those worthy beings practising misconduct by body, speech, and mind, insulters of the noble ones, of wrong view and undertaking deeds in consequence of wrong view, when the body perishes have been reborn after death in a state of misery, a bad bourn, a state of ruin, hell. But those worthy beings practising good conduct by body, speech, and mind, not insulters of the noble ones, of right view and undertaking deeds in consequence of right view, when the body perishes, have been reborn after death in a good bourn, a heavenly world.' Thus he sees this with the divine eye and he understands how beings pass on according to their deeds. This is the second knowledge attained by him. Ignorance is dispelled, knowledge has arisen; darkness is dispelled, light has arisen, as happens in one who lives diligent, ardent, and resolute.

"Then again, bhikkhus, a bhikkhu, through realization by his own direct knowledge, here and now enters and abides in the mind-release and wisdom-release that is taintless by the destruction of the taints. This is the third knowledge attained by him. Ignorance is dispelled, knowledge has arisen; darkness is dispelled, light has arisen, as happens in one who lives diligent, ardent, and resolute.

"Thus, bhikkhus, do I declare that it is through the Dhamma that one becomes a brahmin possessing the threefold knowledge; (I do not say this) of another merely because he can talk persuasively and recite."

He who knows his former lives,
Who sees heaven and states of woe,
Who reaches the end of birth,
A sage and master of direct knowledge—

By these three ways of knowing one becomes
A brahmin having the threefold knowledge.
That is what I call the threefold knowledge,
Not another's babbling and reciting.

This too is the meaning of what was said by the Lord, so I heard.

CHAPTER 4

THE SECTION OF THE FOURS
(Catukkanipāta)

1–13 The Dhamma-offering *(Brāhmaṇadhammayāga Sutta)*

This was said by the Lord….

"Bhikkhus, I am a brahmin, ever accessible to entreaties, open-handed,[1] one bearing his last body, an unsurpassed physician and surgeon.[2] You are my own legitimate sons, born from my mouth,[3] born of Dhamma, fashioned by Dhamma, heirs of Dhamma, not heirs of material things.

"Bhikkhus, there are these two kinds of giving: the giving of material things and the giving of the Dhamma. Of these two kinds of giving, this is the foremost, namely, the giving of the Dhamma. There are these two kinds of sharing … these two kinds of help … these two kinds of offerings:[4] the offering of material things and the offering of the Dhamma. Of these two kinds of offering, this is the foremost, namely, the offering of the Dhamma."

The Tathāgata has made the Dhamma-offering,
Unselfish, compassionate towards all beings;
Living beings revere such a one,
Gone beyond being, as chief of devas and humans.

2–13 Easily Obtained *(Sulabha Sutta)*

This was said by the Lord….

"These four, bhikkhus, are trifling things, easily obtained and blameless. What four? A robe made of cast-off rags is a trifling thing, easily obtained and blameless. Food gathered on alms round is a trifling thing, easily obtained and blameless. The root of a tree as a dwelling place is a trifling thing, easily obtained and blameless. Medicine consisting of putrid cow urine is a trifling thing, easily obtained and blameless.[5] These, bhikkhus, are the four trifling things, easily obtained and blameless. When a bhikkhu is content with these things that are trifling and easily obtained, I say of him that he has the requisites for recluseship."

One content with what is blameless,
Things trifling and easily obtained,
Does not become vexed in mind
When not obtaining a place to live,
A robe to wear, and food and drink;
He has no resentment in any quarter.

These are the things declared to be
Suitable for a recluse's life
By possession of which a bhikkhu
May abide content and diligent.

3–13 The Destruction of the Taints (*Āsavakkhaya Sutta*)

This was said by the Lord....

"For one knowing and seeing, bhikkhus, I say there is the destruction of the taints, not for one not knowing and not seeing. But for one knowing what, seeing what, is there the destruction of the taints? For one knowing and seeing, 'This is suffering,' there is the destruction of the taints. For one knowing and seeing, 'This is the origin of suffering' ... 'This is the cessation of suffering' ... 'This is the course leading to the cessation of suffering,' there is the destruction of the taints. Thus it is, bhikkhus, that for one knowing and seeing there is the destruction of the taints."

For a learner who is training
In conformity with the direct path,
The knowledge of destruction arises first,
And final knowledge immediately follows.[6]

To one freed by that final knowledge,
The topmost knowledge of freedom,
There arises the knowledge of destruction:
"Thus the fetters are destroyed."

Certainly not by the lazy person
Nor by the uncomprehending fool
Is Nibbāna to be attained,
The loosening of all worldly ties.

4–13 Recluses and Brahmins *(Samaṇabrāhmaṇa Sutta)*

This was said by the Lord....

"Bhikkhus, whatever recluses and brahmins do not understand as it actually is: 'This is suffering'; 'This is the origin of suffering'; 'This is the cessation of suffering'; 'This is the course leading to the cessation of suffering'—these recluses and brahmins are not considered by me to be true recluses among recluses, to be true brahmins among brahmins. These venerable ones live without having realized and achieved here and now by their own direct knowledge the aim of being a recluse, the aim of being a brahmin.

"But, bhikkhus, whatever recluses and brahmins understand as it actually is: "This is suffering'; 'This is the origin of suffering'; 'This is the cessation of suffering'; 'This is the course leading to the cessation of suffering'—these recluses and brahmins are considered by me to be true recluses among recluses, to be true brahmins among brahmins. These venerable ones indeed live having achieved and realized here and now by their own direct knowledge the aim of being a recluse, the aim of being a brahmin."

Those who do not understand suffering,
Or how suffering is produced,
Or where suffering finally stops
Altogether without remainder,
And who do not know that path
Leading to relief from suffering—
They are destitute of mind-release
And lack release by wisdom too;
Unable to make an end of it,
They fare on in birth and decay.

But those who understand suffering,
And how suffering is produced,
And where suffering finally stops
Altogether without remainder,
And who also know that path
Leading to relief from suffering—
They possess that mind-release
And the release by wisdom too;
Able to make an end of it
They never come back to birth and decay.

5–13 Excelling in Virtue *(Sīlasampatta Sutta)*

This was said by the Lord....

"Bhikkhus, as to those bhikkhus who excel in virtue, excel in concentration, excel in wisdom, excel in release, excel in the knowledge and vision of release, who are advisors, instructors, and demonstrators, who can exhort, inspire, and encourage, and who are competent teachers of the true Dhamma—seeing those bhikkhus is very helpful, I say; listening to those bhikkhus, approaching them, attending upon them, remembering them, and following their example in going forth into homelessness is very helpful, I say. For what reason?

"By following such bhikkhus, by associating with them and attending upon them, the aggregate of virtue as yet incomplete reaches completion of development, the aggregate of concentration, of wisdom, of release, and of knowledge and vision of release as yet incomplete reaches completion of development. Such bhikkhus as these are called teachers, caravan-leaders, fault-abandoners, dispellers of darkness, light-bringers, makers of radiance, luminaries, torch-bearers, bringers of illumination, noble ones, possessors of vision."

For those who are knowledgeable
This is a state making for joy—
Living the life of Dhamma
Under the noble ones perfected in mind.

They clarify the true Dhamma,
Shining forth and illuminating it,
Those light-bringers, heroic sages,
Endowed with vision, dispelling faults.

Having heard their teaching,
The wise with perfect understanding
By directly knowing the end of birth
Come no more to renewal of being.

6–13 Arousing Craving *(Taṇhuppāda Sutta)*

This was said by the Lord....

"Bhikkhus, there are four things that arouse craving whereby the craving that has arisen in a bhikkhu arises. What are the four? Because of robes, because of almsfood, because of a dwelling place, because of gaining this or losing that[7] the craving that has arisen in a bhikkhu arises. These, bhikkhus, are the four things that arouse craving whereby the craving that has arisen in a bhikkhu arises."

A person companioned by craving
Wanders on the long journey
In this state of being or another
And cannot go beyond saṃsāra.

Having understood the danger thus,
That craving is the origin of suffering,
A bhikkhu should wander mindfully,
Free from craving, without grasping.

7–13 With Brahmā *(Sabrahmaka Sutta)*

This was said by the Lord....

"Living with Brahmā are those families where, within the home, mother and father are respected by their children.[8] Living with the early devas are those families where, within the home, mother and father are respected by their children. Living with the early teachers are those families where, within the home, mother and father are respected by their children.[9] Living with those worthy of adoration are those families where, within the home, mother and father are respected by their children. 'Brahmā,' bhikkhus, is a term for mother and father. 'Early devas' and 'early teachers' and 'those worthy of veneration' are terms for mother and father. For what reason? Because mother and father are very helpful to their children, they take care of them and bring them up and teach them about the world."

Mother and father are called
"Brahmā," "early teachers"
And "worthy of veneration,"
Being compassionate towards
Their family of children.

Thus the wise should venerate them,
Pay them due honour,
Provide them with food and drink,
Give them clothing and a bed,
Anoint and bathe them
And also wash their feet.

When he performs such service
For his mother and his father,
They praise that wise person even here
And hereafter he rejoices in heaven.

8–13 Very Helpful *(Bahukāra Sutta)*

This was said by the Lord....

"Bhikkhus, brahmins and householders are very helpful to you. They provide you with the requisites of robes, almsfood, lodgings, and medicine in time of sickness. And you, bhikkhus, are very helpful to brahmins and householders, as you teach them the Dhamma that is good at the outset, good in the middle, and good at the end, with its correct meaning and wording, and you proclaim the holy life in its fulfilment and complete purity. Thus, bhikkhus, this holy life is lived with mutual support for the purpose of crossing the flood and making a complete end of suffering."

Householders and homeless alike,
Each a support for the other,
Both accomplish the true Dhamma—
The unsurpassed security from bondage.

From householders the homeless receive
These basic necessities of life,
Robes to wear and a place to dwell
Dispelling the hardships of the seasons.

And by relying on one of good conduct,[10]
Home-loving layfolk dwelling in a house
Place faith in those worthy ones[11]
Of noble wisdom and meditative.

Practising the Dhamma in this life,
The path leading to a good bourn,[12]
Those wishing for pleasure rejoice
In the delights of the deva world.

9–13 Deceitful *(Kuha Sutta)*

This was said by the Lord....

"Bhikkhus, whatever bhikkhus are deceitful, stubborn, mere talkers, frauds, arrogant, and unconcentrated, these bhikkhus are no followers of mine. They have turned aside from this Dhamma-and-Discipline and will not achieve growth, progress, or development within it.

"But whatever bhikkhus are not deceitful, not mere talkers, wise, adaptable, and well concentrated, these bhikkhus are indeed my followers. They have not turned aside from this Dhamma-and-Discipline and will achieve growth, progress, and development within it."

Deceitful, stubborn, mere talkers,
Frauds, arrogant, unconcentrated—
These make no progress in the Dhamma
Taught by the Fully Enlightened One.

Undeceitful, not talkative, wise,
Adaptable, well concentrated—
Such as these progress in the Dhamma
Taught by the Fully Enlightened One.

10–13 The River Current *(Nadīsota Sutta)*

This was said by the Lord....

"Suppose, bhikkhus, a man was being borne along by the current of a river that seemed pleasant and agreeable. But upon seeing him, a keen-sighted man standing on the bank would call out to him: 'Hey, good man! Although you are being borne along by the current of a river that seems pleasant and agreeable, lower down there is a pool with turbulent waves and swirling eddies, with monsters and demons.[13] On reaching that pool you will die or suffer close to death.' Then, bhikkhus, upon hearing the words of that person, that man would struggle against the current with hands and feet.

"I have made use of this simile, bhikkhus, to illustrate the meaning. And this is the meaning here: 'The current of the river' is a synonym for craving. 'Seeming pleasant and agreeable' is a synonym for the six internal sense-bases. 'The pool lower down' is a synonym for the five lower fetters.[14] 'Turbulent waves' is a synonym for anger and frustration. 'Swirling eddies' is a synonym for the five strands of sensual pleasure. 'Monsters and demons' is a synonym for womenfolk. 'Against the current' is a synonym for renunciation. 'Struggling with hands and feet' is a synonym for instigating energy. 'The keen-sighted man standing on the bank' is a synonym for the Tathāgata, the Arahant, the Fully Enlightened One."

Desiring future security from bondage
One should abandon sensual desire
However painful this may be.[15]
Rightly comprehending with wisdom,
Possessing a mind that is well released,
One may reach freedom step by step.

One who is a master of knowledge,
Who has lived the holy life,
Is called one gone to the world's end,
One who has reached the further shore.

11–13 While Walking *(Cara Sutta)*

This was said by the Lord....

"Bhikkhus, if while walking a sensual thought or a thought of ill will or an aggressive thought arises in a bhikkhu, and if he tolerates it and does not reject it, does not dispel it and get rid of it and bring it to an end, that bhikkhu—who in such a manner is lacking in ardour and unafraid of wrongdoing—is called constantly lazy and indolent. If while standing ... If while sitting ... If while lying down a sensual thought or a thought of ill will or an aggressive thought arises in a bhikkhu, and if he tolerates it and does not reject it ... that bhikkhu is called constantly lazy and indolent.

"But if while walking ... standing ... sitting ... lying down a sensual thought or a thought of ill will or an aggressive thought arises in a bhikkhu and he does not tolerate it, but rejects it, dispels it, gets rid of it, and brings it to an end, that bhikkhu—who in such a manner is ardent and afraid of wrongdoing—is called constantly energetic and resolute."

Whether walking or standing,
Sitting or lying down,
Whoever thinks such thoughts
That are evil and worldly,
He is following a wrong path,
Infatuated with delusive things—
Such a bhikkhu cannot reach
Enlightenment which is supreme.

Whether walking or standing,
Sitting or lying down,
Whoever overcomes these thoughts,
Delighting in the quelling of thoughts—
Such a bhikkhu is able to reach
Enlightenment which is supreme.

12–13 Perfect in Virtue *(Sampannasīla Sutta)*

This was said by the Lord....

"Bhikkhus, you should live perfect in virtue, perfect in the practice of the rules of discipline, and be restrained by the restraint of the rules. Perfect in conduct and resort, seeing danger in the slightest faults, you should train in the rules of training you have undertaken. Living perfect in virtue, bhikkhus, ... and training in the rules of training you have undertaken, what is there further that should be done?

"If while he is walking, standing, sitting, and lying down a bhikkhu is free from covetousness and ill will, free from sloth and torpor, free from restlessness and worry, and has abandoned doubts, his energy becomes strong and unflagging, his mindfulness is alert and unclouded, his body is calm and undistressed, his mind concentrated and one-pointed. A bhikkhu who in such a manner is ardent and afraid of wrongdoing is called constantly energetic and resolute."

Controlled while walking,
Controlled while standing,
Controlled while sitting,
Controlled while reclining,
Controlled in bending and
Stretching his limbs—
Above, across, and below,
As far as the world extends,
A bhikkhu observes how things occur,
The arising and passing of the aggregates.

Living thus ardently,
Of calm and quiet conduct,
Ever mindful, he trains in the course
Of calm tranquillity of mind—
Such a bhikkhu is said to be
One who is ever resolute.

13–13 The World *(Loka Sutta)*

This was said by the Lord, said by the Arahant, so I heard:

"Bhikkhus, the world has been fully understood by the Tathāgata; the Tathāgata is released from the world.[16] The origin of the world has been fully understood by the Tathāgata; the origin of the world has been abandoned by the Tathāgata. The cessation of the world has been fully understood by the Tathāgata; the cessation of the world has been realized by the Tathāgata. The course leading to the cessation of the world has been fully understood by the Tathāgata; the course leading to the cessation of the world has been developed by the Tathāgata.

"Bhikkhus, in the world with its devas, māras, and brahmās, with its recluses and brahmins, among humankind with its princes and people, whatever is seen, heard, sensed, cognized, attained, sought, and reflected upon by the mind—that is fully understood by the Tathāgata: therefore he is called the Tathāgata.

"Bhikkhus, from the night when the Tathāgata awakened to unsurpassed full enlightenment until the night when he passes away into the Nibbāna-element with no residue left, whatever he speaks, utters, and explains—all that is just so and not otherwise: therefore he is called the Tathāgata.

"As the Tathāgata says, so he does; as the Tathāgata does, so he says: therefore he is called the Tathāgata.

"In the world with its devas, māras, and brahmās, with its recluses and brahmins, among humankind with its princes and people, the Tathāgata is the conqueror, unvanquished, all-seer, wielding power: therefore he is called the Tathāgata."

By knowledge of the whole world,
The whole world as it truly is,
He is released from all the world,
In all the world he is unattached.

The all-conquering heroic sage,
Freed from every bond is he;
He has reached that perfect peace,
Nibbāna which is free from fear.

Rid of taints, he is enlightened,
Trouble-free, with doubts destroyed,
Reached the final end of deeds,[17]
Released by clinging's full destruction.

The Enlightened One, the Lord,
A lion is he, unsurpassed;
For in the world together with its devas
He set the Brahma-wheel in motion.[18]

Thus those devas and human beings,
Gone for refuge to the Buddha,
On meeting him pay homage to him,
The great one free from diffidence.

Tamed, of the tamed he is the best;
Calmed, of the calmed he is the seer;
Freed, of the freed he is the foremost;
Crossed, of the crossed he is the chief.

Thus do they pay him due homage,
The great one free from diffidence:
"In the world together with its devas
There is no person equalling you."

This too is the meaning of what was said by the Lord, so I heard.

The Book of the Buddha's Sayings is finished

NOTES TO THE UDĀNA

CHAPTER 1

1. See Introduction for a brief explanation of dependent arising and the meaning of its key terms. "Forward order" (*anuloma*) means the order of origination; "reverse order" (*paṭiloma*), dealt with in the next sutta, means the order of cessation. In MN 26, in the passage describing the Buddha's solitary meditation immediately after his enlightenment, dependent arising is identified with the Dhamma that is "profound, difficult to perceive, difficult to comprehend" realized by the Buddha in his enlightenment.
2. *Dhammā*, meaning here the Four Noble Truths (Comy.).
3. A brahmin is a person born into the privileged, priestly caste of the Indian social system, but in Buddhism it is used to denote an arahat, one who has realized enlightenment. It is in this sense that the Buddha refers to himself as a brahmin. See Dhp 385–423, and Ud 1.4.
4. Māra is the Tempter in Buddhism, who personifies those forces that prevent progress in the spiritual life. He is depicted in Buddhist art as the head of a hostile army arrayed against the future Buddha on the eve of his enlightenment. For an explanation of Māra's army, see Sn 436–39.
5. *Huhuṅkajātiko brāhmaṇo*: one who says "hum hum," condemning others out of pride (Comy.).
6. *Vedantagū*: This is an instance of the Buddha adapting brahmanic terminology for his own purposes. Comy.: He is called thus because he has come to Nibbāna, the consummation of formations, by the "Vedas" consisting in the knowledge of the four paths, and because he has gone to the end of the Vedas.

   Brahma means highest, supreme or divine; it is also the name for one of the highest type of gods. The "holy life" (*brahmacariya*), the highest or best conduct, is the celibate spiritual life of the bhikkhu.

7. The "swellings" (*ussadā*) are passion, hate, delusion, conceit, and views (Comy.).
8. PTS ed. includes "the Venerable Devadatta" among the elders who arrive, but this hardly makes sense, as Devadatta was the Buddha's evil-minded, ambitious cousin. He is not included in the Burmese or Sinhalese editions. I follow the Burmese ed. in taking the last monk to be Nanda rather than Ānanda, who did not become an arahat until after the Buddha's parinibbāna.
9. An alternative and enlarged version of this episode occurs at Ud 3.7.
10. Comy.: He is described as "not supporting another" (*anaññaposī*) because he is solitary, without anyone else whom he must maintain; this is said to show how easy he is to support. The phrase can also mean that he is "not maintained by another," since he is not bound to any donor for his requisites. He is called "unknown" (*aññāta*) because he does not make himself known out of a desire for gain, honour, and fame. The word can also mean "well known," i.e., for his good qualities.
11. *Dosa*. It here probably means "fault" or "blemish"; but it can also mean "bodily humour," so there is an implied reference to his being rid of his sickness. "One with taints destroyed" (*khīṇāsava*) is another name for an arahat, one who has destroyed the taints of sensuality, being, and ignorance.
12. A goblin, *pisāca*, is in Indian folklore a sort of flesh-eating demon. *Yakkha* is a more general term for a non-human spirit inhabiting trees and woodland glades, not necessarily malignant. Shrines were set up for them where offerings were made by villagers for favours and the protective influences they gave in return.
13. *Sakesu dhammesu pāragū*. Comy.: The "things pertaining to himself" are the five aggregates of his own individuality. He has gone beyond these by the full understanding of them, by abandoning their cause (craving), by realizing

their cessation (Nibbāna), and by developing the path to their cessation. Or else, the things pertaining to himself are the states of purification—virtue, concentration, wisdom, and deliverance, etc.—which he has "gone beyond" by perfecting them.

14. *Imaṃ evarūpaṃ vippakāraṃ*. Comy.: This ugly action, namely, placing the son in his lap, which is unseemly for renunciants.
15. *Saṅga*: ties or attachments. There is a pun here on Saṅgāmaji's name. He is freed from the five ties of lust, hate, delusion, conceit, and views (Comy.).
16. *Gayāsīsa*: a hill a mile to the southwest of the town of Gayā.
17. *Antaraṭṭhaka*: the coldest eight days of the North Indian winter when snow falls, around the full moon of January or February. These ascetics were called Jaṭila because they wore their hair long and matted (*jaṭā*).
18. The commentarial background story to the present sutta is found in *Buddhist Legends*, 2:222–26. This story forms the background to Dhp 101: "Though a thousand verses are made of meaningless lines, better the single meaningful line by hearing which one is at peace."
19. According to Comy., the devatā was actually a fellow-monk of Bāhiya during the dispensation of the former Buddha Kassapa. At that time seven monks, anxious to reach liberation quickly, used a ladder to ascend a precipitous mountain, then kicked the ladder away and devoted themselves to meditation. The eldest in the group quickly achieved arahatship and the next eldest the fruit of a never-returner, but the other five, refusing to eat the almsfood that the former two obtained through their psychic powers, died after seven days. The never-returner was reborn in the Brahmā world and now appeared to Bāhiya as the "former blood-relation." The five monks who perished, after a rebirth in the heavenly worlds, were reborn as human beings in the time of the present Buddha. One was Bāhiya. Dabba the Malla, who also appears in the Udāna (8.9, 8.10) was another.

20. Comy. explains the phrase *sabbattha ekarattiparivāsena* to mean that Bāhiya completed the entire journey (of 120 yojanas, with a yojana equivalent to about six miles) in one night, adding that he was able to cover such a great distance so fast because he was aided by the supernormal power of the devatā. It is difficult to see how this meaning can be derived from the Pali phrase, and I prefer to translate it in accordance with its apparent meaning, which also corresponds to common sense.

21. This is a difficult passage. An explanation of it derived from Comy. would be something like this: "In the seen is merely what is seen" without adding one's own views, opinions, concepts, personal likes and dislikes, etc.: that is, just seeing what is there as it actually is. "You will not be with that," bound by that view, by attraction or repulsion, etc. "You will not be in that" situation of being deluded and led astray by views and emotions. "You will be neither here nor beyond nor in between the two": neither in this world nor another world. This means the experience of Nibbāna or enlightenment, which is a stepping out of the mundane world.

22. Bāhiya's sudden attainment of arahatship upon the mere hearing of a brief discourse, a most rare occurrence, is a testimony both to the profundity of the Buddha's cryptic statement and to the maturity of Bāhiya's own faculties. Though Bāhiya died within minutes of meeting the Buddha, the Buddha ranked him as the bhikkhu disciple foremost in quickness of understanding (*etadaggaṃ khippābhiññānaṃ*).

23. Woodward mistranslated this sentence, taking it to mean that it was a young calf that attacked Bāhiya; the phrase *gāvī taruṇavacchā*, however, actually means "a cow accompanied by her young calf," which is more plausible. Normally gentle and inoffensive, a cow can become dangerous and unpredictable when it has a calf to protect. The same fate befell Suppabuddha the Leper in Ud 5.3.

24. This utterance gives a description of the experience of the arahat, the moment of illumination that outshines even the sun and moon. Comy. takes the first four lines to refer to

Nibbāna as it is experienced by the sage with the wisdom of the supreme path (of arahatship). He is then freed from "form and formless," that is, from the form and formless planes of existence; and "from pleasure and from pain," that is, from the sense-sphere planes.

CHAPTER 2

1. Nāgas are a class of semi-divine beings in Indian folklore. They inhabit the ocean, rivers, and pools, and are considered to be the guardians of hidden treasure. They have the form of cobras and are portrayed in art as half-human, half-serpent. Mucalinda's name is derived from the tree growing beside the pool that was his abode.
2. Comy. explains "noble silence" (*ariyo tuṇhībhāvo*) as not talking while engaged in developing serenity and insight. It paraphrases the Buddha as advising the monks that when they are living in seclusion for the purpose of gaining mental detachment, if they meet they should either help each other by discussing Dhamma or avoid impeding each other by abiding in the attainment of jhāna.
3. *Phusanti phassā upadhiṃ paṭicca,* lit. "contacts touch one depending on clinging." Comy. takes *upadhi* here to mean the five aggregates, explaining that contact occurs only while the aggregates exist. The context, however, seems to require taking *upadhi* as clinging or attachment, and interpreting the word "touch" metaphorically as meaning "affect." There may be a double meaning intended.
4. It was the custom to perform a ritual bathing and cleansing after a funeral. "In the middle of the day" means at an unsuitable, wrong, or unusual time to visit.
5. *Maccurājā,* identical with Māra personified as the Lord of the (spiritually) Dead.
6. Also called Kuṇḍadhana, Kuṇḍikāna, etc.
7. *Mūḷhagabbha*: difficulty in giving birth, "complications." Malalasekera suggests the "seven years" refers to a series of miscarriages.

8. His actual name is not given. Comy. says he was the son (*putta*) of the Koliyan king as Suppavāsā was the daughter (*dhitā*) of the king, meaning that they were of the Koliyan nobility, not that they were brother and sister.
9. Comy. devotes thirty pages to elucidating the meaning of the word "Tathāgata." For a translation of the first set of explanations from a different commentary, see Bhikkhu Bodhi, *Discourse on the All-embracing Net of Views* (Kandy: BPS, 1978), pp.331–44.
10. I.e., the womb. He was to become the Elder Sīvalī. His ability to hold a conversation as a new-born baby was only one of a number of remarkable qualities he had.
11. *Dhammasenāpati*: a title of Sāriputta, one of the two chief disciples of the Buddha, the other being Moggallāna.
12. Although Visākhā was actually Migāra's daughter-in-law, he honoured her by calling her his mother as it was through her that he became a devotee of the Buddha and a stream-enterer. The story is to be found in *Buddhist Legends*, 2:74–75.
13. Comy.: "As a deer, living in a forest where men do not travel, stands, sits, and sleeps confidently, and goes wherever it wants unimpeded in its movements, so do I live."
14. Comy.: "Except for those who have attained the path (of arahatship), none of those reborn as gods are capable of seeing him; they cannot see him even if they try, in the sense that they cannot see the course of his mind (*cittacāra*). Much less can humans do so. For like worldlings, even trainees (*sekha*) do not understand an arahat's mental process." Compare with Dhp 92: "Those who do not accumulate and are wise regarding food, whose object is the Void, the unconditioned freedom—their track cannot be traced, like that of birds in the air."

CHAPTER 3

1. The arahat has "left behind all action" in that he has abandoned all deeds liable to cause rebirth in the future. He has no need to talk of his illness to people in order to get medicines and personal care. Comy. explains the word

tādino, rendered here as "stable one," by reference to the arahat's "six-factored equanimity," i.e., his imperturbability when faced with pleasant and painful sense objects.

2. They were half-brothers having the same father but different mothers. Nanda's mother was said to have been Mahāpajāpatī, the Buddha's aunt and foster-mother.
3. *Hīnāya*: i.e., the status of a householder.
4. Though *janapadakalyāṇī* means "the loveliest girl in the land," and is used elsewhere in the Canon in that sense (see M II 33), Comy. takes it to be the personal name of Nanda's fiancée. According to the traditional story, on the morning of Nanda's wedding, the Buddha came to his house for alms. After giving his almsbowl to Nanda, without receiving it back he turned around and started to walk towards his monastery. Nanda followed him intending to return the bowl, and as he was about to leave the house his bride-to-be—perhaps anxious about losing him—urged him to return quickly. The Buddha proceeded straight to the monastery without stopping. When Nanda approached him to hand back the bowl, the Buddha asked him if he wished to become a monk. Though Nanda wanted only to return to the wedding, out of deference to his older half-brother he answered that he did. Thus the Buddha gave him ordination, and Nanda subsequently was overcome by discomfort. See *Buddhist Legends*, 1:218–19.
5. *Paluṭṭha*: the word implies the cauterization of a stump after amputation.
6. The traditional three-month retreat during the Indian rainy season, from mid-July to mid-October, when bhikkhus are prohibited from undertaking extensive travel. It is intended to be a period of intensive training in mind-development and meditation.
7. The knowledge of past births, of the arising and passing away of other beings, and of the destruction of the taints.
8. *Āneñja-samādhi*. A term for the concentration of the fruition of arahatship based on the fourth jhāna or any of the four

immaterial jhānas (Comy.). See MN 106, Vism XII,16–17 (377).

9. Comy. states that the cause for this habit was a *vāsanā*, a term which might be rendered "disposition." Comy.: "A *vāsanā* is a mere capacity to behave in certain ways similar to the behaviour of those who still have defilements; it is engendered by the defilements that had been harboured in the mind through beginningless time, and remains in the mental continuum of the arahat even after the defilements have been abandoned, as a mere habitual tendency. The *vāsanās* are not found in the mental continuum of a Buddha, who removes the defilements by abandoning the obstruction to omniscience, but they are found in the minds of disciples and paccekabuddhas."
10. Cf. Ud 1.6.
11. *Sapadānaṃ*: going to each house in succession without passing any one by.
12. Kosiya, "the owl," is Sakka's clan name.
13. See Ud 2.2 and Chapter 2, note 2.
14. *Muddā-sippan*: by hand gestures (Comy.). Perhaps it has military significance as do the previous crafts, i.e., directing the course of a battle by signaling commands.
15. *Lokāyata*: the art of philosophical debate employing reasoning and logic, originally a branch of learning for brahmins. Examples of the subjects for debate are the pairs of views such as those found in Ud 6.4: "The world is eternal/not eternal," "the world is finite/infinite," etc. In later times this word became the name for a purely materialistic philosophy.
16. Some texts have *khettavijjā* (lit. "science of fields," that is locating suitable sites for building) instead of *khattavijjā* (political science). There is also a possible reading of *nakkhattavijjā* (astrology).
17. Compare this with the famous Fire Sermon: "All is burning, bhikkhus. The eye is burning, visible objects are burning.... The mind is burning, mental objects are burning. Burning with what? Burning with the fire of passion, with the fire of hate, with the fire of delusion; it is burning with birth,

ageing, and death, with sorrow, lamentation, pain, grief, and despair, I say" (Vin I 34; S IV 19; also S III 71).

18. The five aggregates—form, feeling, perception, mental formations, and consciousness—are referred to as "disease" since they are fundamentally unsatisfactory, the basis of suffering. But because of ignorance, wrong views, and craving, ordinary people, "the world," (mis-) conceive them as permanent, eternal, and pleasurable, as a "self," as "I" and "mine." However, whatever they conceive—
being impermanent, unsatisfactory, and not-self—is different from the deluded way in which it is misconceived.
19. These two sentences can be understood to refer, respectively, to the eternalists and the annihilationists, the former affirming the permanence of a self, the latter accepting a temporary self bound for eventual annihilation. The "middle way" of dependent arising and conditionality avoids these two extremes.
20. Here *upadhi* is rendered as "clinging," *upādāna* (equivalent in meaning but from a different root) as "grasping."
21. 21. The key words of this *udāna*—being, craving, grasping, etc.—are all to be found in the formula of dependent arising (see Ud 1.1–1.3 and Introduction), of which this discourse is an exposition centred upon the aspect of the suffering inherent in "being."

CHAPTER 4

1. Apparently this sutta must date from a period before Ānanda became the Buddha's permanent attendant.
2. According to Comy., in five hundred successive births Meghiya had been a king. His royal park was located where that mango grove now stood, and he used to sit together with his dancing girls at the very spot under the tree where he had sat down for meditation. Thus, when he sat down at that spot, he felt as if his monkhood had left him and his mind was overrun by fantasies of beautiful dancing girls. Also, in his lives as a king, at that same spot he had ordered the execution and imprisonment of bandits, and thus when

he sat there as Meghiya, malevolent and cruel thoughts arose in him.

3. Pātimokkha: the code of disciplinary rules of the Buddhist monastic order.
4. *Asubha*: this is the contemplation of the unpleasant aspects of the body and its functions, undertaken to remove attachment and lust.
5. "Body" (*kāya*), according to Comy., here refers to the six "bodies of consciousness," that is, the senses and mind-consciousness, which are guarded by mindfulness so that defilements do not arise with respect to sense data. There is an alternative reading of mind (*citta*) instead of body, but this makes little or no difference to the meaning.
6. The bad destinations (*duggati*) are usually the three realms of misery: the hells, the animal realm, and the sphere of ghosts (to which a fourth, the asura realm, is sometimes added). Comy., however, here explains that from the highest standpoint all renewed being is unfortunate, and therefore the Buddha's statement should be understood as an injunction to put a complete end to rebirth.
7. The divine abiding (*brahmavihāra*) of equanimity, according to Comy. Some teachers say the attainment of the cessation of feeling and perception (*nirodhasamāpatti*), others the attainment of fruition (*phalasamāpatti*), for only these three are capable of protecting the body.
8. *Paṃsupisācakaṃ*: a small ghost or demon haunting swamps and dunghills (Comy.). Comy. explains that Sāriputta, who had reached the height of attainments and modesty, said this in the sense that he did not see them because, at that time, he had not adverted to them, as the word "now" (*etarahi*) suggests.
9. Comy. explains that the Buddha was living surrounded by these eight assemblies, not out of gregariousness, but out of compassion, because he desired their welfare, in accordance with his vow to liberate others and to rescue them from the four floods.
10. *Nāgassa nāgena*. The "perfected one" or arahat and the bull-elephant, as well as the serpent deity, are all termed *nāga*.

11. *Adhicittamanuyutto.* The higher mind can be understood as possession of the eight attainments (four fine-material and four immaterial jhānas) or as possession of the fruition attainment of arahatship; but here, they say, the fruition of arahatship is meant (Comy.). *Adhicitta,* the training in concentration (*samādhi*), is the second of the three higher trainings, preceded by the higher moral discipline (*adhisīla*) and followed by the higher wisdom (*adhipaññā*). Comy. takes *adhicitta* in the verse to follow as meditation aimed at attaining the eight attainments.
12. *Etaṃ buddhāna(ṃ) sāsanaṃ.* When the plural "buddhas" occurs in these texts it probably does not refer to Sammāsambuddhas appearing in past ages but to the Buddha and his chief enlightened disciples, *sāvaka-buddhā,* also called *anubuddhā,* "the Buddha's like," or "enlightened by following (*anu-*) instruction." It would apply especially to those disciples who gave discourses, such as Sāriputta, Mahākassapa, Mahākaccāna, and who were regarded originally as being on an equal footing with the Teacher in respect of their liberation from defilements. Possibly the counterpart of *anubuddha* is *paccekabuddha,* one enlightened without instruction.
13. *Sakyaputtiyā.* "Son of the Sakyans" was one of the names by which the Buddha was known, Sakya being the clan from which he came.
14. *Abhūtavādī.* Most translations of this verse (also found at Dhp 306) render the first line, "The liar goes to hell." However, this does not clearly differentiate this subject from the person of the next line. The translation here is suggested by the story, also to be found in *Buddhist Legends,* 3:189–91.
15. *Sapanti. Sapati* means to swear, to be on oath, to make (a truth-) assertion.
16. Compare with Dhp 320.
17. This Upasena was said to be the younger brother of Sāriputta. The manner of his death, after he was bitten by a snake, is recorded at S IV 40.

18. *Diṭṭhapado*: who has seen or realized Nibbāna. *Pada* means "state," "place," or "standpoint," and is used as a term for Nibbāna, the ultimate state.
19. *Upasamaṃ*: this refers to his being an arahat with all defilements gone.
20. Phrase in parenthesis suggested by Comy.

CHAPTER 5

1. This passage is included in MN 123 amidst a series of statements relating to the birth of a bodhisatta (the Buddha-to-be). The prose portion here does not really match the verse the Lord utters.
2. The arising of the Dhamma-vision (*dhammacakkhu*, lit. "eye of Dhamma") signifies the attainment of the first supramundane path, the path of stream-entry. By attaining this stage, the disciple cuts off three fetters binding him to *saṃsāra*—view of self, doubt, and clinging to rules and vows—and limits his future existences to a maximum of seven.
3. As with Bāhiya in Ud 1.10.
4. Paccekabuddhas, "privately enlightened ones," are individuals who awaken to the essential truths of Dhamma by themselves, without the guidance and instruction of a Supreme Buddha, but are not capable of leading others to enlightenment. See Ria Kloppenborg, *The Paccekabuddha: A Buddhist Ascetic* (BPS Wheel No. 305/307). For another reference to Tagarasikhī, see S I 92.
5. Compare Ud 2.3.
6. Uposatha or "observance day" is the occasion for the bhikkhus to recite the Pātimokkha, the disciplinary rules of the Order. It falls twice monthly, on the days of the full moon and the new moon.
7. A *timi* is a large fish of uncertain species. Woodward translates it as "leviathan." *Timiṅgala* means a "timi-swallower" and a *timirapiṅgala* is able to swallow even a *timiṅgala* (Comy.). However, the Mahāsutasomajātaka

(J-a V 462) says all three live on seaweed (*pāsāṇa-sevāla*). For the other types of beings, see Introduction.

8. *Yojana*: a measure of distance, about six miles.
9. For a step-by-step exposition of the gradual training, see MN 107. The gradual training may be briefly explained as the sequence of morality, concentration, and wisdom, each resting on its predecessor and all developing towards final knowledge.
10. *Anupādisesā nibbānadhātu*. The "residue" (*upādi*) refers to the arahat's five aggregates, the mind-body complex which ceases only at his death. At the moment he becomes an arahat the defilements are extinguished but the aggregates remain, thus this aspect is called "the Nibbāna-element with residue left." Since he harbours no more craving leading to future birth, at his death even these finally cease. As the "residue" of the five aggregates then no longer exists, this is called the "Nibbāna-element with no residue left."
11. These are the thirty-seven constituents of enlightenment (*bodhipakkhiyadhammā*) in which the Buddha summed up the practice of his teaching.
12. According to Comy., this riddling verse means a bhikkhu should not conceal (cover up) an offence, otherwise the defilements (rain) will stay within him and accumulate. By revealing the offence to his fellows it is expiated and he learns to avoid committing further offences in the future.
13. *Dasavaggaṃ bhikkhusaṅghaṃ*. According to the Vinaya, an Order consisting of at least ten bhikkhus is required to perform the ceremony of *upasampadā*, higher ordination, which elevates a novice (*sāmaṇera*) to the status of bhikkhu. On Mahākaccāna's request this number was reduced to five for those living in the outlying countries. See Vin I 194f., where this story of Soṇa Koṭikaṇṇa is included and which was the occasion for the modification of the rule concerning ordination. However, the "going forth" as a sāmaṇera can be given by a single senior bhikkhu without any other bhikkhu being present. Thus Soṇa would have received the going forth soon after his teacher gave his consent, and

lived as a sāmaṇera for three years before receiving the higher ordination.

14. This is now the fourth chapter of the *Sutta-nipāta*. From this passage it can be deduced that it once existed as a separate work. "Aṭṭhakavagga" means "The Octad Chapter" and is so called because four of its sixteen suttas have *aṭṭhaka* in their titles, for the reason that they consist of eight verses each. It is regarded as one of the oldest Pali canonical works extant, which makes it of considerable interest.
15. *Vassa*, literally, "rains retreat." Seniority is reckoned by the number of rains retreats a bhikkhu has observed since his higher ordination. If Soṇa had been ordained at the beginning of the rains, this conversation probably occurred about six months later, allowing two months for the journey from Avantī to Sāvatthī.
16. At Vin I 197 this verse has the alternative ending: "A pure one delights in the teaching."
17. This is the fourth of the seven purifications. See MN 24 and Vism Chapter XIX. Before he became an arahat, it is said that Revata was very much plagued by doubts, hence he was given the appellation "the Doubter."
18. It is interesting to note that the text omits *āyasmā*, "the Venerable," before Devadatta's name, presumably because of what occurs.
19. *Bhindissati*, i.e., will cause a schism. Cf. Vin II 198, where this episode is included as part of the story of the Devadatta schism.
20. Cp. Dhp 163. Dhp 163–64 were spoken in reference to Devadatta.
21. Readings of this word vary among the different editions, but the most authentic is probably the Burmese ed.'s *sadhāyamānarūpā*, as against PTS ed.'s *saddāyamānarūpā*. This would represent the Sanskrit verb *śardhati*, to mock, to ridicule, which is supported by Comy.
22. This verse occurs at Vin I 349 and M III 154 where it is uttered by the Buddha in condemnation of the quarreling factions at Kosambī, when there was a serious rift in the Order. It is interesting that this discourse immediately

follows one referring to Devadatta's schism, though there is no obvious connection between them. In the first edition I had rendered *paṇḍitābhāsā* as "wise speech," but I now follow Comy., which takes *ābhāsā* in the sense of "(mere) appearance" and glosses the phrase as *paṇḍitapaṭirūpakā*.

23. In his early days as a bhikkhu he could not learn by memory even a single stanza. The Buddha taught him to rub a piece of cloth reciting, "Removal of dirt, removal of dirt," and while doing so he attained arahatship. He excelled in the supernormal power of multiplying his body. See Vism XII,60–66 (387–89); *Buddhist Legends*, 1:299–306.
24. Comy.: Successive distinctions by way of calm (*samatha*) should be understood as the sequence of form and formless jhānas; by way of insight (*vipassanā*); as the sequence of insight knowledges culminating in arahatship.
25. 25. This expression is also found at Dhp 46. The King of Death (*maccurājā*) is another name for Māra, as at Ud 2.7.

CHAPTER 6

1. What follows also occurs at D II 102f., S V 258f. and A IV 308f. It is an important episode in the life of the Buddha, marking the beginning of the events leading up to his parinibbāna, the final Nibbāna or passing away.
2. The shrine of the yakkha named Cāpāla. Yakkhas were originally local guardian gods who were worshipped and given offerings in exchange for various material benefits, but after or just prior to the advent of Buddhism they rapidly degenerated and became thought of as malignant demons, as at Ud 4.4. Many Buddhist vihāras were built on the sites of what were originally yakkha shrines.
3. These were probably all yakkha shrines around Vesālī.
4. *Iddhipādā*, often translated as "bases of supernomal power." The four are: the power of will, of energy, of mind, and of investigation. They led to the accomplishment of the various supernormal powers possessed by the Buddha and his disciples.

5. *Kappa*. When used alone in the suttas, with reference to time, this word always denotes a world-aeon, the lifespan of a world-system; its duration is difficult to count, but illustrated by similes (see S II 181–83). Comy., however, explains the word here as the natural lifespan of human beings (*āyukappa*), i.e., the maximum human lifespan of 120 years. In the first edition I followed Comy., but as this explanation is not supported by any suttas I have now chosen to translate the word according to its apparent meaning.
6. Comy.: Māra distracted his attention by causing a fearful sight to appear.
7. The actual occasion is not to be found, either in the Vinaya Mahāvagga or in the Māra-saṃyutta, where it might have been expected. However, in the Mahāparinibbāna Suttanta, the Buddha explains to Ānanda that it occurred when he was staying beneath the Goatherd's Banyan Tree soon after the enlightenment (cf. Ud 1.4).
8. *Pattayogakkhemā*. Omitted by Comy. and in D II 104, so possibly an interpolation.
9. *Tulam atulañ ca sambhavaṃ*: Comy. offers several explanations: *Tulaṃ* (the measurable) is sense-sphere kamma, *atulaṃ* (the immeasurable) is sublime kamma (i.e., of the jhānas); or *tulaṃ* is sense-sphere and fine-material-sphere kamma, *atulaṃ* is immaterial-sphere kamma. Or *tulaṃ* is what yields limited results, *atulaṃ* what yields abundant results. *Sambhavaṃ* is the cause of origination, that which produces rebirth. Or else: *tulaṃ* is (the present participle) "measuring," weighing in mind. *Atulaṃ* is Nibbāna, and *sambhavaṃ* is being. The Buddha-sage measured the five aggregates as impermanent, and their cessation, Nibbāna, as permanent. Having seen the danger in being and the advantage in Nibbāna, he had rejected—by the supreme path (of arahatship)—kamma, the force of being, which is the root of the aggregates.
10. For the Jaṭilas, see Ud 1.9. The naked ascetics are often identified as Ājivakas, the single-garment ascetics as a kind of Jain. The expression "with hairy bodies and long nails" implies being dirty, smelly, and unwashed.

11. A region of India famous for its fabrics and perfumes; its capital was Benares.
12. Purity is threefold: bodily, verbal, and mental.
13. *Corā*: literally, "thieves," i.e., they steal the offerings of food given to them in good faith as ascetics because they are not ascetics at all (Comy.). However, *corā* is possibly a wrong reading for *carā*, which has the sense of spies or undercover agents. Informer is *ocaraka*.
14. White is the traditional colour of the layman's garb.
15. A bhikkhu should not emulate the bad actions of these king's men by doing the work of a spy. As an ascetic is able to travel about freely, he could be misguided into doing such work. The Buddha apparently is warning the bhikkhu against wrong livelihood and also expressing his disapproval of misusing the outward signs of religion for such a wrong purpose as gathering information for a king to use for military and political ends.
16. According to Comy., the first line of the verse refers to the defilements, which formerly existed and then ceased at the moment of enlightenment. The second refers to those virtuous and faultless qualities present at that moment. And the final two lines refer to the noble path as an unrepeatable experience, i.e., the path-moment (*arahatta-magga*) which occurs but once and is then immediately followed by its fruition (*arahatta-phala*). The latter, however, is repeatable throughout the remainder of life.
17. For the Buddha's attitude towards these various views see, for example, MN 72. According to Comy., "Tathāgata" here means the "self" or "soul" (*attā*).
18. The perpetual wandering on in the round of birth and death.
19. He was the younger brother of Anāthapiṇḍika. The Buddha declared him the foremost disciple of those who dwell peacefully (*araṇavihārīnaṃ*) and of those worthy of offerings (*dakkhiṇeyyānaṃ*).
20. According to Comy., Nibbāna is here referred to as the formless (*arūpa*), in the sense that it lacks the nature of form

and is free from mutability, the essential characteristic of form. Nibbāna is perceived by the perceptions of the paths and fruits. The four bonds (*yogā*) are sensual desire, being, views, and ignorance. We should read the last phrase as *na jātum eti*, not as *na jātim eti*. Comy.: He does not return to further being (*punabbhavāya*).

21. The first extreme mentioned here is that of self-mortification (*attakilamathānuyoga*), the second is indulgence in sensual pleasures (*kāmasukhallikānuyoga*). Both were rejected by the Buddha as unbeneficial in his First Sermon, where they occur in the opposite order. "What is attained" by them is suffering both now and in the future. The "cemeteries" are ignorance and craving, which merely serve to reinforce wrong views. "Some hold back," by attachment to existence and sensual pleasures or by adoption of the eternity view. "Some go too far" by engaging in self-mortification or by the adoption of an annihilation view. (See It Sutta 49.) Those who penetrate these extreme views with path knowledge and insight practise the Middle Way. Those who "were no more found among them" are those who have abandoned these views. They "did not conceive them" by way of craving, wrong view, and conceit, and thus, when they attain final Nibbāna without clinging, there is no threefold round (of defilements, kamma, and results) coming to manifestation.

22. *Adhipātakā*: moths and grasshoppers (Comy.).

23. Comy.: Being bound by craving and views, some recluses and brahmins are attached to what they have seen with eye-consciousness or to their own views ("what is seen") or to what they have heard transmitted by oral tradition ("what is heard"). Thus they adhere to their eternalist views, etc., and not knowing the genuine escape, like insects falling into a flame they fall into the three realms of existence which are like a pit of hot coals, and they are burnt by the fires of lust, etc.

24. *Takkikā*: those theorists whose teachings are based on reasoning and argument, as opposed to direct experience.

CHAPTER 7

1. *Lakuṇṭaka Bhaddiya.* This Bhaddiya is a different person from Bhaddiya, Kāligodhā's son, referred to in Ud 2.10. Bhaddiya the dwarf had been a wealthy resident of Sāvatthī who was very short, ugly, and unsightly. He had heard the Buddha preach, gained faith, and became a bhikkhu. After he had attained the fruit of stream-entry he approached Sāriputta to ask for a teaching that would help him gain the higher paths.
2. This implies the absence of conceit and wrong views, which have both been uprooted by the arahat; or it implies the contemplation with insight of all conditioned things as "This is not mine, this is not I, this is not my self," by which one attains arahatship.
3. Comy.: While Sāriputta was teaching the Dhamma to him, Bhaddiya attained arahatship right in his seat. Sāriputta, however, was unaware of this and continued to speak, thinking Bhaddiya was still a learner.
4. Comy.: The round (*vaṭṭa*) referred to in the first line is the round of defilements (*kilesavaṭṭa*), and when that is cut the round of kamma is also cut. The desireless (*nirāsa*) is Nibbāna. The stream (*saritā*) is craving, which has been entirely dried up by the achievement of the fourth path. "The severed round does not revolve": with the eradication of the round of defilements, the round of kamma is interrupted and no longer occurs, because it has been brought to a state of non-arising and cannot yield results. "Just this is the end of suffering": the absolute non-arising of the round of results in the future is itself the end, the termination, the stilling, of all the suffering of saṃsāra.
5. This discourse omits the word "excessively" found in the previous one.
6. *Okoṭimakaṃ*: deformed, misshapen, i.e., hunchbacked and pot-bellied.
7. *Neḷaggaṃ*, translated as "faultless," is derived from "not having the fault of slavering or drooling," according to Comy. The whole verse subtly contrasts the purity and

beauty of Bhaddiya's enlightened mind with his outward appearance. In S IV 291 the householder Citta gives an explanation of this riddling verse as a description of the arahat: "Faultless" refers to the moral virtues, "white awning" means release or the fruit of arahatship, "one-spoked" signifies mindfulness, "the chariot" is the body, "the stream" is craving, and "no more bondage" refers to the arahat being free of all fetters.

8. Koṇḍañña was one of the group of five ascetics to whom the Buddha addressed the First Sermon and the first of the disciples to gain insight into the Dhamma. When the Buddha realized this he said, "Koṇḍañña has understood." Thereafter, he became known as Aññāta Koṇḍañña, "Koṇḍañña who has understood."

9. Comy. reads the second line (*paṇṇā natthi kuto latā*) as *natthi latā kuto paṇṇā*, "There are no creepers, how then leaves?" It explains that ignorance is the root of the tree of individual existence and the taints, hindrances, and unwise consideration are called "soil" because they are the causal basis for ignorance. These do not exist in the noble individual referred to, because they have been eradicated by the supreme path (of arahatship). Such a one has no more "creepers," i.e., conceit and arrogance, whence then "leaves," i.e., vanity, negligence, hypocrisy, cunning, etc.? Comy. also admits that the second line can be read as it stands, explaining that the leaves appear first when the sprout is growing and the creepers come later. On this reading, kamma is the seed, consciousness is the sprout, name-and-form are the leaves, and the six sense spheres, etc., are the creepers.

10. *Papañca-saññā-saṅkhā-pahāna.* This is a very difficult phrase of profound import and in the various contexts where it occurs it has been translated very differently. The stumbling block has been the important term *papañca*, which even the ancient commentators found difficult to define. I follow here Bhikkhu Ñāṇananda's interpretation of it, in his *Concept and Reality*, as "conceptual proliferation." Through craving, conceit, and views we conceptualize what is perceived through the senses and by mind, distorting with

fixed labels what is naturally a fluid "living" situation. The ordinary person measures and evaluates, chooses and rejects, the contents of his perceptions from the viewpoint of the ego or "self," the ultimate concept to be dissolved when enlightenment is realized. The Buddha, by abandoning craving and so forth, no longer conceptualizes in this way (see Dhp 195, 254).

11. Comy. explains *ṭhiti* as "stagnation in saṃsāra caused by the proliferations," which are the factors that delay one in saṃsāra. But it also points out that in *Netti* (p.37) *ṭhiti* is glossed as *anusaya*, latent or dormant tendencies to the defilements. Comy. identifies the tether (*sandāna*) as craving and views, which are like a tether in causing bondage. The bar, or cross-bar (*paligha*), is ignorance, which is similar to a cross-bar in preventing entrance to the city of Nibbāna.
12. Mahākaccāna, who excelled in elaborating upon the Dhamma, was Soṇa's preceptor in Ud 5.6.
13. This cryptic saying can be paraphrased with the help of the Comy. thus: "If there had not been" impure deeds (*kilesa-kamma*) that I had done in the past, then "there would not be for me" now, in this life, the experience of their ripening (*vipāka*). And since "there will not be" any impure deeds when he is an arahat, so "there will not be" anything to ripen in the future.
14. The name of a people and a country at the time of the Buddha.
15. *Muṇḍakā samaṇakā*: this is a term of abuse.
16. Sāmāvatī, one of the consorts of King Udena, was the woman lay-follower of the Buddha foremost in loving-kindness (*mettā*). According to Comy., the fire was deliberately caused by Māgandiyā, another consort of the king. She hated the Buddha and also Sāmāvatī because of the latter's devotion to the Buddha. The full story can be found in *Buddhist Legends*, 1:274–93.
17. These are the first three stages of the noble disciple's path, the final and fourth being the arahat or perfected one.
18. Of being able to act freely and independent of delusion.

CHAPTER 8

1. *Tadāyatanaṃ*: that base, sphere, place, region, position, etc., meaning Nibbāna. Parinibbāna (of the title) means "complete" or "final" Nibbāna. (See the conclusion of Ud 8.5.)
2. The four elements are the primary qualities of matter. The four "formless realms," or subtlest aspects of perception, are experienced in the most advanced stages of calm meditation, but are still "mundane" and "other" than Nibbāna. "Sun and moon" may stand for the entire physical universe.
3. It has no support, i.e., it is unconditioned. This whole utterance is one of the most complete statements on Nibbāna to be found in the Pali Canon.
4. The introductions to Ud 8.1–8.4 are identical.
5. Some eds. read *anattaṃ*, presumably understood as "non-self," but Comy. supports *anataṃ*: "It is craving that is called *natā* (inclining) because of its inclining to the various sense objects and to the various types of being, and also because, by its occurrence bent in that direction, it makes beings incline there. Where there is no such inclining is *anata*, 'the uninclined,' meaning Nibbāna." The word *nati*, in the same sense, occurs at Ud 8.4.
6. Comy.: Supported by craving and views with regard to formations such as form, etc.
7. Comy.: When craving, which is called inclination (*nati*), no longer exists at all, that is, when it has been brought to a state of complete non-arising in one who has expelled defilements by the succession of paths.
8. Comy.: "Coming" is coming by way of rebirth; "going" is going to the other world, passing away. "Decease-and-uprising" is the succession of deaths and rebirths. On the rest of the formula, see Ud 1.10 and Chapter 1, note 21.
9. What follows is also found in the Mahāparinibbāna Suttanta (DN 16). It is a part of the story of the Buddha's last days near the end of the three-month period foretold in

Ud 6.1. For a translation see Sister Vajirā *Last Days of the Buddha*.

10. From the earliest times the nature of this dish, the Buddha's last meal, has been the subject of continuing controversy; thus it has been left untranslated. *Sūkara* means a pig or young hog, and *maddava* means soft, tender, succulent, etc. The commentaries give various speculations: the tender parts of a pig carefully prepared; or a soft boiled rice dish; or a plant or mushroom loved by pigs (hence it has been translated elsewhere as "truffles"); or again, bamboo shoots trampled by pigs, etc. It has also been suggested that the dish was an infusion of an alchemical elixer prepared by Cunda the (gold-)smith.
11. The narrative verses in this sutta were evidently added by the ancient compilers to emphasize the importance of the events being described.
12. The Buddha decides before going to sleep how long he will sleep and the moment when he will awaken. This is an aspect of the practice of mindfulness.
13. *Bhagavā'dha dhamme*: the Lord as embodying the Dhamma.
14. This was the bowl of milk-rice given by the lady Sujātā.
15. The people of a republic bordering the kingdom of Magadha. Not long after the passing away of the Buddha the two countries went to war and Magadha eventually conquered and absorbed the territory of the Vajjīs.
16. The seat of the Buddha and Buddhism, namely, northeast India.
17. Pāṭaliputta was the name given to the city which became great during Emperor Asoka's reign, fulfilling the Buddha's prophecy. It is the modern Indian city of Patna.
18. According to Comy., the bridge is the noble path, the flood is saṃsāra, and its flow is craving. The last two lines imply that without the knowledge of the noble path, there is no effective way of escaping from saṃsāra. While still having attachments ("binding a raft") people experience sorrow (flounder in the "swampy pools") and are unable to extricate themselves from saṃsāra ("cross over the river

flood"). That the path-moment is immediately followed by its fruit is indicated by the instantaneous crossing by "the wise," i.e., the Buddha and his disciples.

19. This episode must have occurred early in the Buddha's ministry, before Ānanda became his permanent attendant and before Nāgasamāla became an arahat. Cp. Ud 4.1.

20. *Koñco khīrapako va ninnagaṃ.* Comy.: As a heron (*koñcasakuṇa*), if presented with milk mixed with water, drinks the milk without taking up the water, so a wise man, though he must stand and sit with fools, abandons them by his conduct; he never mixes with them. See K.R. Norman, "The Milk-drinking Heron in Pali Literature," in his *Collected Papers*, 5:100–106. Norman quotes a verse from a twelfth century Sanskrit work, the *Subhāshita-ratna-kosha*: "The wise man takes the right and leaves the wrong, for such discrimination is natural to the great. Mix milk and water, yet the wild goose will sunder them to drink the milk and leave the water" (trans. by Daniel H.H. Ingalls).

21. See Ud 2.7 and Chapter 2, note 4.

22. He entered into concentration (*samādhi*) based upon the fire element, one of the ten *kasiṇa* exercises (cf. Vism Chapter V), and then emerged from that concentration. Dabba Mallaputta is mentioned elsewhere as having psychic power of control over the element of fire or heat and in Vin III 76–80 he guides the bhikkhus to their quarters by producing light from his fingers. He is said to have become an arahat when he was a child of seven.

23. These are the five aggregates (*khandha*), the groups of unstable and impermanent components that constitute what we call "a being." They continue in process through the round of rebirths but cease at the parinibbāna or passing away of an arahat.

24. The simile, in the Pali, is rather obscure and the translation is only tentative regarding its actual intention.

NOTES TO THE ITIVUTTAKA

The Section of the Ones

1. The introductory and concluding words found in each sutta are omitted after this first discourse to avoid unnecessary repetition. *Attha*: both the meaning (significance and intention) of the Buddha's words, and the aim or goal of the Teaching.
2. Non-returning (*anāgāmitā*) is the third stage of the noble path, above stream-entry and once-returning but below arahantship. One who has reached this stage has eradicated the fetters of sensual desire and ill will and is reborn in one of the five celestial realms called the Pure Abodes (*suddhāvāsa*), there to attain arahantship. Comy. points out that greed (*lobha*) here bears the narrower meaning of sensual lust (*kāmarāga*). While the non-returner abandons sensual lust, greed for being is eliminated only by the arahant.
3. This refers to the three subhuman realms of existence: hell, the animal realm, and the world of hungry ghosts (*peta*).
4. In contrast to greed, hate (*dosa*) is eliminated in its entirety by the path of the non-returner. According to the Comy., among the unwholesome qualities mentioned in the following suttas, anger and contempt are fully eradicated by the non-returner, while delusion and conceit are eliminated only in part, their full eradication requiring attainment of the path of arahantship.
5. According to the Comy., the "All" refers to *sakkāya-dhammā*: the factors of personality, that is, the five aggregates of grasping (*upādānakkhandha*)—form, feeling, perception, mental activities, and consciousness. These comprise the "all" or totality of our experience. Comy. explains "direct knowledge" (*abhiññā*) as knowing things in a superior mode by way of their undistorted characteristics. "Full understanding" (*pariññā*) is explained as the investigation of conditioned things as

impermanent, suffering, and not-self, culminating in the abandonment of attachment.

6. Or repeated birth, *punabbhava*. See Ud 3.10. *Bhava*: being, becoming, or existence, is one of the factors in the formula of dependent arising (*paṭicca-samuppāda*). Being arises from grasping and leads to birth, death, and suffering.
7. These five discourses have been abbreviated as they merely repeat the previous one, substituting greed, etc., for conceit. The verses are identical with those of 1–5.
8. Ignorance (*avijjā*)—synonymous with delusion (*moha*)—about suffering, its origin in craving, its cessation, and the noble eightfold path that leads to its cessation. *Saṃsāra* is the perpetual wandering on from birth to birth, the cycle of rebirths.
9. *Aṅga* means a limb or constituent part, hence, as here and in the next discourse, an essential factor or requirement for gaining release. Wise attention (*yoniso manasikāra*) means attending to aspects of a thing or situation in a way that is helpful to the practice of the path. The commentaries mention considering things as impermanent, unsatisfactory, not-self, and foul rather than the opposites, and the avoidance of fruitless speculation.
10. A learner (*sekha*) is a noble disciple who has not yet become an arahant but is training himself for that goal. The arahant or perfected one is called an *asekha*: one who has no more to learn, who has completed the training. Supreme security from bondage, *anuttara yogakkhema*, is release from the four bonds (*yogā*): sensual desire, desire for being, views, and ignorance.
11. In Vism Chap. III the good friend (*kalyāṇamitta*) is a teacher, the giver of the meditation subject, and at SN 3:18/S I 88 it is said that good friendship encourages one to develop and cultivate the noble eightfold path. In this same discourse the Buddha says: "It is because of my being a good friend, Ānanda, that beings liable to birth are released from birth, that beings liable to old age are released from old age, that beings liable to sickness … death … sorrow … suffering … despair are released from despair."

12. The fetters (*saṃyojana*) are ten in number: personality view, doubt, clinging to external observances, sensual lust, ill will, craving for form, craving for the formless, conceit, restlessness, and ignorance. The stream-enterer has cut off the first three; the once- returner has also weakened the fourth and fifth; the non-returner has removed the first five; and the arahant has destroyed all ten.
13. Comy. refers to the schism in the Sangha created by Devadatta, the Buddha's cousin. Concerning Devadatta see Sutta 40 and notes. Maliciously creating a schism in the Sangha leads to immediate rebirth in hell for an aeon.
14. Those ordinary people whose faith is as yet undeveloped (Comy.), that is, those people who, without committing themselves, have shown an interest in the Buddha's teaching.
15. A *kappa*, an aeon or world-cycle, is in Buddhist cosmology a vast period of time during which the universe evolves and declines, expands and contracts. These periodic cycles continue without beginning or end.
16. "(He) is not deprived": he is not excluded from attaining security or freedom from the four bonds and thus becoming an arahant. See note 10 above.
17. This is a difficult idiomatic phrase that occurs in several places in the Pali Canon. Comy. explains: "Just as something that has been carried is cast aside, so he is placed in hell, having been conveyed there by his own (bad) deeds." That this is intended is made clearer in the third verse.
18. *Netti*, pp. 130–31, has a somewhat different version of this (and the next) discourse, both in the prose and the verse. See *The Guide*, pp. 177–78. *Netti* adds some extra lines of verse and in the first stanza replaces "the Buddha" by "the Teacher" (*satthā*), the more usual epithet in such contexts.
19. *Pasannacitta*: a clear, bright, purified, and confident mind. According to the Comy., it means having faith in the Three Jewels and in actions (*kamma*) and their results.

20. He knows from personal experience by remembering his former lives.
21. Loving-kindness (*mettā*) is the first of the four "divine abidings" (*brahmavihāra*) or boundless states, the other three being compassion, sympathetic joy, and equanimity.
22. The plane of Streaming Radiance (*ābhassara*) is not destroyed at the end of the aeon. When a new universe begins, beings come from there to inhabit it. The first to be born is the Great Brahmā, a high divinity in the Buddhist cosmos.
23. Sakka is the chief god or deva of the Tāvatiṃsa (the heaven of the "Thirty-three"), one of the heavens of the sensuous world (*kāma-loka*), which is below the form world (*rūpa-loka*) inhabited by the brahmās.
24. The *cakkavatti-rājā* or righteous Wheel-turning Monarch is the worldly counterpart of the Buddha. It was prophesied of the Bodhisatta, the Buddha-to-be, that if he remained a householder he would become a Wheel-turning Monarch, but if he went forth into homelessness he would become a Fully Enlightened One and turn the "Wheel of Dhamma" instead of the "Wheel of Conquest." The seven jewels are emblems of royalty: the wheel-jewel, the elephant-jewel, the horse-jewel, the woman-jewel, the gem-jewel, the steward-jewel, and the counselor-jewel. See MN 129.
25. *Dāna*, giving or generosity, is traditionally the most basic source of "merit" in all Buddhist lands. Self-mastery (*dama*) is control of the mind and the senses so that passion, etc., do not overwhelm one. Refraining (*saññama*) is control of bodily actions and speech. Thus these three cover all possible ways of performing voluntary actions.
26. Diligence (*appamāda*) means being energetic and ever mindful in cultivating what is good and wholesome; it is the foundation for all progress. Its opposite is negligence (*pamāda*) by which the mind is distracted from the good and becomes overwhelmed by defilements.
27. This refers to the stream-enterer, who is reborn at most seven more times before attaining release.
28. "If they were to enjoy, as I now enjoy" (Comy.).

29. *Bhuñjati* means both to eat and to enjoy, to make use of something.
30. The "three grounds for making merit" (*puññakiriya-vatthu*) are giving, virtue, and mind-development; see Sutta 11. Comy. glosses "productive of a future birth" (*opadhikāni*) as meaning productive of a successful individual existence, yielding results at conception and during life. The term is contrasted with grounds for making merit aimed at release from future birth, such as by developing insight.
31. Mind-release (*cetovimutti*) is the culmination of the mind's purgation of emotional impurities by the practice of tranquillity (*samatha*). There are various kinds of mind-release, and although they are very exalted, the only one that is irreversible is the unshakeable mind-release (*akuppā cetovimutti*) possessed by an arahant. The practice of loving-kindness, the first of the four divine abidings, culminates in the boundless mind-release (*appamāṇā cetovimutti*) in which all ill will or malice (*vyāpāda*) is removed from the mind.
32. It is by being practised towards all beings equally and without exception, not just towards one person, that loving-kindness becomes boundless and the basis for mind-release.
33. This refers to the legendary kings of the past who ruled righteously and made sacrifices to the gods and gave abundant alms to the needy after their victories. Later they abdicated to become seers (*isi*), hermits or holy men, and then went to heaven. The sacrifices are mentioned at Sn 303 as having been initiated by corrupt brahmins desirous of accumulating wealth. *Soma* is the sacrificial drink offered in libations to the gods.

The Section of the Twos

1. The senses are regarded as "doors" by which sense objects as well as unwholesome states enter the mind. They are guarded by mindfulness. Being immoderate in eating (literally, "not knowing the measure in food") is eating

without wisely reflecting and for purposes other than merely the upkeep of the body and physical health.

2. *Akatabhīruttāna*. Comy. explains: "He has not done what gives protection to oneself from danger." Hence this phrase has been rendered "(not done) what is beneficial."
3. "Bad behaviour" (*pāpaka sīla*) refers to immoral conduct, uncontrolled behaviour that is considered wrong (Comy.). "Bad view" is of various kinds, such as the view that actions (*kamma*) do not produce results (*vipāka*).
4. The restraint of wrong behaviour by moral conduct and of unwholesome states of mind by mindfulness, and the abandoning of the defilements by meditation and wisdom.
5. *Anītiha*: not handed down by tradition or based upon hearsay as is the Vedic lore of the brahmins. The Buddha teaches from his own direct experience of enlightenment.
6. Direct knowledge (*abhiññā*) includes various kinds of supernormal powers, such as the recollection of past lives, and also the knowledge of the destruction of the taints, which is the attainment of arahantship. Full understanding (*pariññā*) is penetrative insight into phenomena and their characteristics as impermanent, unsatisfactory, and not-self. Here, according to the Comy., the two terms mean knowledge and penetration of the four noble truths.
7. This verse is identical with that in Sutta 8.
8. That is, he has a reason for beginning to exert himself.
9. He is moved by a sense of urgency (*saṃvega*) on seeing the suffering inherent in the saṃsāric round of birth, old age, and death, and he makes a proper endeavour (*yoniso padhāna*), wise or skilful endeavour or right effort, to attain release.
10. *Tathāgata* is a term often used by the Buddha when referring to himself. Briefly, it means "He who has thus come" or "thus gone" (to enlightenment). The commentaries give a long and detailed explanation. For a translation, see Bhikkhu Bodhi, *The Discourse on the All-embracing Net of Views* (BPS, 1978), pp.331–44. See also Sutta **13**.

11. Comy.: The thought of security (*khemavitakka*) is especially connected with compassion (*karuṇā*), though it also occurs connected with loving-kindness and sympathetic joy. It is the forerunner and concomitant of the Buddha's attainment of great compassion as well as of his attainment of loving-kindness, etc. The thought of solitude (*pavivekavitakka*) is the forerunner and concomitant of his attainment of fruition, though it also occurs in connection with the jhānas, etc.
12. Non-ill will (*avyāpajjha*) is a synonym for loving-kindness (*mettā*).
13. Or "movable or immovable" (*tasaṃ vā thāvaraṃ vā*). According to the Comy. it means those with craving and those without craving (i.e., arahants). This is the first thought, the thought of security, indicative of the Buddha's great compassion.
14. Comy. identifies solitude here with the eradication and subsiding of defilements that occurred with the Buddha's attainment of enlightenment, and also with the ultimate solitude of Nibbāna, the escape from all conditioned things.
15. Comy.: He endured or carried the entire equipment for supreme enlightenment and the undertaking of great compassion, which no one other than a great Bodhisatta could endure or carry; and he conquered Māra, whom no one else could conquer; and he performed the tasks of a Buddha, which no one else could perform.
16. *Vissantara* (PTS ed.), *vessantara* (Sinh. ed.), *visantara* (Burmese ed.). Comy. explains etymologically: "He is called thus because he has expelled unrighteousness (*visamassa vantattā*) such as unrighteous bodily conduct, etc.; or because he guides others across after he himself has crossed over (*taritvā*) the poison (*visa*) of all defilements, or the poison of all the suffering of the round."
17. Māra is the Evil One, the personification of all that prevents our attainment of enlightenment. The

commentaries explain Māra as the defilements, the five aggregates, and death, also as the Tempter, an evil deity.

18. This verse also occurs at MN 26 (I 168).

19. On shame and fear of wrongdoing, see Sutta 15 and note 22.

20. Clinging to name-and-form (*nāmarūpa*), or the five aggregates, ordinary people (mis-)conceive them as being a self or as belonging to a self.

21. Penetration of the four noble truths.

22. *Sukka* means bright, pure, good, and refers to those qualities that are virtuous and wholesome, by which the mind is cleansed and purified and made radiant. "Shame" (*hiri*) is the inwardly arisen disgust with evil, the voice of conscience which inhibits one from doing wrong; "fear of wrongdoing" (*ottappa*) is the outwardly directed fear of the painful consequences of evil and fear of being blamed by others. The two are said to be the foundation of morality.

23. The prose portion to follow is identical with the inspired utterance in Ud 8.3. This discourse contrasts the unconditioned, Nibbāna, with what is caused and conditioned. The verses continue the contrast by listing synonyms for each of the two terms, concluding with the appropriate evaluation of each.

24. Nutriment is fourfold: material food, contact, mental volition, and consciousness. All are essential to support life. Thus, according to the Buddha, "mental food" is as important for the mind as material food is for the upkeep of the body. "Craving's cord" (*netti*) is craving for being—see note 29 below.

25. The taints (*āsava*) are sensual desire, desire for being, and ignorance; see Sutta 7. "One whose taints are destroyed" (*khīṇāsava*) is another name for an arahant.

26. The attainment of arahantship consists in the extinction of the defilements (*kilesa-parinibbāna*)—attachment, hate, and delusion—and while the arahant continues to live out his life, his freedom from defilements is called "the Nibbāna-element with residue left" (*sa-upādisesa-nibbānadhātu*). The

"residue" is the five aggregates—the mind and the body and the senses—that continue to function.

27. As there is no craving and clinging ("delight"), at the arahant's death, when the body perishes, there is nothing to be projected into a future birth. Thus there takes place the final extinction of the aggregates (*khandha-parinibbāna*), which is "the Nibbāna-element with no residue left" (*anupādisesa-nibbānadhātu*).

28. *Tādi*: "stable," is a term for an emancipated one, the arahant, and refers to his equanimity towards agreeable and disagreeable sense objects.

29. The "cord of being" (*bhavanetti*) is craving for being (*bhavataṇhā*), so called because it keeps living beings attached to the round of existence.

30. *Paṭisallāna*. Comy. explains as physical solitude (*kāyaviveka*), the prerequisite for mental seclusion achieved by meditation.

31. Comy. glosses insight (*vipassanā*) as the sevenfold contemplation: of impermanence, suffering, not-self, dispassion, detachment, cessation, and relinquishment.

32. Comy.: The five aggregates as impermanent, etc.

33. Māra, the Evil One, is conceived as leading a large army (of defilements) which must be faced and defeated to gain enlightenment.

34. This refers to the cultivation of insight and understanding after establishing mindfulness, clarity, and tranquillity of mind as a basis. Comy. also mentions the cultivation of the *bojjhaṅga*, the seven factors of enlightenment: mindfulness, investigation, energy, rapture, tranquillity, concentration, and equanimity.

35. These verses are found at Dhp 306–308.

36. The cessation of being (*bhavanirodha*) is Nibbāna.

37. Those who strongly crave for being and delight in it incline towards the eternalist view which posits a self existing eternally in some form after death. Thus they "hold back" from Nibbāna as the cessation of being.

38. Those who crave for non-being or personal annihilation "overreach" in adopting an annihilationist view. Both the eternalist and the annihilationist fall into the trap of thinking in static terms about the "self," i.e., that there is a permanent self which continues forever (eternalism) or else is permanent only for a fixed period during life and stops at death (annihilationism).
39. The correct attitude of "those with vision," according to the Buddha, is to avoid thinking in terms of "self" and to tackle the root of the problem by eradicating the ignorance and craving that give rise to both wrong views.

The Section of the Threes

1. *Tacasāraṃ.* Comy. explains that this is a name for the bamboo, so called because its pith is exposed outside rather than concealed within. These plants die after seeding.
2. The form element (*rūpadhātu*) is the realm of subtle form, the worlds of the brahmās and the jhānas that lead to rebirth into that realm. The formless element (*arūpadhātu*) is the formless realm and the formless jhānas that lead to rebirth there. The element of cessation (*nirodhadhātu*) is Nibbāna.
3. The point is not to settle in "form" or in the "formless," which are blissful and peaceful states attained through meditation, but to realize that they are still subject to impermanence and death. Only in Nibbāna is perfect freedom to be found. The attainment of jhāna can be such a profound experience that it may easily be mistaken for the ultimate goal. In fact, entire religions and theologies have been founded upon and reinforced by such experiences.
4. *Kāyena phassayitvā.* Literally, "having touched with the body." According to the Comy., "body" (*kāya*) in this context denotes the mind or mental factors (*nāmakāya*) rather than the physical body (*rūpakāya*).
5. By penetrative understanding of feelings according to the method of the four noble truths and by attaining the noble

path of the arahant. Feelings are seen as the truth of suffering, as is shown in the next sutta (No. 4). They originate in contact (*phassa*) and lead to craving, as stated in the formula of dependent arising (*paṭicca-samuppāda*).

6. Because it is unstable and liable to change.
7. Search (*esanā*) is a questing or seeking and a form of longing that arises through ignorance and craving.
8. According to the Comy., "the search for a holy life" means seeking and holding various wrong views such as eternalism and annihilationism, various theories about the soul and the world, etc. See Ud 6.4–6.6.
9. Māra is depicted leading his army into battle while mounted upon an elephant.
10. Māra's domain is the whole of conditioned existence over which he exercises control.
11. A non-learner (*asekha*) is an arahant, one who has no more to learn, who has completed the course of training.
12. Virtue, concentration, and wisdom that are complete and perfected. These three are called the three trainings (*sikkhā*) and form the threefold division of the noble eightfold path.
13. These verses are identical with those in Sutta 18.
14. The fleshly eye (*maṃsa-cakkhu*) is the physical sense-organ, the vision of which is limited in comparison to the other two. The divine or heavenly eye (*dibba-cakkhu*) is one of the direct knowledges (*abhiññā*) by which one sees the arising and passing away of beings according to their deeds. The wisdom eye (*paññā-cakkhu*) is that which penetrates the four noble truths.
15. Comy. states that the occurrence of the fleshly eye is the path, or basis, for the divine eye; for the divine eye arises in one whose natural sight is unimpaired, since he arouses the divine eye by extending the light of the *kasiṇa* object, and he cannot do so without having first acquired the learning sign (*uggahanimitta*) in the *kasiṇa* disc.

16. Comy.: The knowledge of the destruction of the taints arises from the wisdom eye. By arousing and developing the eye of noble wisdom, one is released from all the suffering of the round (of existence).
17. They are faculties (*indriya*) in the sense of ruling, controlling, and dominating other factors associated with themselves. There are altogether twenty-two faculties arranged under various groupings of which the three listed here are exclusively supramundane.
18. Comy.: The first is the wisdom pertaining to the path of stream-entry. It is so called because it arises in one who had, prior to the attainment of the path, practised with the determination, "I shall know what I have never known before in this beginningless saṃsāra—the deathless state (i.e., Nibbāna), or the four noble truths." The second is the faculty of wisdom in the six supramundane states from the fruition of stream-entry through the path of arahantship. And the third is the consummate knowledge of the four noble truths which arises in the arahant with the attainment of the final fruition.
19. *Ujumagga*: the noble path leading directly to Nibbāna.
20. Comy. gives two interpretations of this couplet: (1) first arises the knowledge of the path of arahantship, called "destruction" because it destroys all defilements; and immediately after there arises arahantship itself, here called "final knowledge" (*aññā*); (2) first there arises the knowledge of the path of stream-entry, called "destruction" because it destroys the defilements coexisting with wrong views; and immediately afterwards there arises the faculty of final knowledge, which persists through the path of arahantship.
21. The arahant, endowed with the third faculty, delights in the peaceful state (*santipada*), Nibbāna.
22. According to the Comy., beings identify one or the other of the five aggregates as the "self," and from that standpoint they proceed to speculate with regard to the three times: "Was I in the past?... Having been what, what did I become in the past?... What will I become in the future?" And in the present they think: "Where has this

being come from, where will it go?" (M I 8, etc.). The concept of a "self," of an "I," is the basic fallacy.

23. He does not misconceive or imagine that there is a permanent self that speaks, acts, and exists in the three times. Through full understanding (*pariññā*) he has realized phenomena to be impermanent, suffering, and not-self.
24. He takes his stand on Dhamma, on Nibbāna (the state of peace), which is timeless (*akāliko*) and stands outside the three periods of time.
25. Comy.: The arahant does not come to renewed being in any state of existence, and thus he no more enters into the range of concepts specifying his personal identity. He goes to the indescribable state, the unconditioned Nibbāna.
26. These verses and those of the following sutta appeared in Suttas 3 and 4.
27. There is a play on words here which is lost in translation: *moneyya*, translated as "perfection," is the state of a *muni*, a sage, a perfect or silent one, one who has *mona*: wisdom, self-possession, silence (the silencing of all imperfections). Thus *moneyya* is the silencing or stilling of activities (*kamma*) of body, speech, and mind, imperfections that lead to a future birth.
28. By the development of virtue, concentration, and wisdom.
29. "Supreme" here is *brahma*, which Comy. explains as the best (*seṭṭha*), i.e., the fruit of arahantship. Comy. also explains "Tathāgata," usually an exclusive epithet of the Buddha, in a way applicable to all arahants: like other arahants, so (*tathā*) this noble person has come along (*āgata*) endowed with excellent supporting conditions from the past and has gone (*gata*) to Nibbāna along the middle way.
30. The symbolic meaning of these terms is explained in Sutta **10**. In the case of bhikkhunīs (Buddhist nuns) "womenfolk" should be replaced by "menfolk." M I 460–62 offers a partly different interpretation of the metaphor.

31. This statement is an idiomatic phrase and is apparently a quotation from an unknown source describing one who has attained his goal. It is found elsewhere, e.g., at SN 35:197/S IV 175, as a designation for an arahant. See *Saṃyutta Nikāya Anthology,* Part I (BPS Wheel No. 107/109), p.67.

32. The King of Death (*maccurāja*) is a name for Māra. The arahant, by not being reborn, vanishes from Māra's sight; he steps outside Māra's domain so that the "Evil One" can neither locate nor define (delimit, measure, *pamāṇa*) him.

33. The terms "recluse" and "brahmin" often occur together and denote those leading a life involved with religion. A recluse (*samaṇa*) is defined as anyone who has gone forth from the house life and in the Indian context could be called "a holy man." A brahmin is a priest who performs rituals and sacrifices and is usually a householder. The Buddha is sometimes called the "Great Recluse" (*mahāsamaṇa*).

34. Renunciation (*nekkhamma*) refers here to the first absorption (*jhāna*), which is the entry into the form realm (*rūpāvacara*) by leaving behind the realm of sensual desires (*kāmāvacara*); it is attained when the mind is "isolated" (*vivicca*) from sensual desires and other unwholesome states. The "formless" (*āruppa*) is a formless-sphere meditative attainment. "Cessation" (*nirodha*) is Nibbāna. See Sutta 2 and note 3.

35. *Sabbasaṅkhārasamatha*: the cessation of all conditioned things, of the whole of conditioned existence; this is Nibbāna, the unconditioned state.

36. The second verse appears also in Sutta 4.

37. The second and third verses are identical with those in Sutta 2, except for a slight variation in the first line of the second verse.

38. These are the Five Precepts which, together with the Three Refuges, are the basic rules of conduct and belief for all Buddhists.

39. He himself gives and enjoins others to do likewise.

40. *Tagara*: a sweet-scented powder obtained from the *tagara* shrub.

41. "Element" (*dhātu*) here means disposition or temperament (*ajjhāsaya*).

42. *Kamma*: here, various kinds of work, such as robe-making and so forth.

43. *Anavaññatti*: wanting to be well regarded by others, a form of arrogance or pride.

44. *Parānuddayatā*. Ordinarily, this might mean having sympathy or compassion for others, but in this context it must mean a love of socializing and an emotional involvement with others leading to loss of independence.

45. *Bodhipakkhiyadhammā*. The seven groups are: the four foundations of mindfulness; the four right efforts; the four bases of successful accomplishment; the five faculties; the five powers; the seven factors of enlightenment (see The Twos, note 34); and the noble eightfold path. See Ledi Sayādaw, *The Requisites of Enlightenment* (BPS Wheel No. 171/174, 1971).

46. Wisdom-release (*paññāvimutti*) is the knowledge associated with the fruition-attainment of the arahant (*arahattaphala*). Mind-release (*cetovimutti*) is the arahant's freedom from the negative emotions of greed and hate, etc. See also Sutta 23 and the accompanying note concerning mind-release.

47. Reading here *tanhi tassa na passanti yena maccuvasaṃ vaje*. The PTS edition is surely mistaken in reading, in the third line, *namassanti* instead of *na passanti*.

48. By reason of the attainment of the noble path (*ariyamagga*).

49. *Opadhikam*. As a foundation or basis for future births. See The Ones, note 30.

50. Contemplating foulness (*asubha*) is reflecting on the body in various ways so as to overcome physical attachment and sensual lust. The most common method is by mentally dissecting the body into its (traditional) thirty-two parts: head hair, body hair, nails, teeth, skin, etc. The practice of

the cemetery contemplations is also used. See Vism VI and VIII,44–144.

51. The practice of *ānāpānasati*, or mindfulness of in-and-out breathing, is the most effective way to control the wandering thoughts that prevent the attainment of tranquillity and concentration.

52. The practice of speaking and thinking what is not in accordance with Dhamma.

53. Or non-ill will (*avyāpāda*). In Pali, unlike English, negative words are actually synonyms of their positive counterparts. Thus "non-blindness" is a synonym for sight, "non-ill will" for friendliness or loving-kindness (*mettā*), "harmlessness" for compassion, etc. This makes it difficult to find exact equivalents for all these terms.

54. These three are called the three unwholesome roots (*akusala-mūlāni*) in Sutta 1.

55. Devadatta was the Buddha's cousin who attempted to usurp his position as leader of the Sangha. According to the Comy., because of pride in his attainments, Devadatta reasoned thus: "The Buddha is a Sakyan, I too am a Sakyan; the Buddha is a recluse, I too am a recluse; the Buddha possesses supernormal powers (*iddhi*), I too possess supernormal powers;... I will be a Buddha and take care of the Order of bhikkhus." When this bid failed he attempted to create a schism within the Sangha and plotted to have the Buddha murdered. See Bhikkhu Ñāṇamoli, *The Life of the Buddha*, pp.258ff.

56. The "trifling attainment" refers to Devadatta's acquisition of supernormal powers, which led to his downfall.

57. The first line of this verse is translated following the Burmese-script edition, *samānam anuciṇṇo*, in preference to the PTS reading, *pamādam anuciṇṇo*.

58. The Unremitting Hell (*avīci-niraya*) is the lowest and most painful of the several Buddhist hells (both hot and cold).

59. *Aggappasāda*: foremost (highest, best) faith, confidence, devotion.

60. Enabling one to enter the noble path (*ariyamagga*) and so gain release.

61. "States": *dhammā*, all phenomena that exist, Nibbāna alone being the unconditioned (*asaṅkhata*) state.

62. Each of the four kinds of noble disciple is considered as either being on the path (*magga*) or as having attained the fruit (*phala*) of that path; thus there are four pairs or eight individuals.

63. *Piṇḍolya* (lit., food-balls or lumps) means the almsfood a bhikkhu collects from house to house.

64. This verse appears also in Sutta 21. The Burmese-script edition includes here also the preceding verse of Sutta 21, though the PTS edition, which I follow, excludes it.

65. *Nibbuto*: quenched or cooled. One who has extinguished the three fires of lust, hate, and delusion (see Sutta 44) has attained Nibbāna, the state of extinction or being "quenched."

66. *Macce*: those subject to death (*maccu*) and rebirth; or those under the sway of Māra, the Evil One, of *maccurāja*, the King of Death.

67. *Sakkāya*: the group of factors constituting individual existence, conceived by the ignorant to be permanent, pleasurable, and the "self." It is identified as the five aggregates of grasping (*upādānakkhandhā*).

68. These are the four bad bourns. The *asuras*—an addition to the usual set of three bad bourns—are a type of titan or demon obsessed by the urge for power.

69. See above, note 50.

70. Penetration (*nibbedha*) is the direct understanding of the four noble truths. See the verse in Sutta 14.

71. In the Uddesavibhaṅga Sutta (MN 138) this highly compressed statement by the Buddha is explained by the Venerable Mahākaccāna and forms the subject matter of that sutta. Briefly, "externally not distracted" means guarding the senses so that the mind is not overwhelmed and carried away by the variety and details of sights, sounds, etc., that impinge on the senses. "Internally not fixed" is not being fascinated by the rapture and joy, etc., experienced in the jhānas. Such fascination is a subtle form

of craving which leads to grasping, being, birth, and so forth, that is, to the whole process of future suffering and the perpetuation of saṃsāra. Investigating (examining, probing) these experiences is the practice of insight meditation (*vipassanā-bhāvanā*).

72. The seven ties (*saṅgā*) are: craving, views, conceit, anger, ignorance, defilement, and misconduct. The "cord" is the cord of being (*bhavanetti*), i.e., craving for being. See The Twos, note 29.

73. Humans and most devas are surrounded by objects that can become objects of desire—this is the first way. The second and third refer to two classes of devas in the world of sense (*kāmadhātu*): the *nimmānarati-devas* ("those delighting in their own creations") and the *paranimmita-vasavatti-devas* ("those who control what others have created"). The verse also mentions "others who enjoy sense objects"; according to Comy., this refers to some beings in the subhuman realms of existence, such as animals.

74. PTS ed. omits this line and the next (*saṃsāraṃ nātivattare etam ādīnavaṃ ñatvā*). The translation follows the Burmese edition.

75. Though pleasurable, sensual pleasures are bound up with danger (*ādīnava*) in that they are impermanent and never fully satisfying. Thus they lead to frustration and to the perpetuation of the "round." The "danger" in them is to be seen as the noble truth of suffering.

76. The bond of sensual desire is what holds living beings to the sense-sphere realm (*kāmadhātu*), the bond of (desire for) being is what holds them to saṃsāra. All those from the worldling through the once-returner (*sakadāgāmī*) are still bound by both bonds; the non-returner (*anāgāmī*) has eradicated the sensual bond but not the desire for being; the arahant has eradicated both bonds.

77. The Pātimokkha, the disciplinary rules of the Order of bhikkhus.

78. See Sutta 5 and note 45.

79. On the "All" see Sutta 7 and The Ones, note 5. The last line also appears in Suttas 17 and 19.

80. Comy. explains that the first verse refers to the giving of material things; the second—by the mentioning of "proclaiming" and "hearing"—refers to the gift of the Dhamma.

81. *Lapitalāpana*. The Buddha is referring pejoratively to the brahmins' practice of reciting from the Vedic scriptures. The threefold knowledge (*tevijjā*) traditionally meant knowledge of the three Vedas, but the Buddha redefined this from the standpoint of the Dhamma as the knowledge leading to enlightenment and release from the round of births. The idea of persuasive talk or "patter" is a beggar's ploy to cajole people into giving alms.

The Section of the Fours

1. Accessible to entreaties (*yācayoga*), that is, always ready to teach the Dhamma when asked; and open-handed (*payatapāṇi*), being in constant readiness to give a gift, here the gift of the Dhamma, in the appropriate manner.
2. The Buddha is called "the great physician" as he offers the treatment to cure the suffering inherent in the round of birth and death. And he is a surgeon (*sallakatta*) who has the method for excising the poisoned arrows (*salla*) of lust, hate, and delusion embedded in the minds of beings.
3. This is the Buddha's variation on the brahmins' claim to be born from the mouth of the god Brahmā.
4. *Yāga*: a sacrificial offering or alms-giving.
5. The first three are included among the allowable ascetic practices (*dhutaṅga*). All four constitute the minimal requisites for living the bhikkhu life, taught as such in the ceremony of higher ordination (*upasampadā*).
6. See Sutta 13 and notes.
7. *Itibhavābhavahetu*: "by reason of being or not being thus." Explained by the Comy. as gain or loss, success or failure, increase or decrease.

8. *Brahmā* means the highest, best, foremost (of beings), and a brahmā god exemplifies the state of one who maintains the practice of the *brahmavihāra*, the "divine abidings" of loving-kindness, compassion, sympathetic joy, and equanimity. It is parents too who maintain these attitudes of love towards their children.
9. One's parents are like the earliest or first devas, divinities in the sense of being powerful guardians and protectors. They are also one's first teachers, teaching the most basic things, how to walk, talk, eat, etc., and about the people and objects in one's environment.
10. *Sugata*. Here meaning the disciples of the Buddha, according to the Comy., which glosses the word with *sammā paṭipanna*.
11. Arahants.
12. Comy.: Those home-loving layfolk, attached to the household life, practise the worldly (*lokiya*) Dhamma of alms-giving, etc., which leads to heaven.
13. *Gaha*, literally "seizer," is also another name for the crocodile, although translated in Sutta 20 as "sharks," because of the ocean setting. *Rakkhasa* is, in Indian mythology, a kind of flesh-eating demon living in lakes and pools and in the ocean.
14. *Orambhāgiya-saṃyojana*: "the fetters belonging to the hither shore" or "lower fetters" are the first five fetters—personality view, doubt, clinging to external observances, sensual craving, and ill will. They are called thus because they bind one to rebirth in the lower world, the sense-sphere realm. They are finally overcome at the stage of the non-returner.
15. *Sahāpi dukkhena jaheyya kāme*. Comy. explains this by reference to one who attains jhāna and the path with painful progress (*dukkhapaṭipadā*), i.e., one who can suppress the defilement of sensuality only with trouble and difficulty.
16. By "the world" is meant the noble truth of suffering, the world of experience consisting of form, feeling, perception, mental formations, and consciousness. These

are the five aggregates, equated with suffering in the exposition of the four noble truths.

17. He has finished with *kamma,* deeds which will produce a result in a future birth.
18. "Brahma-wheel" (*brahma-cakka*) is synonymous with Dhamma-wheel. The commencement of the Buddha's teaching career is referred to as "the setting in motion of the Dhamma-wheel," which is also the title of the famous sutta containing the first sermon proclaimed in the Deer Park at Benares.

PARALLEL PASSAGES AND REFERENCES IN THE UDĀNA

1.1	Nett 145; Vin I 1; S II 1
1.2	Nett 145 (151); Vin I 2
1.3	Vin I 2
1.4	Nett 150; Vin I 2
1.5	Nett 150
1.6	Ud 3.7; S V 79; Sn 65
1.7	Nett 150
1.8	Nett 150
1.9	Nett 151; Dhp 261, 393
1.10	Nett 150; S I 15; cf. S IV 72; Dhp-a 209
2.1	Peṭ 50; Vin I 3; J-a I 80
2.2	Nett 65; Peṭ 55; M I 161; S II 273; S V 342; Dhp 178
2.3	Nett 130, 134; Dhp 131-32
2.5	S IV 210
2.8	J-a I 407; Dhp-a IV 192; It 1
2.10	Vin II 183; J-a I 10
3.2	Dhp-a I 118; Th 157
3.3	M I 456-57
3.4	Th 651
3.5	Peṭ 16; S IV 72
3.6	Peṭ 10; Sn 469, 494
3.10	Nett 156f.; Peṭ 26f.
4.1	A IV 354
4.2	Nett 47, 85, 103; A I 70; S V 269
4.3	Dhp 42
4.4	Peṭ 24-25; Th 191
4.5	Nett 149; Vin I 352
4.6	Dhp 185; D I 50
4.8	Dhp 306; Sn 623
4.9	Sn 746
4.10	It 94; S III 190
5.1	Nett 164; S I 75; J-a III 405
5.2	Nett 164; Peṭ 55; M III 122
5.3	Nett 7; D I 110; M I 380
5.4	S I 209; Thī 246; Pv. 21
5.5	Nett 153; Peṭ 25; Vin II 236; A IV 204; Dhp 14; Th 447
5.6	Vin I 194; Th 365
5.8	Vin II 198; Dhp 163
5.9	Vin I 349; J-a III 488; M III 154; Th 275
6.1	Nett 60; D II 102; S V 259; A IV 308
6.2	S I 77
6.3	S III 55; Th 180
6.4	D I 150; M I 484; S IV 393
6.7	Sn 7, 527
6.8	Nett 173-74
7.1	Nett 63, 143; Peṭ 24
7.3	Peṭ 10
7.4	Nett 36, 128-29; Peṭ 24
7.5	Peṭ 50; S IV 291; S II 279
7.6	Dhp 230; A II 8
7.7	Nett 37
7.9	M I 39; Vv-a 46
7.10	Nett 62; Dhp-a I 161
8.3	Nett 62; It 37
8.4	Nett 65; Peṭ 18; M III 266; S II 67; S IV 59
8.5	Peṭ 28; D II 126
8.6	D II 84; D III 209; Vin I 226; M I 354; S IV 183
8.8	Nett 67; Peṭ 14; Sn 862-63

Bibliography

Editions of the Udāna consulted:

Udāna, edited by Paul Steinthal. Pali Text Society, reprinted 1948 (Roman script).

Khuddakanikāya, Part I. Ceylon Government Buddha Jayanti Tripiṭaka Series, Vol. 24, 1960 (Sinhala script).

Khuddakanikāya, Vol. I. Nālandā Devanāgarī Pāli Series. Bihar Government, 1959 (Devanāgarī script).

Khuddakanikāya I. Chaṭṭhasaṅgāyana edition of the Tipiṭaka, 1956 (Burmese script).

Editions of the Udāna Commentary (*Paramatthadīpanī*) consulted:

PTS: Edited by F.L. Woodward, reprinted 1977.

Sinhalese: Simon Hewavitarne Bequest Edition, Colombo 1920.

Editions of the Itivuttaka consulted:

Itivuttaka, edited by Ernst Windisch. PTS reprinted 1975 (Roman script).

Khuddakanikāya, Vol. I, Chaṭṭhasaṅgāyana edition of the Tipiṭaka, 1956 (Burmese script).

Khuddakanikāya, Part I, Ceylon Government, Buddha Jayanthi Tripiṭaka Series, Vol. 24, 1960 (Sinhala script).

Khuddakanikāya, Vol. I, Nālandā Devanāgarī Pāli Series, Bihar Government, 1959 (Devanāgarī script).

Editions of the Itivuttaka Commentary (*Paramatthadīpanī*) consulted:

Paramatthadīpanī of Dhammapālācariya, edited by M.M. Bose, 2 vols. PTS, reprinted 1977.

Other works consulted:

Coomaraswamy, A.K. *Yaksas*. New Delhi, 1971.

Bodhi, Bhikkhu. *The Discourse on the All-embracing Net of Views*. BPS, 1978.

Burlingame, E.W. *Buddhist Legends*, 3 volumes. Harvard Oriental Series, Vols. 28–30. London: PTS, reprinted 1969. (Translation of Dhammapada Commentary.)

Horner, I.B. *The Middle Length Sayings*, 3 volumes. PTS, 1954–59. (Translation of Majjhima Nikāya.)

Ireland, John D. *Saṃyutta Nikāya: An Anthology*, Part I. Wheel No. 107/109. BPS, 1967.

——. *The Udāna: Inspired Utterances of the Buddha*. BPS, 1990.

Malalasekera, G.P. *Dictionary of Pāli Proper Names*. London: PTS, reprinted 1960.

Masefield, Peter. *The Udāna*. Sacred Books of the Buddhists. Oxford: PTS,1994. —. *The Udāna Commentary*, 2 vols. Sacred Books of the Buddhists. Oxford: PTS, 1994–95.

Ñāṇamoli, Bhikkhu. *The Guide*. PTS, 1962. (Translation of *Nettippakaraṇa*.) *The Life of the Buddha*. BPS, 1972.

—. The Minor Readings and the Illustrator of Ultimate Meaning. London: PTS, 1960. (Translation of Khuddakapāṭha and Commentary.)

——. *The Path of Purification*. Colombo, 1956. (Translation of *Visuddhimagga*.)

Ñāṇananda, Bhikkhu. *Concept and Reality in Early Buddhist Thought*. BPS, 2nd ed., 1976.

Norman, K.R. "The Milk-drinking Heron in Pāli Literature," in *Collected Papers*, Vol. 5. Oxford: PTS, 1994.

Nyanaponika Thera. *Anguttara Nikāya, An Anthology*, Part I. Wheel No. 155/158. BPS, 1981.

Vajirā, Sister. *Last Days of the Buddha*. Wheel No. 67/69. Kandy: BPS, 1964. (Translation of Mahāparinibbāna Suttanta.)

Woodward, F.L. *Minor Anthologies of the Pāli Canon*, Part II. London: PTS, 1935. (Translation of Udāna and Itivuttaka.)

——. *The Book of the Gradual Sayings*, Vols. I and II. PTS, 1932–33. (Translation of Aṅguttara Nikāya, Books 1 to 4.)

Of related interest from the BPS

THE DHAMMAPADA
The Buddha's Path of Wisdom
Translated by Ācariya Buddharakkhita

The Dhammapada is the best known scripture of Theravada Buddhism, and one of the most beloved spiritual testaments of all time. An anthology of 423 verses spoken by the Buddha, the Dhammapada serves as a perfect compendium of his teachings for study, reflection and contemplation.

The translator, Ācariya Buddharakkhita, ably transmits the spirit and content as well as the style of the original. A long introduction by Bhikkhu Bodhi shows how the work embodies the essential teachings of early Buddhism.

This compact, handy volume is not only ideal for personal use, but will also make a beautiful gift which can bring to others the light of the Dhamma in one of its most inspiring expressions.

BP 203 116 Pages

THE LIFE OF THE BUDDHA
According to the Pali Canon
by Bhikkhu Ñāṇamoli.

Among the numerous lives of the Buddha that have been written, this work with its comprehensive material and original method of presentation claims a place of its own. Composed entirely from texts from the Pali Canon, the oldest and most intact authentic record, it portrays an image of the Buddha which is vivid, warm and moving. An inspiring and informative work.

BPS 101 375 Pages

Of related interest from the BPS

BUDDHA, MY REFUGE

Contemplation of the Buddha based on the Pali Suttas

Bhikkhu Khantipalo

This book weaves together a rich variety of texts from the Pali Canon illustrating each of the Buddha's nine outstanding virtues. The result is a beautiful and inspiring anthology of suttas on the personality of the Blessed One.

BP 409 126 Pages

THE VISION OF DHAMMA

Nyanaponika Thera

This volume brings between two covers the author's original writings from the BPS's Wheel and Bodhi Leaves series such as essays on kamma, the four nutriments, and the roots of good and evil. These writings offer one of the most mature, comprehensive, and authoritative expressions of Buddhism by a contemporary Western monk.

BP 414 340 Pages

GREAT DISCIPLES OF THE BUDDHA

Their Lives, Their Works, Their Legacy

by Nyanaponika Thera and Hellmuth Hecker.

A masterly compilation of twenty-four life-stories of the closest and most eminent of the Buddha's personal disciples. The profiles, set against the colourful social and cultural background of ancient India, bring to life legendary names such as Sāriputta and Moggallāna, Ānanda and Mahākassapa, and many more, enabling us to participate in their great breakthroughs, achievements, and activities in spreading the Dharma.

BP 417 411 Pages.

THE BUDDHIST PUBLICATION SOCIETY

The BPS is an approved charity dedicated to making known the Teaching of the Buddha, which has a vital message for all people.

Founded in 1958, the BPS has published a wide variety of books and booklets covering a great range of topics. Its publications include accurate annotated translations of the Buddha's discourses, standard reference works, as well as original contemporary expositions of Buddhist thought and practice. These works present Buddhism as it truly is—a dynamic force which has influenced receptive minds for the past 2500 years and is still as relevant today as it was when it first arose.

For more information about the BPS and our publications, please visit our website, or contact:

Administrative Secretary
Buddhist Publication Society
P.O. Box 61
54 Sangharaja Mawatha
Kandy • Sri Lanka

E-mail: bps@bps.lk
web site: http://www.bps.lk
Tel: 0094 81 223 7283 • Fax: 0094 81 222 3679